NUCLEAR STABILITY IN SOUTHERN ASIA

NUCLEAR STABILITY IN SOUTHERN ASIA

Edited by

P.R. CHARI
SONIKA GUPTA
ARPIT RAJAIN

KONRAD ADENAUER FOUNDATION

INSTITUTE OF PEACE AND CONFLICT STUDIES

MANOHAR
2003

First published 2003

ISBN 81-7304-520-8

Published by
Ajay Kumar Jain for
Manohar Publishers & Distributors
4753/23 Ansari Road, Daryaganj
New Delhi 110 002

Typeset by
Kohli Print
New Delhi 110 051

Printed at
Lordson Publishers Pvt. Ltd.
Delhi 110 007

Contents

Appendices

Acknowledgements

This book would not have been possible without the support of several people who contributed academically and in many other substantive ways to the project.

We especially thank the Konrad Adenauer Foundation (KAF) for being the co-organiser and particularly Prof. Gert W. Kueck for the excellent co-operation in the successful completion of this project. Mr. Pankaj Madan at the KAF handled the administrative details and we would like to thank him for his endeavours.

We are grateful to Dr. Ashley J. Tellis, Special Advisor to the US Ambassador, New Delhi, for taking up in a very thorough manner the general issue of nuclear stability in Southern Asia.

For the several papers that were presented for this book, we are specially grateful to the authors from India as well as Germany whose names and respective contributions are duly incorporated in this volume. Furthermore, we are deeply obliged to Prof. Kanti Bajpai, Dr. Arvind Kumar, Prof. Surjit Mansingh, Dr. Placid Rodriguez, Dr. Varun Sahni and Ambassador Dr. Walter Schmid, Deputy Commissioner for Disarmament and Arms Control of the German Federal Government, whose critical remarks helped in the review of the papers presented by the authors. We are also grateful to Dr. P.K. Iyengar and Dr. K. Santhanam for chairing the sessions.

We would also like to thank the strategic and diplomatic community in New Delhi, who are not being individually recognized here, for their active participation in the deliberations, which greatly enriched the discussions and added new perspectives for consideration of the paper writers.

At the Institute of Peace and Conflict Studies (IPCS), we wish to thank Maj. Gen. Ashok Krishna, former Deputy Director, for his guidance in conducting the project. We are particularly grateful to

R. Radhakrishan and Aisha Khan for their assistance in conducting the conference. Finally, a word of thanks to Vijay Chauhan and Surinder Singh for taking care of the various last minute logistical details during the conference

EDITORS

1
Introduction

Sonika Gupta and Arpit Rajain

The nuclear tests by India and Pakistan in May 1998 have radically altered the strategic landscape in Southern Asia.[1] The strategic triangle comprising Pakistan, India and China presents new challenges to Southern Asian security. The nuclear dimension of this triangular relationship developed in the 1960s following China's entry into the Nuclear Club in 1964, and the steady nuclearization of India and Pakistan over the early 1970s and 1980s, culminating in their reciprocal nuclear tests in May 1998. Following these tests there is an urgent need for the South Asian states to stabilize their relationship, despite their past history of bilateral conflict. Since the Indo-Pak nuclear tests cannot be undone, both countries need to decide what strategic interests they should pursue in order to serve their own and regional interests. However, China, India, and Pakistan have adopted different political approaches to arms control and nuclear disarmament, as well as issues like general and complete disarmament that subsume nuclear disarmament.

India and Pakistan need to deal now with the political and military issues involved in nuclear weaponization and deployment, establishing command and control arrangements over their nuclear holdings, evolving a doctrine for the possible use of nuclear weapons and the military strategy to guide such usage. There is an asymmetry between these three countries—India *vis-à-vis* China and Pakistan *vis-à-vis* India—in conventional and nuclear weaponry. This is an obstacle to

[1] In this book, unless otherwise defined, Southern Asia refers to the region comprising South Asia plus China.

the establishment of a plausible nuclear restraint regime or the evolving of credible nuclear risk reduction measures between the three nuclear weapon powers in the region. Hence the possibility of escalation of regional conflict from the sub-conventional level to a minor skirmish to a major conventional conflict and further to crossing the nuclear threshold cannot be ruled out.

Some part of the difficulty in establishing nuclear restraint and risk reduction regimes in Southern Asia arises from the differing political systems in the three states, ranging from a practising democracy to an authoritarian regime and a praetorian state. This has implications for the maintenance of checks and balances on the political executive and the military, which has great salience for command and control structures and ensuring nuclear safety. In India, the military is more or less out of the decision-making circuit on nuclear issues with absolute civilian control existing over the nuclear arsenal; in Pakistan, on the other hand, the Army has always been primarily concerned with all decisions relating to the production of or control over the bomb; whilst in China it is believed that release authority or the ultimate decision to use nuclear weapons rests with the Chairman of the Central Military Commission after its top leaders have reached a consensus.

The question of the risk of war and the issue of strategic stability in Southern Asia is also complicated by the fact that India has a nuclear adversarial relationship with Pakistan and China. Historically, this is an unprecedented situation where a triangular nuclear competition has been constructed, which is qualitatively different and more dangerous than the bilateral nuclear rivalry that had existed between the United States and the Soviet Union during the Cold War. From the Indian perspective, its military calculations need to plan for a situation where it might need to simultaneously deter Pakistan and China, apart from the need for deterring Pakistan supported by China. For its part, Pakistan needs to decide on whether it wishes to remain China's surrogate in South Asia, despite its relationship with the United States having improved considerably after 11 September, and the collaborative role played by it to advance US interests in Afghanistan and the Central Asian region. India would also need to decide on whether it wants to enter into an arms race with China, which would be highly detrimental to Asian security.

At present, India and Pakistan face an invidious choice between proceeding further to weaponize and deploy their nuclear weapons, or rest content with their present capabilities, or creep along to ultimate weaponization and deployment in the fullness of time. Should India and Pakistan proceed towards weaponization and deployment, and China continue with its nuclear modernization plans, there are several risk-reduction measures that could be contemplated in the interests of nuclear stability. Some of these were included in the ill-fated Lahore Declaration,[2] including advance notification of missile tests, moratorium on nuclear tests, upgrading existing communication links, undertaking measures to reduce the risk of accidental or unauthorized use of nuclear weapons, agreement to prevent incidents at sea, establishing a consultative machinery to ensure effective implementation of confidence-building measures (CBMs), and bilateral consultations on security, disarmament, and non-proliferation. These measures need to be fleshed out. Most importantly, India and Pakistan have to discuss what exactly are their strategic concepts pertaining to the utility of nuclear weapons. Risk-reduction measures must also include exchange of information on steps to ensure safety of stockpiles, and the establishment of hotlines between their respective Air Forces and nuclear establishments. Finally, risk-reduction should also contemplate an agreement to avoid inflammatory statements, especially in times of crisis. The lack of any dialogue between India and Pakistan has prevented these vital questions from being discussed.

Treating nuclear stability in Southern Asia in its totality, this book explores all the above issues. The existing literature on nuclear issues in Southern Asia deals with the evolution of the nuclear programmes of China, India, and Pakistan or with bilateral nuclear dyads.[3] No attempt

[2] The Lahore Declaration was signed on 21 February 1999 between the Indian and the Pakistani Prime Ministers following the Indian Prime Minister's much publicized bus trip to Lahore. The text of the Lahore Declaration can be seen in *The Hindu*, 22 February 1999.

[3] Robert A. Manning, Ronald Monaperto and Brad Roberts, *China, Nuclear Weapons and Arms Control* (New York: Council on Foreign Relations, 2000); Li Daoyu, 'Foreign Policy And Arms Control: The View From China', *Arms Control Today*, December 1993. Banning N. Garrett and Bonnie S. Glaser, 'Chinese Perspectives on Nuclear Arms Control', *International Security*, Winter 1995-6, pp. 64-5; Alastair Iain Johnston, 'Prospects for Chinese Nuclear Force Modernization: Limited Deterrence Versus Multilateral Arms Control', *The China Quarterly*, June 1996, pp. 552-8; Jonathan D. Pollack and Richard H. Yang (eds.), *In China's Shadow: Regional Perspectives on Chinese Foreign Policy and Military Developments* (Washington: RAND Corporation, 1998); David Shambaugh and Richard H. Yang (eds.), *China's Military in Transition* (Oxford: Clarendon Press, 1997); Dingli Shen, 'Towards a Nuclear Tiger: The Search for Security in South Asia', *Arms Control Today*, Vol. 23, No. 5, June 1993; Srikanth Kondapalli, *China's Military: The PLA in Transition* (New Delhi: Knowledge Books, 1999); Zhao Xiaowei, 'The Threat of a New Arms Race Dominates Asian Geopolitics'. *Global Affairs* (Summer 1992), pp. 29-40;

has been made to examine the triangular nuclear equation existing in Southern Asia. While the China-Pakistan nuclear relationship is co-operative, the adversarial Sino-Indian and Indo-Pak nuclear equations are linked through a common denominator, India. Furthermore, the

---

Di Hua 'China's Security Dilemma to the year 2010' (Stanford: CISAC Working Paper, 1997); Ming Zhang, *China's Changing Nuclear Posture: Reactions to the South Asian Nuclear Test* (Washington: Brookings Institution Press, 1999); Ching-Pin Lin, *China's Nuclear Strategy: Tradition Within Evolution* (Lexington: Lexington Books, 1988); George Perkovich, *India's Nuclear Bomb* (Los Angeles: University of California Press, 2000). P.R. Chari, *The Indo-Pak Nuclear Stand-off: The Role of the United States* (New Delhi: Manohar, 1995). Ashley Tellis, *India's Emerging Nuclear Posture: Between Recessed Deterrent and Ready Arsenal* (Washington: RAND Corporation, 2002); Amitabh Mattoo (ed.), *India's Nuclear Deterrent: Pokhran II and Beyond* (New Delhi, Har Anand, 1999); Bharat Karnad, *Nuclear Weapons and Indian Security: The Realist Foundations of Strategy* (New Delhi: Macmillan, 2002); Raj Chengappa, *Weapons of Peace* (New Delhi: Harper Collins, 2000); Ashok Kapur, *Pokhran and Beyond: India's Nuclear Behaviour* (New Delhi: Oxford University Press, 2001); Sumit Ganguly, 'India's Pathway to Pokhran II, *International Security*, Vol. 23, No. 4, Spring 1999, pp. 148-77; Jasjit Singh, *Nuclear India* (New Delhi: Knowledge World, 1998); Samina Ahmed, 'Pakistan's Nuclear Weapons Programme: Turning Points, and Nuclear Choices', *International Security*, Vol. 23, No. 4, Spring 1999; Akhtar Ali, *Nuclear Politics and the Challenges of Governance* (Karachi: Royal Book Company, 1999); Nasir Ahmad, 'The Atomic Energy Commission', *Pakistan Quarterly*, Vol. 7, No. 3, Autumn 1957; Zalmay Khalilzad, 'Pakistan', in Joseph Goldblat (ed.), *Nuclear Proliferation: The Why and Wherefore* (London: Taylor & Francis, 1985); Samina Ahmed and David Cortright, 'Pakistan's Nuclear Choices', A Special Report by Joan B. Kroc Institute for International Peace Studies and the Fourth Freedom Forum (Notre Dame: Joan B. Kroc Institute for International Peace Studies, 1996); Abdul Sattar, 'Reducing Nuclear Dangers in South Asia', *Regional Studies*, Vol. 8, Islamabad (Winter 1994-5); Herbert Krosney and Steve Weisman, *The Islamic Bomb* (New York: Times Books, 1981); Zafar Iqbal Cheema, 'Pakistan's Nuclear Policies: Attitudes and Posture', in P.R. Chari, P.I. Cheema and Iftekharuzzaman (eds.), *Nuclear Non-Proliferation in India and Pakistan* (New Delhi: Manohar, 1996); General Mirza Aslam Beg, *Development and Security* (Rawalpindi: Foundation for Research on National Development and Security, FRIENDS, 1994); Shahid-Ur-Rehman, *Long Road to Chagai* (Islamabad: Printwise Publication, 1999); Zafar Nawaz Jaspal, 'Reassessing Pakistan's Nuclear Strategy', *Defence Journal*, http://www.defencejournal.com/2001/july/reassessing.htm, accessed on 30 July 2001; Zafar Iqbal Cheema, 'Pakistan's Nuclear Use Doctrine and Command and Control' in Peter R. Lavoy, Scott D. Sagan, and James J. Wirtz, *Planning the Unthinkable: How New Powers will Use Nuclear, Biological, and Chemical Weapons* (London: Cornell University Press, 2000); Ayesha Siddiqa-Agha, 'Nuclear Navies', *Bulletin of the Atomic Scientists*, Vol. 56, No. 5, September/October 2000; Shireen M. Mazari, 'Formulating a Rational Strategic Doctrine', paper available on the website of the Pakistan Institute For Air Defence Studies, available at http://www.piads.com.pk/users/piads/mazari3.html, accessed on 30 August 2001; Lt Gen (Retd) Sardar F.S. Lodi, 'Pakistan's Nuclear Doctrine', *Defence Journal*, available at, http://www.defencejournal.com/apr99/pak-nuclear-doctrine.htm, accessed on 27 July 2001.

question of nuclear stability in Southern Asia cannot be treated in isolation from global nuclear politics. The US-China-India equation constitutes a nuclear chain that has implications for nuclear stability in this region and beyond into the Middle East and North-East Asia. This book attempts to explore the global, regional, and bilateral dimensions of the nuclear issue to understand the fuller dimensions of nuclear stability in Southern Asia.

In this exercise, the role of strategic culture cannot be ignored. While the concept of strategic culture has come under attack from realists,[4] it bears mention that Jack Snyder had introduced the concept of strategic culture in the context of Cold War nuclear deterrence. In a study done for the RAND Corporation, Snyder defined strategic culture as 'the sum total of ideas, conditioned emotional responses and patterns of habitual behaviour that members of the national strategic community share with each other'.[5] Snyder, however, dealt with only strategic decision-making and did not recognize the larger impact of strategic culture on nuclear policy formulation. Ken Booth, in an effort to deepen the concept of security studies, provides a more comprehensive definition of strategic culture. He defined strategic culture as:

> . . . a distinctive and lasting set of beliefs, values and habits regarding the threat and use of force which have their roots in such fundamental influences as geo-political setting, history and political culture. These beliefs, values and habits constitute a strategic culture which persists over time, and exerts some influence on the formation and execution of strategy.[6]

Booth argued that evaluating a nation's strategic behaviour within a purely Realist framework with no input from strategic culture could lead to costly mistakes between rival states. The argument here is for tempering the rational actor theory of nuclear deterrence with a study of policy formulation and decision-making, appreciating local conditions. This is applicable to a discussion on nuclear stability in Southern Asia in the following ways.

Firstly, this is the first triangular nuclear competition in the history

[4] For a critique of strategic culture as a framework for analysing nuclear strategy, see Gerald Segal, 'Strategy and Ethnic Chic', *International Affairs*, Vol. 60, Winter 1984, pp. 15-30.

[5] Jack L. Snyder, *The Soviet Strategic Culture: Implications for Limited Nuclear Operations* (Santa Monica, California; RAND Corporation Report R-2154-AF, 1977), p. v.

[6] Ken Booth and Russell Trood (eds.), *Strategic Cultures in the Asia Pacific Region* (London: McMillan, 1999), p. 4.

of international relations.[7] Secondly, the geo-strategic realities of Southern Asia make it imperative that deterrence operates in an assured manner due to the geographical contiguity of the nuclear rivals. Thirdly, sub-conventional conflicts and cross-border terrorism, which did not exist during the Cold War, are new variables in Southern Asia and intrude into nuclear politics. Finally, with the three nuclear weapons states being under three different political dispensations, the direct application of the rational actor paradigm to this region would be simplistic. Their domestic compulsions and different leadership styles need to be factored into analyses of nuclear policy in Southern Asia. Given these four factors, the experience of the Cold War in managing nuclear deterrence, while not irrelevant, needs to be recast within the South Asian context. Rather than dismiss local conditions as aberrations or as exceptions to the rule, these need to be treated as variables to be investigated and integrated into any discussion of nuclear strategy in South Asia.

In this book, the postures of China, India, and Pakistan, deriving from their historical experience and national objectives, are explored in the context of bilateral, trilateral, and global nuclear politics. Rather than have separate chapters on the three nuclear actors in the region, their interrelationship is the enduring theme throughout this book with specific discussions being undertaken on nuclear doctrine, nuclear deterrence, strategic triangle, nuclear strategy, nuclear safety, and limited war in a nuclear setting.

This book collates the papers presented at a conference on 'Nuclear Stability in Southern Asia' held in New Delhi in April 2002 held jointly by the Institute of Peace and Conflict Studies (IPCS) and the Konrad Adenauer Foundation (KAF). The conference was widely attended by the strategic and diplomatic community in New Delhi, with the active participation of academics and think-tanks concerned with South Asian security. Each of the papers presented at the conference was discussed by a designated discussant, and intensive discussions followed each presentation. The papers were revised thereafter by the paper writers in the light of these discussions.

[7] In Chapter 3, Jasjit Singh argues that the Cold War nuclear competition was essentially between the US and the USSR, with China having disengaged itself from this competition by adopting a policy of minimum deterrence in the face of maximalist positions taken by the superpowers.

Structure of the Book

In Chapter two, Ashley Tellis briefly explores the issues constituting *Nuclear Stability in Southern Asia.* Tellis discusses deterrence stability, crisis stability, arms race stability and technical stability. While conceding that there are no easy solutions to stabilizing the nuclear triangle in Southern Asia, Tellis argues that each aspect of this triangle merits attention to safeguard against the dangers of escalation from sub-conventional to conventional to nuclear conflict. The problem of cross-border terrorism has created a situation of endemic conflict; hence sub-conventional conflicts are a threat to both conventional and nuclear peace in the region. Rather than assuming that deterrence will work based on the logic and principles of the Cold War, their re-examination within the Southern Asian context is urged.

In Chapter three, Jasjit Singh explores the *Nature of the Strategic Triangle in Southern Asia.* According to him, the United States, China, and India are the three main players with Pakistan, the Russian Federation and the European Union (EU) playing subsidiary roles in this triangle. He traces the history of the Cold War US-USSR-China strategic triangle to discuss the parameters of the strategic triangle in Southern Asia. He believes that the post 11 September US military presence in South Asia would contribute to stability in the region. Within the US-China-India triangle, nuclear deterrence would work in respective bilateral dyads leading to nuclear stability in the region. Pakistan's nuclear arsenal, being India-centric, only impacts upon the region in relation to India. It is the US-China-India nuclear equation that needs to be explored.

Chapter four by Rajen Harshe, entitled *Indo-Pakistan Ties and Nuclear Confidence Building in Southern Asia*, identifies the fractious relationship between India and Pakistan, especially the Kashmir issue, as the major source of instability in the region. Identifying China, Afghanistan, and Myanmar as parts of the South Asian geo-strategic region, he outlines the CBMs possible between India and China as well as between India and Pakistan to establish regional nuclear stability. He categorizes the existing CBMs between India and Pakistan into the military-strategic and politico-diplomatic spheres, the latter being of greater significance. He relates nuclear CBMs with the totality of Indo-Pak relations and the composite framework of interstate and inter-societal relations.

Chapter five by Rajesh M. Basrur on *Strategic Stability and the*

Evolution of India's Nuclear Strategy posits Indian nuclear thinking as being predominantly politico-strategic rather than military-strategic, deriving from India's strategic culture that abhors the use of nuclear weapons. Basrur argues that this approach encourages nuclear minimalism. However, this alone cannot ensure nuclear stability, and the operational dynamics of nuclear weapons need to be factored into the policy of minimum deterrence. The failure to comprehend these operational dynamics can seriously undermine India's security and nuclear stability in the region.

Delving into the issue of nuclear safety G. Balachandran, in his chapter on *Nuclear Safety*, probes the links between nuclear safety, smuggling of nuclear materials, and nuclear terrorism. He examines these issues against the backdrop of the renewed focus on nuclear safety in post 11 September international relations. Nuclear safety is also discussed in the light of reports of Pakistani scientists having had links with Afghanistan, and of the right wing forces in Pakistan posing a challenge to the authority of President Musharraf. Balachandran asks the question whether India and Pakistan require special attention in the matter of export controls.

Raja Menon's chapter entitled *Nuclear Doctrine in South Asia* provides a comparative analysis of Western and the Indian (draft) nuclear doctrine. Nuclear weapons operate within doctrinal parameters. Is there such a thing as nuclear doctrine? Did the doctrine follow the bomb? Can Western nuclear doctrines be transported to a culturally, strategically, and politically different Southern Asia? In Chapter seven, Menon seeks to answer these questions.

Karl-Heinz Kamp's chapter on *Nuclear Stability, Deterrence, and Terrorism*, highlights the lessons that can be drawn from the Cold War bilateral nuclear relationship and seeks similarities between this dyadic relationship and the nuclear triangle in Southern Asia. The American-Soviet experience with the problems of maintaining strategic stability during the Cold War fills a strategic gap in the nuclear literature and would impact on the thinking regarding these issues in Southern Asia.

In Chapter nine, P.R. Chari outlines the major issues that emerge in debating nuclear stability in Southern Asia. In his chapter entitled *Nuclear Stability in Southern Asia: An Indian Perspective*, he deconstructs 'nuclear stability' and locates the roots of instability in the Southern Asian region in the post 11 September scenario. He establishes the linkages between the political and strategic aspects of nuclear stability in the region and draws on the history of the Indo-Pak relation to focus on its successive crises to situate the unstable nuclear relationship against the backdrop of continued hostility that characterizes the bilateral relationship.

Continued Pakistani support to cross-border terrorism under the umbrella of nuclear deterrence has led Indian strategists to debate the possibility of a limited war beneath the nuclear shadow. Apart from the 1969 Ussuri river clashes between the Soviet Union and China, the Kargil War remains the only case where two declared nuclear weapon states have engaged in armed conflict. The views of General V.P. Malik, former chief of the Indian Army on limited war, drawn from his experience of the Kargil War operations, are presented in Chapter ten in the form of an interview with him. General Malik speaks about the changes in India's strategic environment after Pokhran II, the possibility of launching and winning a limited military strike across the LoC or the international border into Pakistan, and India's nuclear equation with China.

In conclusion, it must be highlighted that, while not subscribing to the thesis of Southern Asia as a nuclear flashpoint, the governments in the region need to be sensitive to the real dangers of escalation of conflict that could lead to nuclear instability. Establishing formal structures to establish nuclear risk reduction measures should be a priority with the nuclear actors in Southern Asia. The crisis behaviour of the nuclear actors in Southern Asia, especially India and Pakistan, suggests an urgent need for a dialogue to evolve these formal structures. The aggressive statements of leaders of both countries during the long troop deployment along the Indo-Pak border were hardly conducive to establishing an atmosphere in which formal deterrence structures could be evolved. Governments need to make a commitment towards maintaining nuclear stability and not make the threat of use of nuclear weapons a part of their political intercourse.

2

Nuclear Stability in Southern Asia

Ashley J. Tellis

The nuclear tests conducted by India and Pakistan in May 1998 altered the strategic landscape in South Asia. As a result, India altered its status from a 'nuclear capable state' to a declared 'nuclear weapon state'. The Indo-Pakistani nuclear tests of May 1998, however, brought about an 'equilibrium change'[1] rather than a radical transformation of the existing regional strategic environment. This evolutionary development has been increasingly manifested by overt reminders in the form of resumed missile testing, continued acquisition of new delivery systems, steady modernization of supporting infrastructure, and vocal references to continued nuclear weaponization in the Southern Asian region.[2]

After the May 1998 tests, many analysts in India and Pakistan adopted a dismissive attitude to the question of nuclear stability in Southern

* Based on the 'Inaugural Address' delivered at the India Habitat Centre in New Delhi on 18 April 2002 at the conference on 'Nuclear Stability in Southern Asia' organized by the Institute of Peace and Conflict Studies and the Konrad Adenauer Foundation, New Delhi.

[1] The term 'equilibrium change' is borrowed from Morton Kaplan's classic work *System and Process in International Politics* (New York: Wiley, 1957), pp. 6-8, where it refers to any movement that contributes to the achievement of new operating levels in an otherwise stable political system. 'Equilibrium change' thus stands in contrast to 'systems change', which refers to the complete transformation of the 'system of action' itself.

[2] Ashley J. Tellis, 'The Strategic Implications of a Nuclear India', *Orbis*, Vol. 46, No. 1, Winter 2002.

Asia, arguing that it was essentially a non-problem that has been fabricated by the United States to further its non-proliferation agenda. Many Indian analysts also downplayed the challenge posed to that thesis by past Indo-Pak hostilities arguing that:

(i) Indo-Pakistani wars are not really serious affairs but merely small scale conflicts or 'communal riots with armor'.
(ii) Indo-Pakistani wars represent localized conflicts between people of a common stock, common background, and similar worldviews; hence they will invariably remain limited, as numerous civilizational factors would assuredly prevent their escalation to the nuclear level.
(iii) Further, structural factors like wind patterns, which can disperse radioactivity over both attacker and victim, makes for robust nuclear stability in South Asia.
(iv) Finally, Pakistan's geophysical weaknesses are so acute that it will be unable to risk total destruction in any nuclear conflict with India and hence would be deterred from nuclear use in the first place.

All these arguments are too facile to be persuasive *a priori.* Nuclear weapons are, at least formally, new entrants into the region. The issue of nuclear security in Southern Asia remains complex with many dimensions that remain to be untangled. First, the region now hosts three declared nuclear weapon powers, and there is some possibility, however remote, of non-state actors armed with weapons of mass destruction eventually appearing on the stage. In such a context, simple dyadic behaviour patterns are not relevant. Further, there are many drivers propelling the acquisition of nuclear weapons, their deployment, and possible use. These include competing grand strategies, differences in national military capabilities, imperfect awareness of adversary capabilities in many issue-areas, and often, poor leadership quality in the regional states. Finally, there is a general weakness of domestic organizational structures, and the continual intrusion of domestic pressures on matters of high politics. The complex interplay of these multiple drivers and forces almost leads one to despair about the intractability of the problem of nuclear stability in Southern Asia. The following sections identify some of the prospective challenges associated with the problem of ensuring nuclear stability in Southern Asia.

WHAT IS NUCLEAR STABILITY?

The issue of nuclear stability should not become a synonym for 'political temperature'. Rather, it should be assessed in terms of specific criteria, and arguably along the following specific dimensions:

(a) Deterrence stability—which refers to a condition where no change in the existing status quo is possible by the use and application of force.
(b) Crisis stability—which refers to a condition where neither side can obtain any decisive military advantage by a pre-emptive or surprise attack.
(c) Arms race stability—which refers to a condition where neither side feels compelled to react automatically to *every* military acquisition by its adversary to ensure its own security.
(d) Technical stability—which refers to a condition where weapons, materials, systems, and facilities are technically safe from accidental or inadvertent use that could have serious political consequences.

Analysing these different dimensions of stability is complicated because there are many interactions between these dimensions as well as positive and negative 'feedback loops' among them. These complications further increase because dyadic calculations have to give way to multilateral matrices that obtain when the triangular dimension of Southern Asian security competition—(a) India *vis-à-vis* Pakistan and (b) India *vis-à-vis* China—is taken into account.

DETERRENCE STABILITY

Exploring the various dimensions of nuclear stability in Southern Asia further, three aspects of deterrence stability operating in the region must be investigated: (a) nuclear deterrence stability; (b) conventional deterrence stability; and (c) the interconnections between nuclear and conventional deterrence stability.

NUCLEAR DETERRENCE STABILITY

How can general nuclear deterrence stability be preserved in a triangular relationship is a difficult question to answer in practice, although it is easier to answer in principle. In general, deterrence stability requires preserving the security of one's retaliatory reserve under all imaginable circumstances, though what this translates to in terms of force structure, under conditions of triangular security competition, is often difficult to judge. It may be argued with some justification that pure deterrence stability, however, is easiest to obtain under conditions of 'minimum deterrence' if the retaliatory forces available on all sides are oriented primarily towards counter-value targeting. The key problem in Southern Asia is that India needs to construct different force levels *vis-à-vis* China and against Pakistan. In this context, what India may consider to be a minimum force against China could become a 'maximum' force in Pakistan's perceptions. Even if a satisfactory solution to this issue can be found, the vexatious problem of the relationship between the requirements for successful prewar deterrence and nuclear use in the event of deterrence breakdown would still remain unresolved, thus leaving us to wonder whether we are inevitably condemned to choose between the unpalatable alternatives of 'limited nuclear use' and various forms of 'damage limitation'. And, if these alternatives, in fact, bound our choices, can a 'minimum deterrent' stay limited in the Southern Asian context when nuclear capabilities are relatively modest, asymmetrical, and opaque, and when nuclear doctrines are still evolving and are perhaps confused?

CONVENTIONAL DETERRENCE STABILITY

In general, conventional deterrence stability obtains if wars cannot be won decisively—fast. Thanks to the presence of nuclear weapons, we can hope that conventional wars to achieve unlimited aims in Southern Asia are obsolete, at least in the first instance. That leaves us with the challenge of managing limited aims and unconventional wars. Theoretically, conventional wars can be fought for limited aims between nuclear-armed states, although Clauswitz's insight that all wars intrinsically tend towards totality must be clearly recognized. Even if the problem can be managed by robust political control, the temptations of escalation still remain, especially for the losing side, which could use all the weapons available at its disposal if it were in fact uncertain about the assailant's larger political–military intentions or if the thresholds of limited war were not commonly accepted by both sides. Further, the challenges of managing limited wars remain enduring when various forms of cognitive closure handicap the political leadership on one or both sides. Today, more than ever before, India is faced with the conundrum of managing deterrence successfully in the face of various psychological threats to stability in Pakistan—an issue that threatens to undermine the successful management of any limited war in practice. The nature of political control and mutual perceptions of offensive and defensive strategies available to both sides are also crucial here, when viewed against the backdrop of fractious domestic politics and possibly inadequate leadership.

INTERCONNECTIONS BETWEEN NUCLEAR AND CONVENTIONAL DETERRENCE STABILITY

The presence of sub-conventional conflicts under the nuclear umbrella make things even more difficult because the interactions between the 'stability-instability paradox' and the 'principal-agent' problem could generate the kind of strategic instability that we almost automatically reject because of the presence of nuclear weapons. The critical issue in the foreseeable future, at least in the Indo-Pakistan context, will be the interconnections between nuclear peace and sub-conventional conflict, mediated through the issue of conventional deterrence stability. This matter, in turn, requires a better understanding of the relationship between limited aims wars and nuclear deterrence breakdown. As far as this problem goes, the Southern Asian situation is unique because security competition, unlike that obtaining during the Cold War, takes place in the homelands of the competing rivals. The questions of escalation control, war termination, and nuclear deterrence stability then become relevant once again in the final analysis.

It is possible to dismiss all these problems as being beyond the pale of analysis, but their significance makes it imperative that they are critically discussed and not dismissed.

Crisis Stability

Southern Asia is a unique case in that there are no 'ready arsenals' in India and Pakistan (although a pseudo-ready arsenal exists in China). There are two competitive, but still evolving, nuclear dyads with weak triangularity in their nuclear deterrence relationships. But—fortunately—there are no tightly coupled nuclear force structures either within or across the dyads and no hard-target kill capabilities in at least two, if not on all three, sides. For these reasons, much of the contemporary Western literature that bemoans the prospect of 'launch-on-warning' or 'launch-under-attack' nuclear postures in Southern Asia is either misplaced or irrelevant. The critical issue of crisis stability in the region is in fact one of cognitive closure affecting the relevant political leaderships, and to the degree that technical factors matter, the general ambiguity of the alerting process. Over the longer term, more significant 'classical' factors affecting crisis stability could emerge: these include the relative rates of force generation; the prospects of asymmetrical intelligence breakthroughs; the acquisition of new kinds of nuclear weapons capabilities; and the capacity for precision targeting, all of which will play a significant role in affecting crisis stability as the nuclear arsenals on all sides mature.

Arms Race Stability

The challenge here consists of knowing 'how much is enough' in the context of a triangular competition between asymmetrically placed states. This competition, which persists in a dynamic security environment, ensures that the question may never be satisfactorily answered as happened during the Cold War. To complicate matters, there is a further need to explore the dynamics of arms race interactions within *and* between any given dyad in the context of three different scenarios: (a) A is and believes itself to be weaker than B and acts accordingly; (b) A is not weaker than B but believes itself to be so and acts accordingly; (c) A is actually weaker than B but believes otherwise and acts accordingly.

Technical Stability

Technical stability involves matters pertaining to the safety of nuclear infrastructure, nuclear materials, and nuclear weapons. The issue of safety comprises, apart from accidents, the threat from state and non-state actors. The latter threat could also arise from within a state: from dissidents, malcontents, and unstable elements.

There are four main areas of concern relating to technical stability—preventing unauthorized use (which requires technical and procedural safeguards); mistaken authorized use (which may require evaluating the patterns of reconstitution relative to strategic or tactical warning); accidental detonation (which requires scrutiny of the technical quality of the weapons design); and, terrorist seizure (which may require technical and procedural safeguards as well as active defences). There are three issues with respect to each of these four problems that merit further research: First, what is the likelihood of each problem in each of the three relevant countries in southern Asia? Second, what are the consequences of each of these dangers for security *in situ*? And, third, what are the challenges posed by each of these dangers from the viewpoint of catalyzing interstate conflict?

Concluding Remarks

The problem of nuclear stability in Southern Asia represents a very complex and difficult cluster of problems. There is general reluctance to admit this for political reasons, but the assertion that it is a non-issue does not imply the absence of a problem. The difficulties of analysis here often derive from the absence of data, as governments, which have the relevant data, may not wish to share it with private institutions that often are the most capable in analysing it. None the less, private institutions have a role to play; even if they cannot undertake true operations analysis, they need to think conceptually about these problems, acting as 'bellringers' to sound alerts, and to provide pertinent advice that contributes to the making of sound public policy.

3

Nature of the Strategic Triangle in Southern Asia

Jasjit Singh

The concept of a strategic triangle appears to be full of many ambiguities. For example, what strategic capabilities or policies would start to define the nature of relations between three centres of power which could then be defined as a strategic triangle? And what would be the characteristics of capabilities and policy of the three countries forming a triangle that would qualify them to be defined as strategic? Would a balance of power paradigm be the defining principle of a strategic triangle? Many more questions emerge from any attempt to answer the preliminary ones. Given that our intention is to focus on issues relating to nuclear stability, it would be rational to assume that the possession of nuclear weapons with ballistic missiles to deliver them would be the defining precondition for a country to be considered a part of a strategic triangle (or any similar grouping).

Conventional wisdom would have us believe that the interrelationship of the strategic capabilities and policies of China, India and Pakistan would form a strategic triangle in Southern Asia.[1] All three are declared nuclear weapon states even if only one of them falls within the definition contained in the Non-Proliferation Treaty (NPT). But the extent to which a strategic triangle may be seen to have evolved requires closer scrutiny. One example that could be drawn upon for consideration of such a triangle in Southern Asia is the strategic

[1] 'Southern Asia' in this chapter is assumed to broadly cover the region encompassing China, Central Asia, Persian Gulf region, South Asia, Myanmar, Thailand, Malaysia, and Indonesia.

triangle of the US, USSR and China in the period from the 1960s to the 1980s. It would be worthwhile to explore the elements of that triangle, if for no other reason than to identify the parameters against which to undertake our present examination before we embark on an assessment of what is perceived be the new strategic triangle.

The Cold War Strategic Triangle

After the Second World War, when the US began its strategy of containment of communism, the Soviet Union and the People's Republic of China (after the Communist Party took over) were military—strategic allies. During the 1950s the Soviet Union assisted the People's Republic of China (PRC) across the board—politically, economically, technologically and militarily. However, by the mid-1950s, this relationship had started to sour, not in the least because of differences on how to deal with India which had set out to remain a non-aligned democracy but was willing to experiment with a mixed economic model under an inclusive consultative democratic dispensation. The forging of military alliances by the United States in Asia brought the issues into sharper focus, adding to the growing polarization between Moscow and Beijing. In short, by the 1960s, signs of a split between the two communist giants began to be noticeable; and by the early 1960s, when the two superpowers came extremely close to a nuclear conflict over the Cuban missile crisis, the Soviet Union and China had fallen apart after the Soviet Union backed off from providing strategic capabilities that could make China independent of the Soviet Union. Progressive deterioration of relations and new rivalries between China and the Soviet Union culminated in the border war across the Ussuri river in 1969. This provided an opportunity for the US to have a rethink on its recognizing the PRC and the subsequent normalization of relations in the beginning of the 1970s. It is only from about that period onward that some sort of a strategic triangle can be considered to have existed.

The key elements in the nature of the strategic paradigm between the two primary players, that is, the two superpowers, and the third leg of the triangle, China, can be summarized as follows. First, a deep rooted *ideological conflict* dominated political relations and foreign policies of the United States and the Soviet Union. In order to reduce the strength of its opposition the United States gave up its ideological opposition to China in the early seventies. In fact, the US was half-hearted in providing any support to India after the Sino-Indian war of

1962 (which itself was triggered not so much for territory from the Chinese side but on ideological grounds). India, on the other side, was willing to give up its policy of non-alignment in the face of severe challenges to its security. China came into the hypothetical strategic triangle, with the United States no longer targeting it under ideological grounds although it was practising a harsher model of socialism that included the ideology of export of revolutions with violence.

Economic-trade competition of mutual exclusivity and denial comprised the second key element. Trade and technology transfer regimes were established through treaty agreements as well through *ad hoc* regimes and national laws. China was not much of a player in global trade and economic affairs till the end of 1980s by which time the very rationale of the strategic triangle had dissipated.

The third key element was *military confrontation* with a qualitative and quantitative arms race, as was symbolized by the deployment of more than 65,000 nuclear warheads on thousands of ballistic missiles, aircraft, and ships, besides the nearly 1,00,000 main battle tanks, tens of thousands of heavy artillery, and millions of troops in Europe. A low- level military confrontation between China and the Soviet Union on the one side and China and the United States on the other continued through the two decades after the Ussuri river clashes between USSR and China in 1969. But China neither had the techno-economic capability nor did it attempt to engage in an arms race with either of the two superpowers even after the mythical triangle had disappeared.

Fourth, *nuclear strategies* of the two superpowers were based on a maximalist doctrine of first (and possibly early) use of nuclear weapons in case of war. With extensive arsenals on hair-trigger alert, concepts of launch-on-warning and launch-under-attack created a balance of terror where the nuclear weapons and strategy of a third party would have played only a marginal role at the very maximum. China, on the other hand, adopted a strategy of minimum deterrence capabilities with a no-first-use posture, thereby disengaging from the nuclear confrontation between the two superpowers. China's nuclear weapons had little role in a trilateral context as the Chinese would not take sides. This is also one of the reasons why the Intermediate Range Nuclear Forces (INF) Treaty included the Soviet missiles in Asia but China's ballistic missiles were simply not factored in by either side. On the other hand, the nuclear weapons of France and the UK did not play an independent role and instead were a part of the nuclear strategy of the United States and its extended deterrence strategy. The strategic triangle between the

United States, Soviet Union, and China, thus, implied three sets of bilateral deterrence equations among three independent nuclear players.

Fifth, the struggle for *political influence and control* over the developed and developing countries marked the US-USSR relations. The US entered into the NATO alliance and established military alliances such as Central Treaty Organisation (CENTO), South East Asia Treaty Organisation (SEATO) and the US-Japan alliance. The Soviet Union established the Warsaw Pact and entered into a series of peace and friendship treaties with a number of developing countries. Both superpowers engaged in proxy wars essentially fought in the territories of the developing countries. At the same time, they tried to formalize and stabilize their respective spheres of influence through initiatives like the Helsinki Process. China, on the other hand, tried to pursue the path to influence and control through the export of revolutions till the early 1970s. But it soon gave way to engagement of developing countries through political moves and did not enter into any military alliances. In fact, China continued to follow an independent (not very different from India's non-aligned) foreign policy after its break with the USSR.

Sixth, mutually *negotiated arms control* for strategic stability and as an instrument of military strategy in search of competitive advantage characterized the superpower military engagement. Most of these were designed to preserve the specific area of superiority of each superpower while seeking to erode the adversary's capabilities. Strategic stability was sought through measures like the Anti-Ballistic Missile (ABM) Treaty to establish and exploit mutual vulnerability; the Strategic Arms Limitation Talks (SALT) treaties, which sought to define the upper limits to which assets could be built up along with the type of reductions that could be introduced; and the INF Treaty between the US and USSR which became necessary due to the greatly heightened risk of management and control passing beyond human control due to the extremely short flight-time between deployed nuclear missiles on hair-trigger alert. China, on the other hand, stayed almost completely aloof from any arms control and non-proliferation measures as long as the Cold War lasted. The international community also made little effort to engage China in any arms control regimes.

Another key element was co-operation in *non-proliferation measures* applicable to other countries in order to preserve their own capabilities. The NPT was the prime example of many other measures agreed between the two countries.[2] China was a non-player in non-proliferation through the two decades we are addressing. China joined the NPT only in the early 1990s and its commitment to non-proliferation has remained highly questionable.[3] There is credible evidence that it assisted Pakistan in its nuclear weapons programme and supplied nuclear-capable ballistic missiles to it.

Where did China fit into this strategic paradigm? While it is true that China's detachment from the Soviet Union was a net gain for the US, this did not automatically translate into a paradigm that could be interpreted as triangular. The reality is that China played hardly any role in this strategic paradigm even after the 1969 war with the Soviet Union and the détente with the United States. It would be tempting to conclude that China's pre-occupation with the Cultural Revolution was a major factor for its policy of isolationism. But the reality is that China was far too weak in its national power to impact in any meaningful way on the equation between the two superpowers. It certainly had nuclear weapons and a missile delivery system which posed a certain level of existential threat. These placed a level of restraint on the degree and extent of any military threat by any superpower.

It can be argued that China's development (and subsequent curtailment) of its tactical nuclear weapon programme was conditioned on the premise of restraining a localized military confrontation with the Soviet Union (across the disputed frontier) and the United States (especially on the Taiwan issue). But China's nuclear arsenal remained too limited to impinge on the large arsenals of the two superpowers except in a limited defence through deterrence. China reinforced this by its stance of no-first-use thus abjuring an offensive posture for which it did not have the wherewithal in any case. Not only did China pursue an independent foreign policy, it also did not join the key non-

[2] A prime example of how the two superpowers tried to preserve their strategic exclusivity was the rejection of Indian requests for nuclear guarantees (to enable it to sign the NPT) by both the United States and the Soviet Union in 1967 at a time when the US treated the PRC as an enemy and the Sino-Soviet split was complete. Recently declassified US government documents provide fascinating details of the parleys which could have led to India remaining non-nuclear. For a partial account of the negotiations for security guarantees, see Joyce Battle, *National Security Archive Electronic Book No. 6: India and Pakistan—On the Nuclear Threshold*, 1998, available on the website of the George Washington University http:www.gwu.edu.

[3] For example, see *China: The Proliferation Primer*, A Majority Report of the International Security, Proliferation, and Federal Services Subcommittee, United States Senate Committee on Government Affairs, Washington, D.C., January 1998.

proliferation and arms control regimes till the early 1990s, by which time the scenario had changed completely.

The US-USSR-China strategic triangle, which was never a clearly definable paradigm, leave alone being a strong one, started to dissipate during the 1980s with the Soviet Union pursuing Perestroika and its withdrawal from Eastern Europe, improvement of Soviet relations with the United States and the West, and with the Soviets seeking closer relations with China. The Gorbachev phenomenon wiped out whatever faint marks of a strategic triangle, if any, that existed. The collapse of the Soviet Union and the bipolar system that defined the dominant global strategic paradigm removed all traces of any such triangle.

China's economic growth and its impact on the rapid build-up of its comprehensive national power, particularly after the collapse of the Soviet Union, has led to renewed focus on China and its future evolution. Russia remains a much weakened player and has moved closer to China. The power equations between the two appear to have reversed from that of the 1950s with China now being, if anything, the stronger partner in the strategic partnership that the two countries have been seeking in recent years. However, its strategic capabilities remain independent of any bilateral strategic partnership like the one claimed between Russia and China whose ostensible political goal is to oppose US 'hegemony'.

Strategic Triangle in Southern Asia

China developed its nuclear weapons capability and missile delivery systems essentially in order to strengthen its comprehensive national power and to acquire capabilities to oppose what it perceived as the hegemony of the United States and, in a different context, that of the Soviet Union. The central role of its strategic capabilities is to deter the threat and use of nuclear weapons against China rather than the whole range of threats especially that of a conventional military attack. Politically, its nuclear weapons have represented a capability to resist any 'nuclear blackmail'. In conceptual terms it is clear that China has seen its nuclear weapons as a political instrument rather than a military tool to fight a war.

Based on the nature and extent of China's nuclear strategy, including the so-called shift from minimum deterrence to 'limited deterrence', it is possible to conclude that China's nuclear arsenal would have no role in any conventional war unless its vital interests are threatened by the progress of such a war. China already has sufficient comprehensive national power and conventional military capability (which is rapidly expanding qualitatively) to be able to successfully deal with such threats, including those made by the United States. It does not visualize a general all-out war and the likelihood of escalation to a nuclear exchange in a 'local border war' would be extremely limited. Actual war could erupt essentially in three contingencies: Taiwan moves toward independence, instability in Tibet, and escalation of the Sino-Indian border conflict. In the Taiwan scenario, China would be unlikely to forgo its option of using nuclear weapons at an early stage, if not being the first to do so, if it saw Taiwan being permanently lost otherwise. Its assertive use of missile firings in March 1996 indicates the resolve behind its stated policy that the use of force for reunification of China is not ruled out.

PAKISTAN AS A STRATEGIC PLAYER?

What role do Pakistan's nuclear capabilities play in Southern Asia? It is clear that Pakistan's strategic posture is totally India-centric. Barring the broader psychological-political image of a Muslim country also having acquired nuclear weapons, Pakistan's nuclear capability plays virtually no role in Southern Asia except in relation to India. And the significance of Pakistan's nuclear-strategic capabilities is grossly exaggerated in that context.

There is substantive credible evidence of China having supplied nuclear technology and material besides ballistic missiles to Pakistan.[4] Pakistan's nuclear and missile programme has already reached a near-

[4] For China's supplies of ballistic missiles to Pakistan see Pakistan Prime Minister Moeen Qureshi's statement on 26 August 1993, cited in *The Nation*, 27 August 1993; and Foreign Minister Abdul Sattar's statement to the Senate, 26 August 1993, cited in *The Nation*, 27 August 1993 where he stated that 'These missiles were bought keeping in mind Pakistan's security needs', which he went on to justify in relation to missile attacks across the borders from Afghanistan. For an earlier confirmation of Chinese supplies of ballistic missiles to Pakistan, see the address of the Chinese ambassador to USA, Zhu Qizhen to the National Press Club, Washington, D.C., Reuters Transcript Report (27 June 1991) cited in John Wilson and Hua Di, 'China's Ballistic Missile Programs', *International Security*, Vol. 17, No. 2, Fall 1992, p. 37, where he stated that, 'We have sold some conventional weapons to Pakistan, including a tiny amount of short-range tactical missiles. . . .' More recently, Pakistani interlocutors have confirmed that China had supplied M-11s to Pakistan, though modified somewhat to bring them technically under the MTCR limits. *China: The Proliferation Primer*, op. cit., fn. 3.

autonomous status which may not require subsequent Chinese support. The general belief, especially in India, is that this was done as part of China's larger strategy of encirclement and containment of India. But if the overall trend in the Sino-Pakistan relationship is objectively examined, the reality appears to be that China has wooed Pakistan since the mid-1950s to reduce its dependency on the United States and the West. The reasons for which China has supported Pakistan are almost a mirror image of the rationale for the United States to befriend Pakistan. These include Pakistan's strategic location in Southern Asia, its potential capabilities as a Muslim state with its own ambitions to be a leader of the Islamic world, the need to encourage it to maintain an adversarial relationship with the USSR/Russia, and to keep India preoccupied in South Asia rather than seek a broader agenda (like that attempted by Nehru in the early years). It is also significant that the United States brushed aside its own non-proliferation policies and laws to support Pakistan as a frontline state with tacit concurrence, if not approval, since 1981 of its clandestine nuclear weapons programme, a precondition made by Pakistan for playing that role.[5] It is difficult to believe that China did not take into account the reality that Pakistan's nuclearization would make India's nuclearization a greater certainty with consequences for China itself.

The central rationale for Pakistan's acquisition of nuclear weapons has been to deter India's conventional forces.[6] Given the contiguous nature of the two countries and availability of vital targets well within the range of even short-range combat aircraft, its acquisition of ballistic missiles serve a political-psychological purpose besides providing a level of assured penetration of Indian defences. It recognizes that India would maintain conventional superiority, which it would not be able to match, if India decides to engage it in a full-scale military offensive. Pakistan had considered the issue of acquiring nuclear weapons in the 1960s, but the government of Field Marshal Ayub Khan had rejected the proposal to acquire them even after the 1965 India-Pakistan war which had clearly demonstrated that Pakistan would not be able to achieve its political goals of annexing Kashmir through military

[5] General K.M. Arif, *Working with Zia: Pakistan's Power Politics 1977-88* (Karachi: Oxford University Press, 1995), p. 431.

[6] General Mirza Aslam Beg, *The Nation*, 13 December 1993. Also see former Foreign Minister of Pakistan Agha Shahi, in Fasahat H. Syed (ed.), *Nuclear Disarmament and Conventional Arms Control Including Light Weapons* (Rawalpindi: FRIENDS, May 1997, p. 421.

force.[7] Considering that Pakistan reversed earlier decision not to acquire nuclear weapons and decided to pursue a nuclear weapons programme within a couple of weeks of its dramatic military defeat by India in December 1971 would indicate that it had serious concerns of Indian superior military capability being used, at the minimum, to coerce Pakistan under its hegemony, and at the maximum, to dismember the country further, especially by reoccupying the occupied territories of the state of Jammu & Kashmir (which has always been seen as the major threat to Pakistan's survival). India's dramatic military victory over Pakistan both in the eastern as well as the western sector had altered the Pakistani myth of its superiority in arms over India.

Like any other nuclear weapon state, Pakistan may be expected to resort to the use of nuclear weapons if its vital interests, especially its survival, are in serious jeopardy. But, realistically, the circumstances leading to such a situation through an external threat are virtually non-existent. However, given the experience of 1971, when its assumption of a superior fighting capability was exposed with drastic results, Pakistan would no doubt be concerned about the risk of an Indian military advance to liberate the occupied territories by it in the state of Jammu & Kashmir. This may have no relationship with the evidence of five decades which confirms the reality that India has taken no serious steps towards that end from the very beginning and in fact formalized Pakistan's control over these territories through the 1972 Simla Agreement where it committed not to use force to alter the mutually agreed Line of Control (LoC) established under the agreement. The 'sanctity' of that LoC was re-emphasized by India in the summer of 1999. On the other hand, this does not rule out the possibility of a conventional war, including one initiated by Pakistan, that could lead to such a situation.

The Pakistani leadership has emphasized that its nuclear weapons are meant to deter war and maintain peace. This is a tall order. But based on this assumption, and its corollary that India would be deterred from responding militarily, it appears to have grossly miscalculated in launching the 1999 Kargil War.[8] It held out nuclear threats during that war, especially on 31 May 1999. These, if anything, indicate

[7] Ashok Kapur, *Pakistan's Nuclear Development* (Kent: Croom and Helm, 1987), p. 80.

[8] For an analysis of the war see Jasjit Singh (ed.), *Kargil 1999: Pakistan's Fourth War for Kashmir* (New Delhi: Knowledge World, 1999).

that the leadership in Islamabad failed to understand the true significance, especially the attributes and limitations, of nuclear weapons. These are not healthy signs in a nuclear weapon state and also do not constitute a meaningful strategic policy.

In substance, therefore, what is the utility of Pakistan's nuclear deterrence? For India, the Pakistani nuclear arsenal poses an existential threat. However, it is not clear if that forecloses any and all military options for India to pursue its political objectives. This is particularly so in the context of Pakistan's use of sub-conventional war through *jihadi* terrorism since 1988 in Jammu & Kashmir below the nuclear overhang. But there is a clear recognition in India that, in concept, a limited conventional war can be fought and won below the nuclear threshold, provided escalation control is managed. India's Defence Minister had declared that: 'We had understood the dynamics of limited war especially after India declared its nuclear weapons status nearly two years ago. Nuclear weapons did not make war obsolete; they simply imposed another dimension on the way warfare could be conducted.'[9] A strategy of salami-slicing could ensure that no single salami would provoke a nuclear response; and yet, over a period of time, it could significantly alter the political and territorial situation in Jammu & Kashmir. This, however, is not to be lightly contemplated because of the obvious risks involved of miscalculation and loss of control over the situation.

The core conclusion, however, is clear: Pakistan's strategic capabilities play no role as long as there is no conventional war (limited or all-out, local-border or full-scale) between India and Pakistan. Nuclearization provides an elusive status not backed by what constitutes comprehensive power. And the simplest way for India to make Pakistan's nuclear weapons irrelevant is to prevent war from breaking out. There are many ways in which military pressure can be applied without necessarily going to war. As long as India does not initiate a war and, in case a war is thrust upon it, does not attempt any deep incursion or try to rapidly destroy major components of Pakistani military power, it would deny Pakistan the opportunity to resort to nuclear weapons. There is no political interest that requires this. And there is no evidence from the past, even when both countries did not possess nuclear weapons, that India would resort to war to resolve its disputes

[9] Inaugural Address by Defence Minister George Fernandes at the national seminar on *The Challenges of Limited War*, organized by Institute of Defence Studies and Analyses (IDSA) on 5 January 2000 at New Delhi.

with Pakistan. In reality, it was Pakistan which initiated all the wars between the two countries in the past. And if a war does break out, India could be expected to keep it limited to levels well below those that may bring nuclear weapons into this equation. The actual experience since 1987, when Pakistan acquired a credible nuclear deterrent, endorses this conclusion.

On the other hand, Pakistan has to be very conscious of the deterrent capability of India's nuclear and missile arsenal in relation to its size and vulnerabilities. In case of deterrence failure, Pakistan could be expected to launch a first strike with its nuclear forces. However, its targeting philosophy would face the challenge of whether it should focus on India's nuclear arsenal, including its command and control assets. Given India's strategy of assured retaliation, sufficient forces would clearly survive to inflict devastating destruction on Pakistan, decimating its state and society. This is the basic flaw in Pakistan's nuclear strategy, which makes it vulnerable in the light of the Indian nuclear doctrine. Further, Pakistan's economic weakness, political instability, and social turmoil have weakened the country to levels not very different from that of China during the 1970s, which does not support the thesis of it being a strategic player in Southern Asia.

The third leg of the assumed strategic triangle, namely China, is unlikely to play a role in the nuclear-missile paradigm between Pakistan and India. While it did adopt an assertive posture in 1965 during the India-Pakistan war, it remained neutral during the 1971 war and the 1999 Kargil war. If anything, from 1991 onwards its position on the Kashmir issue shifted closer to that of India to resolve this issue bilaterally and peacefully. While China has, in effect, been a strategic partner of Pakistan, it is often ignored that this has much to do with supporting Islamabad to retain greater autonomy with respect to the United States and the West, rather than the conventional view that its aim is to contain India.

The Ace in the Pack

The ace in the pack of strategic paradigm and stability in Southern Asia, however, is the United States. As a global power, it was always present in Southern Asia in some form or the other. As noted earlier, its strategy of containing communism and military alliances in the region also led to China befriending Pakistan which was also part of American military alliances, SEATO and CENTO. The US had a small military presence in Bahrain since the end of World War II. Its naval presence in the Indian Ocean began to expand after the UK withdrew from East of Suez in the 1960s; but after the Vietnam War ended in 1975, its involvement with South-East Asia began to reduce. However, in the 1980s, the United States, while retrenching its presence in East/South-East Asia, started to make a strategic forward shift into continental Asia and the Indian Ocean. By 1983, it had formed the Central Command with a direct military role in the countries of Southern Asia extending west to include the Horn of Africa. The closure of its bases in the Philippines reduced its presence and deployment capabilities in the Pacific Ocean. The formation of the Gulf Cooperation Council (GCC) thereafter provided one of the instruments for regional cooperation in strategic affairs where the US would continue to play a major role.

But it was the 1990-1 Gulf War which led to a major upgradation of the US presence in Southern Asia. The war for Kuwait's liberation fought by the US-led coalition and its aftermath left a substantive US military force deployment in Saudi Arabia. In spite of a substantive retrenchment of US military forces and their deployment abroad, besides the closure of a large number of overseas military bases after the end of the Cold War, a new naval fleet was established for deployment in the Arabian Sea/Persian Gulf region. The strategy of dual containment of Iran and Iraq provided political-strategic strength to most of its regional initiatives. In effect, while the US strategic presence in East Asia reduced, its presence and interests in Southern Asia increased. Now, the war against terrorism after 11 September has brought the United States directly and physically into Southern Asia where its engagement and role is likely to remain deep and strategic for the coming decade if not more. Diego Garcia in the North Indian Ocean has been transformed from being a communications facility in the early years to becoming a launch base for strikes by nuclear-capable strategic bombers into Afghanistan. The bulk of the remaining air operations against targets in Afghanistan were carried out by naval forces deployed in the Arabian Sea. The US has established a military presence in the Central Asian countries and even set up a military base in Jacobabad (not far from the nuclear test site at Chagai in Baluchistan) in the heart of Pakistan from where special operations have been launched into Afghanistan. Since the war against terrorism is likely to take a long time, we may expect the present deployment to continue through the coming decade at least. Looking ahead, it is clear that US interests in the region would deepen, largely because of the potential of oil and gas supply routes across Afghanistan to Pakistan and India now becoming a reality with a friendly government in Kabul and US control over the region.

The erstwhile US-USSR strategic axis has already acquired a new US-China orientation. President George Bush had described China as a 'strategic competitor' for the United States during his presidential election campaign. China has strongly protested against the US Nuclear Posture Review listing China explicitly as one of the targets for a nuclear strike along with other 'rogue states'. This does not mean that the two countries are not seeking closer co-operative relations with each other. The war against international terrorism, in fact, has brought them closer to deal with the challenges posed by ethno-religious terrorism, especially of the *jihadi* variety, although there is a recognition of the underlying tensions and strategic competition between the world's sole superpower and the emerging superpower, the bulk of this competition is currently being played out in Southern Asia and its periphery.

THE GEO-STRATEGIC PARADIGM

In the ultimate analysis, the strategic paradigm would be strongly influenced by the broader geo-strategic paradigm, whose main elements in the coming decades can be summed up as follows:

- The international order has been evolving towards a polycentric configuration with the United States, Russia, the European Union (with France and Germany at its core), China, Japan, and India as the pivotal centres.
- Concurrent competition and co-operation obtains between these centres of power based on national interests.
- Techno-economic capabilities are more likely to dominate international relations rather than military (and nuclear-missile) power.
- International coalition making would become increasingly important in solving conflict situations in the world.
- Nuclear weapons would progressively lose their importance with the increase in the vulnerability of states to conventional war.

STRATEGIC ENVIRONMENT IN SOUTHERN ASIA

The strategic environment in Southern Asia is being heavily influenced by the United States and its policies and presence in the region; its central element is the strategic competition between the United States and China. The US withdrawal from the ABM Treaty and its plans to go ahead with missile defences would accentuate the emerging competitive strategic paradigm. China has been the most vocal in the criticism of US policy and has cautioned it regarding the damage to arms control and strategic stability. The semantics may be less harsh than that between the US and USSR during the Cold War, but the dynamics of what is happening is clear. China sees the US missile defence policy as targeted against it. The National Missile Defences would erode, if not completely nullify, China's small offensive nuclear forces composed of an arsenal of perhaps two dozen Inter-continental Ballistic Missiles (ICBMs) which can target the US. At the same time, Theatre Missile Defences could pose a serious challenge to China's goal of Taiwan's reunification with the mainland. Japan, protected by a defence shield, could adopt a somewhat different policy toward China. There are increasing signs of a revival of thinking in Japan on nuclear weapon issues.

At the same time, because of the US missile defence programme, China would no doubt expedite establishing its countermeasures. China has already been giving greater attention to modernizing its military and nuclear-missile capabilities. The country that would be most affected by China's countermeasures programmes would be India. Firstly, the minimum level in India's 'credible minimum deterrence' nuclear doctrine and capabilities would have to shift upwards if China has even a rudimentary defensive capability. Secondly, China is likely to expand its space capabilities both to support its strategic offensive and its projected defensive capabilities. This would impact on the survivability of India's nuclear arsenal. At the minimum, this would necessitate an expansion of Indian nuclear arsenal. Thirdly, as China moves towards its missile defence capability, India would inevitably have to look for a defensive capability of its own. Thus the United States' strategic policy has a direct bearing on those of China and India, the two major powers in Southern Asia. Pakistan, even in the distant future, would be unable to play any meaningful role in this process.

The China-India strategic equation has a substantive stability largely because both countries have, unlike the two superpowers, adopted a minimalist nuclear doctrine and strategy. There is a strong correspondence between the nuclear doctrine and strategy of the two countries, which is a factor promoting strategic stability. Both countries have adopted a no-first-use doctrine. India's doctrine and strategy, of course, goes much further than the Chinese commitment to no-first-use and relies on what has been termed 'recessed deterrence'. This relies completely on assured retaliation against the adversary's strike rather than a first strike strategy. It, therefore, implies a de-alerted and de-targeted arsenal, which also reduces the risks of accidents and miscalculations. The tensions in bilateral Sino-Indian relations have been kept to the very minimum in spite of the 1962 Sino-Indian war and a long-standing unresolved territorial dispute. The 1996 China-India Bilateral Agreement, especially seen in the context of the four decades old Panchsheel Agreement of peaceful coexistence, commits both sides not to use their military power against each other.

US STRATEGIC PRESENCE

The US strategic presence in Southern Asia has increased dramatically after 11 September 2001. This has naturally raised many questions about the short- and long-term implications of its presence and involvement in the region. While the jury may remain out for quite some time, it is possible to reach certain conclusions and trends flowing out of this development.

As noted earlier, the US presence in Southern Asia should be treated as a semi-permanent phenomenon, if not a permanent one. Going by historical experience, this presence is likely to contribute towards polarization and instability in the region, especially with respect to Indian interests. However, nothing could be farther from reality. A great deal has changed in the world during the past decade. We should, no doubt, expect some instability in future, especially where Cold War mindsets have not altered as yet, and reactions to US policies. But, given the dynamics of US interests in the region now, its presence would contribute predominantly to greater stability.

The potential for instability could, however, increase as a consequence of deepening polarization between the US and China. Both countries have important interests in Central Asia, the Persian Gulf region, and South Asia which range from energy resources to the global competition between the two as future superpowers. To a large measure each has been trying to countervail the other. The increasing US presence and involvement in Southern Asia has already increased the incentive for China to move closer to Russia in a new strategic partnership that aims to neutralize US hegemony. So far, China has countered the US strategic shift into Southern Asia by enhancing its relationship with India despite its unhappiness at being defined as the reason for India's nuclearization in 1998. China is also deepening its relations with other countries in the region. Any increased level of polarization between the US and China, however, would lead to countries in the region having to choose sides, thus involving them in the emerging competition between Washington and Beijing. In an extreme case, we could, at least hypothetically, see a new cold war developing, whose epicentre would be Southern Asia.

Another potential source of instability is the reaction of Muslim populations in the region who tend to see the US not only as hegemonic, but also in terms of an infidel in the holy land and as being anti-Islamic. The revival, resurgence, and extremism of religion has deepened these sentiments which have been the central source of motivation for Osama bin Laden and the Taliban in their war against the United States executed through terror. Ironically, the perception of the US (and by extension the West) as anti-Islamic has been nurtured by the clash of civilizations thesis enunciated by Samuel Huntington.[10] The use of terrorism in the name of religion feeds on such a philosophy where terrorism is rationalized as a weapon of the weak against the great superpower. The reality that terrorism actually targets the weaker element (the innocents) in society is often ignored.

Overall, US presence in the region promises to be a factor of stability. Its oft-repeated position that the problem of Kashmir should be resolved peacefully and bilaterally, which would naturally require dialogue between Pakistan and India (besides the domestic measures required by New Delhi), has been a major shift towards stability. This places the policy objectives of the three most powerful forces in Southern Asia, the United States, China, and India, in consonance with each other. An increasing number of countries, especially the UK, have endorsed the same approach. More important, the United States has on more than one occasion, and at senior levels, asserted that it will not mediate in the dispute although it would be willing to help find a solution whenever India and Pakistan seek its help as a facilitator. Pakistan may feel frustrated by this change and would try hard to seek mediation and intervention of the US, which is unlikely to take place. This, in due course, would nudge Pakistan and India to lower their tensions and look seriously for solutions. Over the longer term this would lead to normalization of India–Pakistan relations, which must have a positive impact on stability even in the broader region of Asia.

[10] Samuel Huntington, *The Clash of Civilizations* (New York: Simon and Schuster, 1996).

Another factor leading to enhanced stability as a consequence of the US presence in the region is its support for the stability, reconstruction, and development of weak, vulnerable, and failed states. The decline and collapse of civil society in Afghanistan and some Central Asian states has reinforced religious extremism and violence. The youth in many countries, especially in Pakistan, faced with a choice between jobs or *jihad*, have opted for militant *jihad* since it has provided emotional satisfaction as well as survival subsistence. Economic reconstruction by aid and assistance, reforms in educational systems away from narrowly focused *madrasas*, changes in the political system envisaging greater participation, and a shift towards greater empowerment of the people are part of the assistance being provided as a consequence of the presence of the United States in the region. These would help to plant the roots of future stability, but also provide the environment for energy supply routes (especially from Central Asia to India) to be laid in the coming years with much greater confidence than earlier.

The US military presence in the region would also provide a dampener for revolutionary changes in the state and society of the Arab countries of the GCC. While its policy of dual containment of Iraq and Iran is a factor for instability in the region, its presence is seen by the GCC countries as a bulwark against any future aggression by Iraq, or even Iran. At the same time, the US presence in the region triggers negative responses among Muslim populations in Arab countries, whilst periodically also providing the stabilizing factor for social-political changes through an incremental and evolutionary process, rather than by any violent change.

Above all, US presence in the region is critical to roll back and wind down the *jihadi* terrorist phenomenon. This would take a long time, but the fact that much of this terrorism is targeted against the US and its interests ensures that the US will remain committed to this task. It has already brought to bear all its strength and power to forge an international coalition against terrorism and expanded the war to a global scale to deal with a transnational networked phenomenon. It has been careful to make the distinction of the war being fought against the phenomenon of terrorism and not against a country or religion and this has ensured the support of Muslim countries, including Pakistan, which has been the fount of religious extremist international terrorism.

In the immediate term, the US presence has helped in applying pressure on Pakistan to reverse its decades old strategy to destabilize India through cross-border terrorism that supports separatism. Islamabad's promises have not yet been translated into practice, leave alone leading to the final cessation of cross-border infiltration and terrorism. But the US presence and pressures is forcing Islamabad to clean up the system within Pakistan and alter its decades old policy of war through terrorism. If continued along its present vector, the US presence and its stick and carrot policy toward Pakistan will prove to be the most significant factor contributing to stability in the region.

Concluding Remarks

In the final analysis, it can be affirmed that a strategic triangle has been emerging in Southern Asia for some time and the present trends indicate its deepened etching on its geo-strategic architecture in the coming decade. The main players in this strategic triangle are the United States, China, and India. Pakistan would only play a marginal role (even after its economic recovery) beyond its existential reality in this process. This, however, should be seen within a larger strategic paradigm since the Russian Federation is also an active player in Southern Asia and clearly has a larger role than Pakistan can ever play. The European Union would remain an active player because of its overall comprehensive capabilities and not necessarily because of the strategic capabilities of France and the UK.

4

Indo-Pakistan Ties and Nuclear Confidence Building in Southern Asia

Rajen Harshe

The trajectories of Indo-Pakistan ties have been virtually defining the nature of interstate relations in Southern Asia over the past five decades. Their relationship has been characterized by diverse kinds of conflicts, which have left their shadow over the entire region. Thus, Indo-Pakistan relations, in particular, and the interstate politics in South Asia, in general, have witnessed protracted ethnic tensions, the emergence of separatist movements, migration of populations, clashes over delineation of interstate frontiers, burgeoning cross-border terrorism, and differences over sharing of resources, especially those related to river waters. These conflicts have adversely affected the prospects of peace in South Asia. In fact, harmonious ties between the two major powers in the region, India and Pakistan, constitute a *sine qua non* for peace and stability in Southern Asia. However, the two countries have already fought three major conventional wars and two minor wars since 1948, and the unresolved conflict over Kashmir has entangled India and Pakistan in a web of ceaseless hostility. Furthermore, there has been a qualitative transformation in the nature of interstate politics in Southern Asia with the advent of India and Pakistan as full-fledged nuclear powers since 1998. In the event of the Kashmir conflict escalating uncontrollably, the possibility of nuclear confrontation between the two adversaries could become real. Averting such an eventuality warrants the initiation of a dialogue process involving Confidence and Security Building Measures (CSBMs), encompassing interstate and inter-societal ties between the two countries. At the same time, such measures would remain ineffective without an analysis of the true nature of the Indo-Pak conflict and a dispassionate exercise to search for its resolution.

Keeping these realities in view, this chapter spells out the configuration of powers that affect interstate ties in Southern Asia. In the process, it examines the divergent policy orientations between India and Pakistan on major issues and the significance of Kashmir in this context. After underscoring the importance of China's role in Southern Asian affairs, the chapter further reflects on Sino-Indian and Indo-Pakistan ties by analysing a number of CSBMs that form part of these bilateral relationships. Further, it explores the prospects for peace initiatives in interstate and inter-societal ties between India and Pakistan in post-nuclear South Asia

Configuration of Powers in Southern Asia

It is not easy to resolve the problem of defining Southern Asia in terms of its geo-strategic space. With the formation of regional groupings like the South Asian Association for Regional Co-operation (SAARC) in the 1980s, the Southern Asian region is being identified with the seven member states of the SAARC, namely, India, Pakistan, Nepal, Sri Lanka, Maldives, Bhutan and Bangladesh. However, a more inclusive view of the region could include countries like China, Myanmar, and Afghanistan. Hence, while defending its territorial integrity, India has been apprehensive about the Chinese support to separatist movements in the north-eastern parts of India, on the one hand, and the Chinese occupied portion of Kashmir, ceded to China by Pakistan after the Sino-Indian war of 1962, on the other. Likewise, China is apprehensive regarding the autonomy of Tibet and the secessionist tendencies in Tibet. In this context, China is inevitably concerned about the presence of a sizeable number of Tibetan refugees, including the Dalai Lama, in India, for the past four decades. Like China, Myanmar too influences the political process in north-eastern India as well as Bangladesh. Finally, Afghanistan links West and Central Asia to South Asia due to its location. In fact, the ongoing problem of Kashmir also has political and religious links with the state and society in Afghanistan. The geographical definition of Southern Asia cannot be confined to the seven SAARC states since China, Myanmar, and Afghanistan are important actors in the South Asian theatre. Obviously, the attitudes and policies of the three latter powers, especially those of China, merit consideration whenever the projects of peace building are initiated in Southern Asia, even though the CSBMs between India and Pakistan are being established at bilateral levels.

Any project concerning CSBMs in Southern Asia can hardly be meaningful without India's active participation since South Asia is predominantly an Indo-centric region. India can easily identify itself with the religious, social, and cultural systems of its neighbours due to the obvious similarities between them and those in India.[1] It has something in common with all its neighbours but they do not share similarities of any magnitude or depth between themselves. Being at the centre of Southern Asia, India can use its resources to promote interstate harmony within the region in its own and the overall interests of the region.

South Asia can also be characterized as an Indo-centric region due to India's overwhelming superior power in relation to its neighbours. A combination of the principal elements of national power has made India a regional hegemon. India's power is based on its vast geographical size, large population, abundant natural and mineral resources, wide and reasonably well developed industrial base, an impressive reservoir of trained manpower, size of its economy, capacities to produce nuclear weapons, and a vibrant democracy. The dominant position of India in South Asia became obvious, especially after the disintegration of Pakistan and the emergence of Bangladesh in 1971. This dominance has contributed towards a divergence of perceptions about India's policies between India and its neighbours. For instance, the strategic community in India tends to construe India's military intervention in its neighbouring countries in defensive terms. However, the smaller and weaker neighbours of India have viewed such intervention in terms of the outward projection and demonstration of India's military might. India's military interventions in Bangladesh (1971), Sri Lanka (1987-90), and Maldives (1988) have only added to the insecurity and fears of Indian

[1] To provide some obvious examples, the Hindu religion is common between Nepal and India. Pakistan, India, and Bangladesh have a sizeable Muslim population. The people of Tamil ethnic origin constitute an important ethnic minority in Sri Lanka while Tamil speaking people predominantly reside in Tamil Nadu in India. Furthermore, in addition to the Bengali language, the people of Bangladesh and those from the state of West Bengal in India share common cultural and linguistic ethos. Likewise, the people of Pakistan share the Urdu language with Urdu speaking people in India and there is much in common culturally between the Pakistani and Indian parts of Punjab.

hegemony amongst its neighbours. Apropos Pakistan has shown a relentless determination to resolve the Kashmir question in its favour after its disintegration in 1971 following the birth of Bangladesh. It has gone so far as to use militant outfits to indulge in cross-border terrorism to disturb the post-1971 status quo. In order to appraise the Indo-Pakistan ties, it would, therefore, be necessary to place certain main differences in the policies of India and Pakistan in perspective.

Divergences in Policies of Pakistan and India

There have been several differences between India and Pakistan in their policies towards religion, polity, and external relations. The genesis of the tension-ridden ties between India and Pakistan can be traced to the fundamental issues that led to the partition of the subcontinent in 1947. In essence, Pakistan emerged as a separate state on the basis of the two-nation theory endorsed by the Muslim League. Since religious considerations provided the very *raison d'être* of Pakistan, the Muslim League construed areas with predominantly Muslim population as obvious spaces within which to build Pakistan. Consequently, Pakistan emerged as a geographically non-contiguous Islamic state. Over 1200 miles of Indian territory separated its two wings, namely East and West Pakistan. Till the birth of Bangladesh in 1971, Islam and the paranoia generated by Pakistan's asymmetrical power relationship with India had kept both wings of Pakistan together. With the emergence of Bangladesh, the paranoia of Pakistan towards India became even more acute. Furthermore, Pakistan's military has always played a decisive role in Pakistan's polity. Its mode of governance has alternated between democracy and military dictatorship since its inception. Finally, in its external relations, Pakistan had joined US sponsored pacts like the South East Asia Treaty Organisation (SEATO) and Central Asia Treaty Organisation (CENTO) established in the context of the Cold War and has enjoyed the consistent moral and material backing of the US. After the new Cold War began following the Soviet intervention into Afghanistan in 1979, the US opted to treat Pakistan as a frontline state in its strategy to repel the Soviet presence. Pakistan has now become an important member of the US led coalition against terrorism since October 2001.

In contrast to Pakistan, the socially plural settings of India's secular nationalism had been creatively pressed into service as an effective mode of state and nation building in the initial decades after India's independence. Over the years, its distinguishing features like civilian supremacy backed by a stable democratic polity and secularism have characterized India's polity. However, secularism is becoming an increasingly contested notion over the last decade with the rise of Hindutva forces. Unlike Pakistan, India has been fairly consistently following a policy of non-alignment in its external relations. The policy of non-alignment permitted India to judge every issue on its merits and retain a measure of autonomy in managing its international affairs during the context of the Cold War. But in the post-Cold War world, the policy of non-alignment has lost its former significance; India is now working through international coalitions and multilateral formations to attain its policy objectives, and is collaborating with the US led international coalition to combat terrorism.

In view of the above-mentioned divergences in domestic and foreign policies, conceiving harmonious ties between India and Pakistan has been a difficult task. The interests of the two countries have clashed in several areas including the demarcation of an international frontier, the sharing of water resources, the handling of the question of refugees on either side, and the status of states like Junagadh, Hyderabad and Kashmir. Among these several controversial issues, the eventual resolution of the Kashmir problem has appeared distant. It would be worth underscoring the strategic significance and the stakes of the contending parties in Kashmir to understand the crux of the dissonant ties between India and Pakistan.

Kashmir's Changing Strategic Significance

Being the source of the vital Indus river water system constituting the five rivers of Punjab, namely the Jhelum, Chenab, Ravi, Beas, and Sutlej, Kashmir's significance for the predominantly agrarian economies of South Asia can hardly be underestimated. The Kashmir Valley has also been strategically important because of the communication links that it provides to the regions of Ladakh and Siachen. In fact, Kashmir began to enjoy enhanced strategic significance in the context of the Cold War dynamics, given that, it shared common frontiers with India, Pakistan, Afghanistan, China and the former Soviet Union. Even after the Cold War, due to its location, Kashmir has become a gateway to South, South-West, and Central Asia; Kashmir, therefore, inevitably has been affected by major developments in these regions. They include the flow of arms and drugs, the growth of cross-border terrorism, and the rise of a host of fundamentalist movements that are promoting Islam. Due to these movements, religion based terrorism has become an important feature in the political landscape of several Central, West, and South-West Asian states.

Kashmir has become a hotly contested area between Pakistan and India, and has become an integral part of the state formation and nation building processes in both countries. Pakistan continues to perceive itself as an incomplete state devoid of strategic depth, without the accession of Kashmir, a state with a predominantly Muslim population, being included within its territorial limits. In contrast, India fears that the project of building a secular nation in India would receive an irretrievable setback if India were to lose Kashmir. In addition to Pakistan and India, China has also become an involved actor in Kashmir after acquiring territory ceded by Pakistan following the Sino-India war of 1962. Thus, three nuclear powers, namely India, Pakistan, and China—have developed important stakes in Kashmir. Consequently, any worthwhile attempts at nuclear confidence building in Southern Asia will be shaped by the triangular relationship between India, Pakistan, and China. The section below proceeds to untangle this triangular relationship by identifying the role of China in Southern Asia and underscoring the significance of CSBMs between India and China, quite apart from such measures conceived of in the Indo-Pakistan context.

China's Role in Southern Asia

China, as a major nuclear power in the world, has shaped the contours of interstate ties in Southern Asia. China shares a long frontier with India. A Line of Actual Control (LAC) exists between the two countries although the territorial boundary between them has not yet been demarcated to the mutual satisfaction of the contending parties. For instance, besides occupying a large portion of north-eastern Ladakh in the western sector of India, the Chinese have always treated Arunachal Pradesh in the eastern sector as an integral part of China. Consequently, they protested when Arunachal Pradesh was conferred statehood within the Indian Union in 1986. When Indian army units were deployed in 1986-7 in the Sumdorong Chu valley in Arunachal Pradesh, China, in a retaliatory move, also stationed its troops in the valley, which raised the prospects of a Sino-Indian war. India's major military exercise through

Operation Checkerboard in 1987 and Chinese attempts to reinforce the border kept the relationship between the two countries tense.[2] Furthermore, China has been equally concerned about the status of Sikkim and Tibet. It condemned the merger of Sikkim within the Indian Union in 1975, and securing the Indo-Tibetan border has always been China's important long-term strategic objective. In spite of Tibet's integration with China, the secessionist tendencies among the Tibetans and the presence of the Dalai Lama and a host of Tibetan refugees in India has always been perceived by the Chinese as threats that can undermine China's security and territorial integrity.

Likewise, India is apprehensive of China's role in Kashmir, Tibet, and North-East India on the following counts. First, China has been holding on to a part of Kashmir's territory since 1962. The Sino-Pak understanding on Kashmir has obviously had security implications for India, which needs to hold on to Kashmir to press its claims over the Aksai Chin region of Ladakh and ward off any threats to the Punjab. Conversely, as Ramesh Thakur has put it, the loss of all of Kashmir to India would deprive Pakistan of land links with its most important Asian ally and threaten its presence in the strategically vital regions on the border of Afghanistan and China.[3] Second, China also has provided assistance to Pakistan in its missile programme.[4] It has reportedly supplied M-11, M-9, and Ghauri missiles to Pakistan.[5] In fact, China has not only supplied weapons grade uranium to Pakistan but also deployed, according to the claims of Indian military officials, intermediate range ballistic missiles (IRBMs) in the Tibetan plateau.[6] Thus, aid to Pakistan and deployment of the IRBMs in Tibet has underscored China's military presence on India's doorsteps. Finally, Myanmar has been a beneficiary of Chinese military aid since the advent of the

[2] Kanti Bajpai, 'Conflicts, Cooperation and CSBMs with Pakistan and China: A View from New Delhi', in Sumit Ganguly and Ted Greenwoods (eds.), *Mending Fences: Confidence and Security Building Measures in South Asia* (New Delhi: Oxford University Press, 1997), pp. 15-43.

[3] Ramesh Thakur, *The Politics and Economics of India's Foreign Policy* (New Delhi: Oxford University Press, 1994).

[4] Amitabh Mattoo, 'India's Nuclear Status quo', *Survival*, Vol. 38, No. 3, 1996, pp. 41-57.

[5] P. K. Vasudeva, 'Diplomacy is fine but we need action', *Indian Express*, 4 May 1999.

[6] Waheguru Pal Singh Sidhu, 'Enhancing Indo-US Strategic Cooperation', Adelphi Paper 313 (New York: Oxford University Press, 1997).

military dictatorship in Yangon in 1988.[7] Both Myanmar and China have been abetting the insurgency in the north-eastern parts of India. China also has a defence supply and training links with Bangladesh,[8] via which China can inscribe a naval presence in the Bay of Bengal. Taking note of the presence of China in different sectors of the Sino-Indian border and the growing Sino-Pakistan friendship, India has strived to contain the individual and joint actions of Pakistan and China that could jeopardize its security interests.

While protecting its security interests, initiating a process of détente and entering a dialogue process to counter these adverse ties can also form a viable strategy. In fact, India had initiated a process of détente with China in the 1980s itself. Rajiv Gandhi's visit to China in December 1988 was a landmark event in this process, and it paved the way for the establishment of Joint Working Groups (JWGs) between India and China to resolve the long-standing Sino-Indian border dispute in a mutually satisfactory manner. In the 1990s, both countries were involved in a dialogue. By initiating official level talks they opted to resolve the outstanding border-related differences between the two countries through these JWGs. The CSBMs renegotiated through the JWGs led to agreements between the two countries being reached in 1993 and 1996. For instance, the 1993 Agreement on Peace and Tranquillity on the Border, brought about greater transparency in military positions and activities along the LAC. The 1996 Agreement on Confidence Building Measures in the Military Field along the Line of Actual Control in the India-China Border Areas, promoted CSBMs and both parties decided to refrain from using military force against each other.[9] Due to these CSBMs, the communication channels established between the two countries have brought about military stability and the possibility of the use of conventional or nuclear weapons by either side has become remote. The CSBMs have also offered a forum to resolve the border dispute, albeit at a slow pace.

However, the normalization of Sino-Indian ties achieved by the government under P.V. Narasimha Rao (1991-6) suffered a momentary

[7] Sujit Dutta, 'Developing Confidence and Security in South Asia: A New Political Agenda', in Dipankar Banerjee (ed.), *South Asia Security: Futures* (Colombo: Regional Centre for Strategic Studies, 2000), pp. 13-26.

[8] Ibid.

[9] Alka Acharya, 'India-China Relations: An Overview', in Kanti Bajpai and Amitabh Mattoo (eds.), *The Peacock and the Dragon: India-China Relations in the 21st Century* (New Delhi: Har Anand Publications, 2000), pp. 168-98.

setback after the Pokhran II explosions of 1998 undertaken by the Bharatiya Janata Party (BJP) led regime. While going nuclear, India's then Defence Minister, George Fernandes, explicitly identified China's growing nuclear capabilities as a major source of threat for India's security. The JWG did not meet after May 1998. However, by early 1999, it was clear that the two powers would restore the status quo ante, at the height of the Kargil War (May–July 1999) between India and Pakistan the JWG met and the Chinese also proposed the institution of a security dialogue.[10]

The CSBMs established between India and China have had a positive but slow impact on relations between the two countries. Certain significant factors such as the consistent growth of bilateral trade between India and China since the early 1990s, high-level political visits and meetings, and co-ordination of positions in multilateral forums have continued to sustain the diplomatic engagement between the two countries. Also, their convergence of interests on issues such as the fight against terrorism, apprehensions about the eastward expansion of the US-led North Atlantic Treaty Organisation (NATO), and US humanitarian intervention in former Yugoslavia began to build affinities between the two countries. For instance, the Chinese military strategists drew a direct connection between Kosovo, Taiwan, and Tibet, while India became concerned about Western humanitarian intervention in Kashmir.[11] Thus, India has been able to adequately handle its multi-layered relationship with China after initiating a CSBMs process in the 1990s. However, exploring fresh pathways towards confidence building between India and Pakistan has proved to be a far more challenging task.

Exploring CSBMs between India and Pakistan

Since the independence of India and Pakistan in 1947, the trajectories of India-Pakistan ties have continued to defy prospects of peace and stability in Southern Asia. The deadlock over the Kashmir issue has and is likely to continue and restrict the scope of the CSBMs between

[10] Kanti Bajpai, 'India, China and Asian Security', in Kanti Bajpai and Amitabh Mattoo (eds.), *The Peacock and the Dragon: India-China Relations in the 21st Century* (New Delhi: Har Anand Publications, 2000), pp. 26-49.

[11] Raju G.C. Thomas, 'India's Nuclear and Missile Programs: Strategy, Intentions, Capabilities', in Raju G.C. Thomas and Amit Gupta (eds.), *India's Nuclear Security* (New Delhi: Sage Publications, 2000), pp. 87-122.

the two countries. CSBMs can be explored and initiated only by coming to terms with the reality that their impact on the bilateral ties between India and Pakistan will be gradual. The content of these measures for analytical convenience can be discussed under three interrelated spheres comprising of the military-strategic, political-diplomatic, and developmental spheres.

MILITARY–STRATEGIC SPHERE

In military–strategic terms, a sense of insecurity accompanied by mutual suspicions regarding the intentions of the adversary has fuelled an arms race between India and Pakistan. As the weaker and smaller neighbour, Pakistan has been obsessed with guarding its sovereignty and territorial integrity. Hence, it has obtained weapons from the US, and sought military and technological aid and co-operation from China while building its nuclear programme. For its part India, too, obtained Soviet/Russian military assistance and weapons to counter Pakistan and China. Despite the arms race thus initiated, both countries were prudent enough to initiate nuclear confidence building measures as early as December 1988. For example an agreement was signed between the two countries in Islamabad on 31 December 1988 on 'Prohibition of Attack against Nuclear Installations and Facilities'. Each party is committed thereunder to refrain from attacking nuclear installations or facilities in the other country. The term nuclear installation/facility includes nuclear power and research reactors, fuel fabrication, uranium enrichment, isotope separation, and reprocessing facilities. Further, both contracting parties are required to exchange information on the lists and precise locations of their nuclear installations on 1 January of each year. The agreement came into effect after its ratification in 1992. Each side reportedly left out one enrichment facility each when the lists were exchanged in 1992.[12] In addition to these nuclear CSBMs, some other agreements between India and Pakistan such as the 1991 Agreement on Advance Notification of Military Exercises and Troop Movements, the 1991 Agreement on Prevention of Air-Space Violations and Promoting Over Flights and Landing by Military Aircraft and the 1992 Joint Declaration on Complete Prohibition of Chemical Weapons (now subsumed in the

[12] Shireen M. Mazari, 'Developing and Enhancing CSBMs in South Asia', in Dipankar Banerjee (ed.), *South Asian Security: Futures* (Colombo: Regional Centre for Strategic Studies, 2002), pp. 26-33.

Chemical Weapons Convention) could be viewed as détente promoting measures.

Irrespective of these positive measures, outstanding issues, especially the Kashmir question, have continued to aggravate tensions between the two countries. India has opted to build its nuclear arsenal or minimum credible nuclear deterrent to protect its national interests against possible security threats from China and Pakistan. In fact, India cited the possible threat from China when India went nuclear, while Pakistan went ahead with its nuclear tests as a reaction to India's Pokhran II tests in 1998. Pakistan could balance India's conventional superiority by thus going nuclear. In the case of India, the proponents of an overt nuclear policy claimed that India's going nuclear had strengthened its security in an environment of growing nuclear threats (China and Pakistan) while the critics began to harp on the unaffordable nuclear programme that had opened up avenues of nuclear confrontation, especially with Pakistan.[13] In substance, as India and Pakistan became nuclear powers, the threat of nuclear war became real in the tension-ridden ties between the two countries.

Despite going nuclear, however, the residual and inconvenient questions of the past continue to saddle planners of military strategy in India and Pakistan with anxious moments. For instance, will India, even if it went nuclear due to China, ever be able to match the Chinese in the nuclear sphere in the foreseeable future? Will it ever be able to successfully counter China's possible aggression? Furthermore, has the status of a nuclear power helped India to deal with the ongoing insurgencies, especially in Kashmir and the North East? In fact, the insurgency or sub-conventional war initiated by the terrorist outfits of all hues defies the normal logic of war. This is highlighted by such events as the hijacking of Indian Airlines flight IC-814 from Kathmandu to Kandahar in December 1999, the attack on the Indian Parliament on 13 December 2001, and several other terrorist attacks sponsored by the Inter-Services Intelligence of Pakistan (ISI). The dynamic modes of sub-conventional warfare, as witnessed in a wide variety of terrorist attacks, would require the armed forces personnel to continuously undergo re-training before they could be able to defend civilians against these terrorist onslaughts. Pakistan, apart from gaining the psychological satisfaction of becoming India's strategic equal after its nuclear tests,

[13] Rajesh Basrur, 'Nuclear Weapons and India's Strategic Culture', *Journal of Peace Research*, Vol. 38, No. 2, April-June 2001, pp. 181-91.

has made little headway in achieving its strategic aspirations. Even though Pakistan has patronized diverse terrorist outfits, the government of Pervez Musharraf has been constrained to proclaim a war on the Taliban regime in Afghanistan and forced to follow the US lead by joining the international coalition against terrorism after September 2001. Ironically, the Taliban regime (1994-2001) could only survive due to its sustained support by Pakistan. What is more, the terrorist outfits that had earlier benefited from the ISI support are threatening to undermine the political stability of Pakistan and the Musharraf regime itself. In the long run, creative strategies have to be jointly evolved at the political level by India and Pakistan to fight sub-conventional wars. In essence, the status of India and Pakistan as nuclear powers has not made any material difference to curbing sub-conventional warfare.

In contrast, the negative impact of their newly acquired nuclear status has become evident. Both India and Pakistan have attracted the attention of outside powers including the US, Western Europe, and Japan. While restraining the arms race in the subcontinent, the US, being a guardian of the non-proliferation regime, had gone so far as to impose sanctions against both the countries.[14] Moreover, embracing military strategies such as a massive build-up of sophisticated weapons and the amassing of troops at the border, and even contemplating war as an instrument of national policy highlights the inability of Pakistan and India to normalize their ties at the political level. In the past, the two countries have fought three conventional wars in 1948, 1965 and 1971. They have also been fighting a minor war to gain control over the Siachen glacier since 1986 and have fought a war in Kargil in 1999. In spite of all these wars, the prospects of peace and stability have eluded Southern Asia. Perhaps, the key to peace needs to be sought in the political-diplomatic sphere.

POLITICAL-DIPLOMATIC SPHERE

In the political-diplomatic sphere, the CSBM measures initiated are of utmost importance. In spite of protracted tensions, India and Pakistan have also had a history of resolving disputes through successful negotiations. Some examples of these are the transfer of official assets (1948), Agreement on Refugee Compensation (1950), the Protection of Minority

[14] For US policy towards nuclear India, see Gaurav Kampani, 'In Praise of Indifference Towards India's Bomb', *Orbis*, Vol. 45, Issue 2, Spring 2001, pp. 241-58.

Communities (1950), and settling of territorial claims on the eastern and western borders.[15] Furthermore, the two countries, through the mediation of the World Bank in 1960, effectively decided the issue of the sharing of the Indus waters. Likewise, after the 1965 war, the two countries agreed to normalize their relations by signing the Tashkent agreement mediated by the Soviet Union in 1966. They have also contemplated signing a no-war pact and before the two countries went nuclear in 1998, Pakistan was seeking to transform South Asia into a Nuclear Weapons Free Zone with the support of the international community.[16] Furthermore, after the Peaceful Nuclear Explosion (PNE) conducted by India in 1974, Pakistan offered a series of proposals, viz., joint declaration renouncing nuclear weapons (1978), mutual inspection of nuclear facilities (1979), and simultaneous accession to the Nucler Non-Proliferation Treaty (NPT) and the International Atomic Energy Agency (IAEA) safeguards (1979).[17] India ignored these proposals because they lacked credibility. They also overlooked India's concerns about the Chinese nuclear weapons. Moreover, India has always resisted any formal third party involvement between the two countries, especially after the Simla Agreement of 1972. The Lahore Declaration of 1999 and the Agra Summit of 2001 was sought on this bilateral basis. However, the former was followed by the Kargil War later in 1999, whilst the latter failed to achieve any concrete results. Thus the history of seeking a peaceful resolution of the outstanding problems between the countries has been one of mixed results. It would be pertinent to concentrate here on the Lahore and Agra Summits since they were held in the post-nuclear South Asia.

During the Lahore Summit (1999) both countries had consciously worked to avert any possibility of nuclear confrontation. Their leadership demonstrated an inclination to promote diverse ties between the two countries, symbolized their bus diplomacy.[18] Besides, in Lahore, by paying a visit to Minar-i-Pakistan, a symbol of the permanence of the creation of Pakistan, Prime Minister Vajpayee paid respect to the notion

[15] Kanti Bajpai, 'Conflicts, Cooperation and CSBMs with Pakistan and China: A View from New Delhi', in Sumit Ganguly and Ted Greenwoods (eds.), *Mending Fences: Confidence and Security Building Measures in South Asia* (New Delhi: Oxford University Press, 1997), pp.15-43.

[16] Ibid., p. 20.

[17] Ibid.

[18] The Prime Minister of India went by bus from Delhi to Lahore and inaugurated the transport service, i.e. Delhi-Lahore, Lahore-Delhi bus service between the two countries.

of Pakistan as a state.[19] The declaration signed in Lahore between India and Pakistan identified specific areas to ensure stable peace between the signatories. These areas can be summarized as follows:

1. The two sides will engage in bilateral consultations on security concepts and nuclear doctrines to negotiate CSBMs in the nuclear and conventional fields and to avoid conflicts.
2. The two sides will provide each other with advance notification in respect of ballistic missile flight tests.
3. The two sides committed themselves to reduce the risks of accidental or unauthorized use of nuclear weapons under their control.
4. The two sides would ensure safety of navigation and sign an agreement to prevent the occurrence of incidents at sea.
5. There will be a periodic review of CSBMs and promotion of appropriate mechanisms to strengthen them.
6. The signatories committed themselves to review the existing communication links between their director generals of military operation.
7. The two sides will engage in bilateral consultations on security, disarmament, and non-proliferation issues.[20]

In substance, the Lahore Declaration was a manifestation of intent to build nuclear confidence. Irrespective of these measures, however, India failed to persuade Pakistan to adhere to a no-first-use agreement.[21] As Pakistan has kept open its option of first strike with nuclear weapons, the possibility of a conventional war escalating into a nuclear war cannot be ruled out. This has underscored the imperative to establish comprehensive verification mechanisms to detect any breach in CSBM agreements. In the ultimate analysis, it is the citizens on either side who are going to be affected by the use of nuclear weapons. That is why inclusion of a human security paradigm in the discourse on nuclear

[19] Agreement on the Prohibition of Attack Against Nuclear Installations and Facilities signed on 31 December 1988 in Islamabad between Foreign Secretaries of Pakistan and India See www.acdis.uiuc.edu/homepage_docs/Link.docs/Treaty.docs/nucl hrtml-3k, *Asian Recorder*, Vol. 45, No. 14, 2-8 April 1999, pp. 28018-19.

[20] See the text of Lahore Declaration, 21 February 1999 published in *Peace Initiatives*, Vol. 6, No . 4, July-December 2000, pp. 228-31. See the summary of the Declaration and report on Vajpayee's visit to Pakistan in *Asian Recorder*, Vol. 45, No. 14, 2-8 April 1999, pp. 28018-19.

[21] Stephen Cohen, *India Emerging Power* (New Delhi: Oxford University Press, 2001).

stability in Southern Asia is essential.[22] Establishing appropriate military-to-military links at the political level could strengthen this element of human security. However, owing to the lack of civilian supremacy and the military's preponderance in Pakistani polity, these CSBMs are unlikely to make much headway at this juncture.

Furthermore, the Lahore Declaration stood for the resolution of outstanding issues, including Kashmir; however, complex questions like Kashmir seldom get resolved through declaratory statements. Such questions require a mutual determination on the part of the contending parties to work for the peace-building project on a long-term basis. And, before initiating such a process, the preparatory groundwork needs to be laid down to initiate a dialogue at the interstate and inter-societal level. The Lahore Declaration was not preceded, moreover, by any peace-building initiatives that had taken root in the societies of the two countries.

In fact, the impact of the Lahore Declaration was very short-lived, as it was immediately followed by the Kargil War, which provided a grim reminder of the fact that the crucial issues surrounding Kashmir will continue to escape easy solutions. India could achieve an important gain, however, after the Kargil War, since Pakistan failed to get any sympathy from the international community on its position regarding Kashmir. Even China refrained from supporting Pakistan's misadventure in Kargil as Islamic terrorist outfits were supposedly backing this effort, and China has itself been involved in fighting Islamic fundamentalists in its Xinjiang province. Hence, it could not have supported the Islamic militant groups in Pakistan. The lack of support to Pakistan from the international community, however, has not been able to contain the ISI sponsored cross-border terrorism effectively.

Ever since the Kargil War, India has been anxious to curb cross-border terrorism. It has repeatedly sought to mobilize world public opinion against ISI sponsored terrorist activities into India. During the Indo-Pak summit held at Agra in July 2001, India insisted on the withdrawal by Pakistan of its support to all terrorist activities before a solution to the Kashmir question could be discussed. However, Pakistan

[22] Human security has by now emerged as a paradigm. It is not confined to developmental processes alone but it encompasses comprehensive security from fear, ignorance, poverty, conflict, and social and cultural deprivation. See P.R. Chari, 'International Security Environment', in Dipankar Banerjee (ed.), *South Asian Security: Futures* (Colombo: Regional Centre for Strategic Studies, 2001), p. 22.

held the view that the people of Kashmir are victims of India's state terrorism and that they have launched a war of national liberation against India. General Musharraf has been keen to get the support of the United Nations or mediation of third parties including the US to resolve the crisis,[23] while India wants to confine the resolution of the Kashmir issue within the framework of bilateralism.

The post-Agra deadlock between the two countries has shown signs of change after the terrorist attacks in the US on 11 September 2001 and the attack on the Indian Parliament on 13 December 2001. Ever since, Pakistan, under international pressure, has taken steps to ban the notorious terrorist outfits like the Jaish-e-Mohammed and Lashkar-e-Toiba. The Musharraf regime is ready to resume a dialogue with India on all major issues including Kashmir. The process of de-escalation, according to him, can commence after the announcement of an immediate ceasefire on the Line of Control. However, Musharraf has refused to concede the Indian demand to hand over 20 wanted criminals/terrorists to India on the grounds that the Government of India has not provided sufficient evidence against them.[24]

Indeed, a positive response to Pakistan's offer from the Indian side would set the scene for a dialogue between the two countries. The CSBMs that could be fianlized through this dialogue need to be conceived of in creative ways and by gradually establishing preconditions essential to promoting harmony. After all, the sensitive military issues involved in CSBMs can only be negotiated within a conducive political environment. In this context both parties can contribute to such an environment in their own ways. First, the communal violence in Gujarat in February-March 2002 has once again driven home the point that only secular practices can hold together the socially plural society of India. The Vajpayee regime will have to rise above the narrow confines of the Sangh Parivar to actively promote and revitalize secular causes and forces.[25] However, it may be inappropriate to single out and dub only the BJP and its allies as communal parties in contemporary India. Most political parties, to different degrees and under different conditions, have exploited communal sentiments to bolster their electoral prospects. However, without promoting a secular ambience, India will be unable to negotiate with Pakistan with the required moral strength. It is for

[23] See extensive interview in *The Hindu*, 1 April 2002.

[24] Ibid.

[25] Here secularism would imply disallowing any religious/communal considerations to have an impact on the outcome of any vital decisions.

this reason that civil society organizations will have to confront communal attitudes whipped up by different parties and forces. Second, if Pakistan is unable to deal with Islamic extremism it can at least work towards bringing about military stability. It is in Pakistan's hands to reduce the incidence of military attacks in Kashmir, contain terrorist strikes, and hand over some of the wanted terrorists/criminals out of the list of 20 to India.

Third, the debate on nuclear confidence building needs to be conducted at the level of specialists, but also at the popular level. Nuclear scientists, military leaders, and specialists in strategic affairs are responsible, by and large, for the enunciation of nuclear policies. If specialists in these areas from both the countries are brought to the table they could work out the technicalities of nuclear confidence building measures in a competent manner. At the same time, since the population from both countries would be affected by these nuclear policies, framing them cannot become the exclusive preserve of specialists, for nuclear questions do broadly fall within the realm of governance that is related to human security. Any democratic mode of governance demands accountability and transparency. Admittedly, in sensitive security areas it is not easy to be transparent, but specialists have to simplify the substance of their proceedings to reach out to a larger number of people. The debate on nuclear confidence needs to be taken to the people of both countries through the English and the vernacular press to raise the level of awareness about the likely dangers of escalation of conflicts.

Fourth, intergovernmental relations play a primary and decisive role in shaping bilateral ties. However, inter-societal organizations like the Pakistan-India People's Forum for Peace and Democracy (PIPFPD) have done commendable work by bringing together the people of the two countries since 1994.[26] Such organizations need to be encouraged in terms of being provided resources. It is the people to people contacts, encouraged by mutual relaxation of visa provisions, that will persuade the two governments to sign an agreement on the non-use of nuclear weapons. Finally, media and the press in both countries need to be persuaded to promote and highlight projects of peace and co-operation. This suggestion might sound utopian at this stage, but if the media and

[26] See Vasant Kumar Bawa, 'Foreign Policy in the Post Cold-War Era', *World Affairs*, Vol. 4, No. 2, April-June 2000, pp. 22-31, and L. Ramdas, 'South Asia: A Search for Solutions', *World Affairs*, Vol. 4, No. 4, October-December 2000, pp. 26-33.

the press could refrain from writing only negative reports on relations between the two countries and underscore the need to promote developmental projects between them, relations between the two countries can dramatically improve.

DEVELOPMENTAL AGENDAS

Plausibly, if the designing and execution of developmental projects accompany the discussions, the Kashmir question might find a mutually satisfactory solution. In this context, India can play a responsible role as the dominant regional power. In fact, India, through the Gujral doctrine, has initiated trade ties with its smaller neighbours like Sri Lanka and Bangladesh that are favourable to the latter countries. Besides, the treaty over the sharing of the Ganga waters between India and Bangladesh signed in 1996, and the growth of a connecting road network has already brought the people of the two countries closer.[27] However, the position regarding the intra-regional trade and development co-operation is still dismal in South Asia, largely because of disharmony in Indo-Pak ties. The potential of Indo-Pak co-operation has yet to be explored. Indeed, apart from co-operative ventures in the power sector, the building of oil pipelines via Pakistan from countries like Iran, located in the energy heartland, can bolster India's energy security. Harmonious ties with Pakistan could also provide India with access to the resources of the gas and oil rich countries in Central Asia. In general, the agenda of development, involving a fight against illiteracy, unemployment, poverty, environmental degradation, child labour, cross-border terrorism, and diverse forms of social discrimination, need to be brought to the foreground in South Asia. Both India and Pakistan, at the inter-state and inter-societal levels, can play a constructive role in this regard.

Finally, the thorny issue of Kashmir, which has cost both countries so dear in terms of resources and manpower, can only be solved through a policy of give and take. If India and Pakistan continue to adopt inflexible postures the people living in Kashmir, on either side, would continue to suffer indefinitely. No people can be forced to suffer for such a long time and on such a massive scale. Options like treating the present Line of Control as the *de jure* international frontier can also be debated by involving all the parties concerned. Besides constant efforts

[27] Rajen Harshe, 'South Asian Regional Co-operation: Problems and Prospects', *Economic and Political Weekly*, Vol. 34, No. 19, 8-14 May 1999, pp. 1100-5.

need to be made through first and second track diplomacy to initiate and sustain gradual and cautious dialogue processes to bring peace to the entire region of Kashmir.

Concluding Remarks

The prospects of peace and stability in Southern Asia are primarily dependent on ushering harmony into India-Pakistan ties. Apart from India and Pakistan, China has become another influential actor in Southern Asia. India and China have been able to mitigate the intensity of their adverse ties by initiating CSBMs through the JWG, and by promoting trade and commerce. However, the India-Pakistan ties, despite several attempts at seeking harmony in the past, have been far from peaceful. The intractable question of Kashmir has proved to be the central cause for the ongoing disharmony between the two countries. Since both countries have joined the club of nuclear powers, they would be compelled to restrain their rivalry through a détente. This course of détente could be pursued through CSBMs within a composite framework comprising the military-strategic, political-diplomatic, and developmental spheres. Indeed, nuclear confidence building within such a composite framework can be sought in all the interrelated spheres of interstate and inter-societal relations.

5

Strategic Stability and the Evolution of India's Nuclear Strategy

Rajesh M. Basrur

Clarity of concepts and balanced strategic thinking are the two critical requirements of nuclear thinking and practice. In their absence, nuclear strategy tends to become the creature of 'non-rational' factors that determine its parameters. How else can one explain the gross overkill capability developed by the United States and the Soviet Union during the Cold War years, or indeed the retention of much of it a decade after the end of the Cold War? The Indian strategic outlook with respect to nuclear weapons has strong elements of stability built into it that underpin the commitment to minimum deterrence. However, there is also a significant imbalance that is conducive to instability, and that needs to be corrected in order to develop a more optimal posture. This paper identifies the strengths and vulnerabilities of Indian nuclear thinking and practice, and highlights the need for a balanced nuclear-strategic framework. In essence, the argument is that Indian nuclear thinking has for long been political-strategic rather than military-strategic, as is evident from the prolonged preference for an 'open door' to deterrence without actual weaponization, the shift to covert weaponization by the late 1980s and early 1990s, and the post-1998 posture of deterrence without active deployment. However, an overly political nuclear posture has the negative effect of discounting the risk of escalation to nuclear conflict arising from sub-nuclear military confrontation.

Nuclear weapons have divergent technical and military characteristics that are hard to separate. On the one hand, they are *military* instruments that are, like other weapons, incorporated into national force structures.

In this role, they have operational meaning for military personnel (and for some strategists) whose job is to think of their utility as instruments of war. Like other weapons, they are assessed in terms of their accuracy, speed, reliability, and so on. On the other hand, they are predominantly *political* instruments for decision makers whose paramount objective is to ensure that they are *not* used. The two roles are inextricably linked: the political non-usability of nuclear weapons is the direct consequence of their operational usability. This inherent contradiction can never be satisfactorily resolved. But it would seem fair to say that politics generally comes first, and that, by and large, even those who contemplate nuclear weapons in usable terms would prefer that they not be actually used.

While the contradiction between the political and operational components of nuclear weapons is essentially unresolvable, it can none the less be prioritized, and the way this is done has enormous consequences for nuclear strategy. Where the political meaning of deterrence takes precedence, nuclear weapons, regardless of their operational characteristics, are treated as uniformly dangerous, and the emphasis is on war-avoidance. This perspective induces a minimalist strategy. The fewer the weapons and the less we rely on them, the better. On the other hand, if the operational constituent is accorded primacy, it follows that considerations of a practical character related to the usability of nuclear weapons powerfully influence strategy. This results in a strong focus on weapon characteristics, modes of deployment, vulnerability, reliability, and so on. Such considerations push strategy towards a maximalist position—the bigger and more sophisticated the arsenal, the better. In practice, there is little evidence as yet that this complex and contradictory character of nuclear deterrence has been adequately grasped by policy-makers and strategic thinkers. In consequence, both components of deterrence coexist uncomfortably. For instance, in the United States and Russia, political leaders strive to overlay operationally driven postures with a political approach to their strategic relationships. Actual variations in nuclear strategy among nuclear powers can be explained with reference to a quite different set of variables. The pushes and pulls of political and economic interests noted by many analysts are played out over more deeply embedded causal factors: national economic and technological capabilities, historical experience, and the symbolic value placed on nuclear weapons by strategic elites.

In the Indian case, strategic thinking has been primarily political. Nuclear weapons have not been viewed as usable instruments of national power, or even as the primary components of national security. This approach has important merits. It induces a fundamentally cautious approach to nuclear strategy, inhibits arms racing, and facilitates arms control. On the other hand, an overly political approach to nuclear weapons has a serious drawback: it tends to neglect the operational aspect of the weapons, and is thereby vulnerable to two problems. First, the neglect of operational knowledge and understanding may place actual operational planning, including force planning and acquisition, in the hands of officials who have a predominantly technical and inherently maximalist approach to nuclear weapons. The tendency here is for the centre of gravity of strategy to shift away from the political to the technical and hence from inherent restraint to inherent open-endedness. Second, the relative unfamiliarity of decision-makers with the ground realities of nuclear weapons as military instruments may encourage them to initiate military actions whose nuclear-strategic implications are improperly understood. This paper will focus specifically on the latter problem as it has emerged in India's recent strategic history.

Deterrence without Weaponization: Indian Strategic Culture and Stability

While national leaders and strategists set much store by doctrine, the basic parameters of national nuclear postures tend to be set early. These crystallize over a period of time into set ways of doing things. While bureaucratic and interest-group pressures, the politics of symbolism, and technological imperatives play a role in pushing patterned behaviours this way and that, the basic patterns themselves are resistant to dramatic change. The concept of 'strategic culture' provides useful insight into this reality, and helps understand some puzzling aspects of Indian strategic behaviour.[1] Few analysts have been able to explain, for example, why, over the decades since Independence, India held fast to its nuclear option and yet refused to allocate sufficient resources to make that option more meaningful; why it was by all accounts a reluctant nuclearizer, given the passage of nearly a quarter century between its first and second tests; and why, even well after announcing that it had become a nuclear power, it has been extraordinarily slow to develop its operational capabilities.

Strategic culture may be defined, in Colin Gray's words, as 'the socially constructed and transmitted assumptions, habits of mind,

[1] For a more detailed study of Indian strategic culture in the context of nuclear weapons, see Rajesh M. Basrur, 'Nuclear Weapons and Indian Strategic Culture', *Journal of Peace Research*, Vol. 38, No. 2, March 2001, pp. 181-98.

traditions, and preferred methods of operation—that is, behaviour—that are more or less specific to a particular geographically based security community'.[2] This definition encompasses both habits of mind and habits of practice, with the former conditioning the latter. Viewed as a set of structured preferences, strategic culture at one level entails fundamental understandings about the nature of the strategic environment, the role of force in that environment, perceptions of threat, and the framing of responses to perceived threats. At another level, it involves preferences relating to the organization of those responses in terms of the quality and quantity of military forces considered necessary in order to meet national objectives.

I define Indian strategic culture in relation to nuclear weapons as *nuclear minimalism.* Its chief characteristics are (a) a very limited acceptance of the utility of nuclear weapons as a source of national security; (b) a political rather than a technical understanding of nuclear weapons (nuclear weapons do deter, and are yet 'non-useable'); and (c) restrained responses to pressures either to enhance or reduce national nuclear capabilities. Indian nuclear minimalism acknowledges that power (implicitly, nuclear power too) is a prerequisite for security in an anarchic international system. At the same time, it considers nuclear weapons both morally unacceptable and detrimental to security because of the risks associated with it. This nuclear minimalism was established at the time of Indian independence (a year after Hiroshima) and crystallized over the next two decades. At the turn of the millennium, it has been under some pressure, but its strength belies the warnings of those who stress the risks of arms racing and high spending allegedly inherent in India's decision to 'go nuclear'.

The basic framework of Indian strategic culture with respect to nuclear weapons was established during the Nehru era.[3] The door to nuclearization was kept ajar, but little was done to develop a military programme because of Prime Minister Nehru's belief that nuclear weapons should be abhorred, and could—given sufficient collective

[2] Colin Gray, *Modern Strategy* (Oxford: Oxford University Press, 1999), p. 28.

[3] For useful nuclear-strategic histories of India, see Raj Chengappa, *Weapons of Peace* (New Delhi: HarperCollins, 2000); Stephen P. Cohen, *India: Emerging Power* (Washington, DC: Brookings Institution Press, 2001), pp. 157-97; Sumit Ganguly, 'India's Pathway to Pokhran II: The Prospects and Sources of New Delhi's Nuclear Program', *International Security*, Vol. 23, No. 4, Spring 1999, pp. 148-77; George Perkovich, *India's Nuclear Bomb* (New Delhi: Oxford University Press, 1999); and K. Subrahmanyam, 'Indian Nuclear Policy, 1964-98 (A Personal Recollection)', in Jasjit Singh (ed.), *Nuclear India* (New Delhi: Knowledge World, 1998).

will at the global level—be abolished. At the time, there was no direct nuclear threat to India. Even when the threat did emerge, following China's first test (1964) soon after the India-China war (1962), the governments of both Lal Bahadur Shastri and Indira Gandhi undertook no more than a cautious nuclearization programme. The latter did authorize a test in 1974 (a whole decade after the Chinese test), but its intent was primarily political rather than military-strategic, and no serious effort was made to develop an active military capability. At that time, there was virtually no global non-proliferation regime. Incremental development continued under successive prime ministers. As India's security environment became increasingly adverse, the first weapon was built covertly during the prime ministership of Rajiv Gandhi, though little was done to integrate it into the defence apparatus. While it is arguable that a constraining factor was the threat of international sanctions, it remains true that relatively limited resources were committed to the nuclear weapons programme, and that virtually no effort was made to develop an appropriate infrastructure even after a decision was undertaken to build the bomb. Throughout, the nuclear issue was treated primarily (though not exclusively) as a political-strategic issue rather than as a military-strategic one.

From this perspective, it made sense to adhere to a policy of deterrence without weaponization. Nuclear weapons were viewed as morally abhorrent and strategically without much utility, since they did not yield a true sense of security, as the example of the superpowers made clear. Nor was there a threat perception sufficiently strong to demand a nuclear response. On the other hand, the possibility that nuclear weapons might be required at some point could not altogether be ruled out. The Indian posture, therefore, hovered between abjuration and actual weaponization. The demonstration of nuclear capability as early as 1974 set in place a measure of deterrence that was sustained for the next decade and a half in what might appropriately be labelled a posture of deterrence without weaponization.

At this juncture, it is worth observing the distinction between 'deterrence without weaponization' and 'nonweaponized deterrence'. The latter term was introduced into the vocabulary of nuclear politics by George Perkovich in the early 1990s.[4] Its specific meaning, however, had less to do with deterrence than with non-proliferation. As Perkovich describes the concept,

[4] George Perkovich, 'A Nuclear Third Way in South Asia', *Foreign Policy*, Vol. 91, Summer 1993, pp. 85-104.

> [Non-weaponized deterrence] draws the line at building weapons and deploying missiles, seeking to keep both countries [i.e., India and Pakistan] from moving up the nuclear ladder toward deployed arsenals. At the same time it seeks to build confidence that could ultimately lead both countries to decide it is in their own interests to move down the ladder.[5]

He goes on to add that 'all concerned should aim to improve South Asia's security environment to the point where those countries can sign binding, universal non-proliferation commitments'.[6]

Deterrence without weaponization, on the other hand, is a more neutral concept that leaves open the possibility of moving either up *or* down the nuclear ladder. That India chose to do the former does not mean that weaponization was inevitable. It only means that, for better or worse, the decision to weaponize was made by the political leadership then in power in response to changing conditions at the time.

Pokhran II and Nuclear Politics

The winding down of the Cold War brought a significant deterioration in India's strategic environment. Its Soviet 'card' *vis-à-vis* China vanished; the United States began to exert increasing pressure on it to cap and roll back its nuclear programme; China seemed to be emerging as the next major economic and military power; Pakistan had also developed nuclear capability, and was increasingly active in fomenting terrorist violence in Kashmir; and there was growing evidence that China was aiding Pakistan in the acquisition of advanced nuclear and missile capability. In this context, from a realist perspective, India's nuclearization was scarcely surprising. Yet the built-in constraints of strategic culture (as well as those imposed by the global non-proliferation regime) led to the search for a limited and covert response. India thus developed its first nuclear weapon around the end of the 1980s, but chose not to bare its programme to the rest of the world.[7]

At the time, India's fledgling programme had before it a crucial choice as to the basic character of its deterrence doctrine. It could have opted for *assured destruction*, the doctrine adopted by the United States and the Soviet Union/Russia, which held (and still does) that large, diverse, and sophisticated arsenals are a prerequisite for adequate deterrence. Alternatively, it could have chosen *minimum deterrence*,

[5] Ibid., p. 96

[6] Ibid., p. 97.

[7] Subrahmanyam, 'Indian Nuclear Policy, 1964-98 (A Personal Recollection)', p. 44.

the doctrine of Britain, France, and China, which holds that relatively small and not necessarily varied nuclear forces are sufficient to deter even a much bigger nuclear power. Given its strategic history and culture, it is not surprising that India opted for a variation of the latter: deterrence without deployment.

While the nuclear tests of 1998 have widely been treated as a watershed event, there is a remarkable degree of continuity between the periods before and after them. First, the bomb had already been developed much before 1998, apparently at the turn of the previous decade. Second, there was no effort to integrate nuclear weapons quickly and effectively into the defence apparatus. Nuclear deployment has so far been eschewed. The conception of 'credible minimum deterrence' has yet to be articulated clearly. The Draft Nuclear Doctrine produced by the National Security Advisory Board in August 1999 remained a draft, and was sidelined by External Affairs Minister Jaswant Singh, who explicitly stated that it was 'not a policy document of the Government of India'.[8] Besides, there appears to have been no sense of an urgent need to develop a national security strategy—along with a nuclear component—through the National Security Council. In terms of organization, there is no clear framework of nuclear command and control four years after Pokhran II.[9] On the other hand, political initiatives to counter nuclear threats have not been lacking. The early efforts to stabilize India-Pakistan relations at Lahore (1999) and Agra (2001) stand in stark contrast to the slow emergence of US-Soviet arms control efforts during the Cold War. Notwithstanding its reservations with respect to the Sino-Pakistani nuclear and missile nexus, India has steadily improved its relations with China. At the global level, India has accepted in principle the legitimacy of the Comprehensive Test Ban Treaty and reaffirmed its long-standing commitment to global arms control and disarmament on a non-discriminatory basis.

Overall, it would seem fair to say that nuclear weapons continue to be seen mainly through political-strategic rather than military-strategic lenses. Contrary to the fears of many critics, the Bharatiya Janata Party (BJP)-led government has not displayed undue enthusiasm for nuclear

[8] 'India Not to Engage in a Nuclear Arms Race: Jaswant', (Interview), *The Hindu*, 29 November 1999.

[9] On 5 January 2003, The Government of India's Cabinet Committee on Security (CCS) announced the formation of a Nuclear Command Authority and Strategic Forces Command that comprises of a Political and Executive Council. The Committee also approved the appointment of a Command-in-Chief of the Strategic Forces Command.

armament, nor relegated arms control to the backburner. On the other hand, it is increasingly becoming evident that the present leadership has failed to appreciate fully the strategic implications of nuclear weapons and their role in India's relationship with its adversaries, primarily Pakistan. In the immediate aftermath of Pokhran II, there was an unrealistic expectation that India-Pakistan relations would quickly be stabilized because Pakistan would not risk war and a possible nuclear conflagration over Kashmir. Despite warnings from eminent strategic thinkers such as K. Sundarji and K. Subrahmanyam, the BJP-led government did not anticipate the emergence of the 'stability-instability paradox'.[10] Contrary to its expectations, Pakistan calculated that India's conventional advantage had been overridden by mutual nuclear deterrence, and that Pakistani covert pressure could henceforth be increased without fear of conventional retaliation from India.[11] The result was the Kargil conflict, in which a major covert thrust by Pakistan in the Kargil sector of Kashmir resulted in a near-war between India and Pakistan.

The Kargil conflict had a powerful impact on Indian strategic thinking. First, it brought a deep sense of betrayal because the Indian government and the BJP had invested much political capital in the Lahore 'breakthrough'. From the Indian standpoint, Pakistan's leaders could not be trusted. Second, it followed that, diplomacy having failed, the Pakistanis were henceforth to be engaged only with the instruments of power. Third, the nuclear face-off could not be allowed to give Pakistan the freedom to promote cross-border terrorism at will. The result was the emergence of a strategy designed to project sub-nuclear (i.e. con-vent-ional) force under the nuclear shadow. The current military build-up and confrontation is the consequence of this shift.

The first signs were apparent much earlier during the Kargil conflict itself, when initial moves to mobilize Indian forces for a possible wider war began.[12] The hijacking of an Indian Airlines aircraft in December 1999 and the forced release of terrorists in exchange for the hostages was a traumatic experience. As a result, the beginnings of a fundamental

[10] Michael Krepon and Chris Gagne, (eds.), *The Stability-Instability Paradox: Nuclear Weapons and Brinkmanship in South Asia* (Washington, D.C.: Henry L. Stimson Center, June 2001).

[11] Ayesha Siddiqa-Agha, *Pakistan's Arms Procurement and Military Buildup, 1979-99* (Basingstoke and New York: Palgrave, 2001), pp. 178-83.

[12] V.R. Raghavan, 'Limited War and Nuclear Escalation in South Asia', *The Nonproliferation Review*, Vol. 8, No. 3, Fall-Winter 2001, p. 89.

rethinking appears to have occurred among Indian policy-makers. Defence Minister George Fernandes declared in January 2000 that Kargil had shown that India's forces 'can fight and win a limited war, at a time and place chosen by the aggressor'.[13] He asserted that Pakistan had made a serious error of judgement in assuming that India was deterred by its nuclear capability and would not fight back. He added that a conventional war remained feasible, 'though with definite limitations if escalation across the nuclear threshold [is] to be avoided'.[14] In October 2001, as terrorist attacks continued, Lieutenant General R.K. Nanavatti, head of the Indian Army's Northern Command, warned that 'the nuclearisation of the subcontinent might have altered the situation, but despite that, the stage exists for a limited conventional war'.[15]

11 September, 13 December and the Emergence of Compellence Strategy

The terrorist attacks in New York and Washington on 11 September 2001 created a radically new situation that facilitated the shift in strategy. First, the attacks created a dramatic awareness of the dangers of terrorism in the West, especially the United States. Second, the links between Pakistan and the Taliban, which had sheltered Osama bin Laden, placed a question mark over Pakistan and strengthened India's case against it. Third, the widely supported American military intervention in Afghanistan provided an element of legitimacy to India's own threat of military action. And fourth, the presence of American troops in Pakistan reduced the likelihood of actual conflict breaking out between India and Pakistan. The 13 December attack on the Parliament provided the provocation that led to the Indian military build-up on the India-Pakistan border soon after. C. Raja Mohan, a strategic analyst, noted the 'growing belief in New Delhi that the time has come to call Pakistan's nuclear bluff' lest India place itself 'in permanent vulnerability to cross-border terrorism from Pakistan'.[16]

Indian strategy underwent a significant shift from deterrence to compellence. While it may be said that the demand that Pakistan cut

[13] C. Raja Mohan, 'Fernandes Reveals Limited War Doctrine', *The Hindu*, 25 January 2000.

[14] Ibid.

[15] 'Indian Army General Warns Pak', *The Times of India*, 31 October 2001.

[16] C. Raja Mohan, 'Between War and Peace', *The Hindu*, 12 December 2001.

back on its support to cross-border terrorism is a deterrent threat, it is also a compellent threat because it includes, among other things, the demand for a series of positive actions, including the handing over of terrorists. The threat was 'decomposed' and projected in a calibrated series of actions accompanied by a parallel series of verbal statements designed to keep Pakistan off balance.[17] At the level of action, the first major move made by India (on 22 December) was to recall its ambassador and to end bus and train services between the two countries. Two days later, it was announced that the Indian Army had 'moved,' but not 'deployed,' the nuclear-capable short-range *Prithvi* missile, normally stored at Secunderabad in the south, to the border region.[18] Another two days later, Defence Minister George Fernandes said India had deployed fighter jets at bases along the border and that its missiles were 'in position'.[19] The following day, Pakistani civilian aircraft were prohibited from overflying India, and India ordered the strength of its mission in Islamabad, as well as that of the Pakistani mission in New Delhi, reduced by half. By this time, the Indian army was laying land mines, constructing bunkers, and positioning tanks and heavy field artillery—all signs of preparation for large-scale conventional conflict. Exchanges of fire were occurring regularly.[20] Yet another signal from New Delhi, albeit an oblique one, came in the form of a missile test: on 25 January 2002, a Pakistan-specific version of the intermediate-range missile, *Agni*, with a declared range of 700–900 km, was tested.

On the verbal plane, Indian rhetoric was strong. The consistent aim was to drive home the point that India stood by its plank of no first use, but that if Pakistan were to use nuclear weapons first, it would be devastated by a counter-strike from India's larger arsenal. In short, Pakistan's nuclear capability would no longer deter India from taking military action. The nature of India's response was left unspecified but, given the extent of its deployment, conceivably included a major conventional thrust. The threat of nuclear desolation came regularly

[17] On the decomposition of threats for greater effectiveness, see Thomas C. Schelling, *Strategy of Conflict* (Cambridge, MA & London: Harvard University Press, 1990), pp. 41-3.

[18] Vishal Thapar, 'Prithvi Missiles Moved near Border in Punjab', *Hindustan Times*, 25 December 2001.

[19] Terry Friel and Jane Macartney, 'India Deploys Planes as Tensions with Pakistan Rise', *Washington Post*, 26 December 2001.

[20] Celia W. Dugger, 'India and Pakistan Add to War Footing', *New York Times*, 28 December 2001.

and from diverse sources. On 25 December, Jana Krishnamurthy, the President of the BJP, warned that if Pakistan attempted to use nuclear weapons, 'its existence itself would be wiped out of the world map'.[21] On 29 December, Defence Minister George Fernandes repeated the warning:

> Pakistan can't think of using nuclear weapons despite the fact that they are not committed to the doctrine of no first use like we are. We could take a strike, survive, and then hit back. Pakistan would be finished. I do not really fear that the nuclear issue would figure in a conflict.[22]

Two days later, while acknowledging Pakistan's action in arresting the founder of the Lashkar-e-Toiba (Army of the Pure) leader, India again raised the stakes by demanding that 20 individuals accused of terrorist acts in India be handed over to it by Pakistan. On 11 January, India's Army Chief, General S. Padmanabhan, when asked how India would respond to a Pakistani first strike, declared that 'the perpetrator of that particular outrage shall be punished so severely that their [*sic*] continuation thereafter in any form of fray will be doubtful'.[23]

Many observers did see the whole exercise as a bluff, but the scale of India's military mobilization, combined with the heated rhetoric, had the effect of creating a level of uncertainty: one could never be sure what would happen. Inherent in the situation, whether intended or not, was the classic 'threat that leaves something to chance'.[24] The recipient of the threat could never be certain if the threatener did indeed have full control over events, with the implication that nuclear conflict might occur without it being intended. Even after discounting for both bluff and style, the aggressive rhetoric emanating from the Indian leadership would have accentuated the problem. As Schelling has pointed out, the less cool and collected one is, the greater the credibility of such a threat.[25]

India's central aim was to show that nuclear weapons are not simple

[21] 'Pak would be Wiped Out if it Uses Nuclear Bomb: BJP', *Hindustan Times*, 30 December 2001.

[22] 'We Could Take A Strike and Survive. Pakistan Won't: Fernandes', *Hindustan Times*, 30 December 2001.

[23] Celia W. Dugger, 'Indian General Talks Bluntly of War and a Nuclear Threat', *New York Times*, 12 January 2002.

[24] Schelling, *Strategy of Conflict*, pp. 187-203.

[25] Thomas C. Schelling, *Arms and Influence* (New Haven & London: Yale University Press, 1966), pp. 36-43.

equalizers, and that asymmetry does matter. It was not so much an affirmation that nuclear asymmetry in itself is significant as an assertion that *the combination of nuclear asymmetry and conventional asymmetry* gave India a distinct advantage. The cost of a nuclear war would be disproportionate: India would be hurt, Pakistan would not survive. In short, Pakistan was not in a position to resort to a first strike: it was effectively deterred from nuclear use altogether. The nuclear freeze, however, left India at an advantage because of its superior conventional force, which could be used to carry out operations without fear of a Pakistani nuclear first-strike. Indeed, even in a conventional war, Pakistan would be continuously inhibited by the fear of a possible uncontrolled escalation leading to nuclear war. There was thus space for a limited war to inflict costs on an economically and politically unstable Pakistan. So long as its core interests were not jeopardized, Pakistan would have no incentive to launch nuclear weapons.[26] Behind this thinking, of course, lay a conception of nuclear weapons that was eminently political. As India's Navy Chief, Admiral Sushil Kumar, pointed out, 'The nukes are for negotiations, they are not weapons of war.'[27]

Does asymmetry actually work in this way? There is only one example of an actual conventional conflict between nuclear powers, and that provides food for strategic thought. The situation preceding the Sino-Soviet border conflict of 1969 at Damansky island on the Ussuri river bears a remarkable resemblance to the recent South Asian confrontation.[28] It also points to the possible course of events if an actual outbreak of fighting were to occur between India and Pakistan. As with the Kashmir problem, the border dispute between China and the Soviet Union was a problem that had its roots in the colonial era. Like Pakistan today, China was then in a state of considerable internal instability as a result of the Cultural Revolution. Minor skirmishes had occurred at other places in the region before the first Damansky incident

[26] This logic was stated to a newsman by Uday Bhaskar, Deputy Director of the Institute for Defence Studies and Analyses. Rajiv Chandrasekaran, 'For India, Deterrence May Not Prevent War', *Washington Post*, 17 January 2002. What exactly Pakistani core interests are, and whether these are truly knowable, is a far more problematic question.

[27] Gaurav C. Sawant, 'Nuclear Wars are Not Meant to be Fought, Especially between Nuclear Powers' (Interview), *Hindustan Times*, 6 January 2002.

[28] Thomas W. Robinson, 'The Sino-Soviet Border Conflict', in Stephen S. Kaplan (ed.), *Diplomacy and Power: Soviet Armed Forces as a Political Instrument* (Washington, D.C.: Brookings Institution, 1981).

on 1 March 1969. At the time the fighting broke out, the Soviet Union had overwhelmingly superior conventional as well as nuclear forces. Following the first clash, it mounted a massive mobilization of conventional forces and resorted to coercive diplomacy through a series of threats as well as actual military engagements between March and August 1969. Unlike the South Asian case, however, there were hints of a nuclear first strike. Eventually, China agreed to come to the negotiating table, signed a one-year navigation agreement with respect to the disputed river, and dropped its insistence that the 'unequalness' of the old treaties, that had determined the Sino-Soviet border, had rendered them worthless. Up to a point, the Soviet strategy seems to have worked, though in the long run, it did not. Once the crisis had been resolved, the Chinese backed away from negotiations 'they had no intention of carrying to conclusion on Soviet terms'.[29] In effect, the Soviet strategy failed because the Chinese concessions were reversible.

The Indian experiment with compellence in a nuclear context is subject to criticism on two grounds. First, while such a strategy may work (and in this case, to a considerable degree, did), it also may not. The possibility of loss of control over an action-reaction process and of accidental war caused by unforeseen events remains a serious risk. The possibility of escalation was evidently discounted. A senior Indian official is reported to have said that 'we've found there is a lot of strategic space between a low-intensity war waged with Pakistan and the nuclear threshold,' and hence 'we are utilizing military options without worrying about the nuclear threshold.'[30] Evidently, Indian leaders did not take into consideration the possibility of a process of action and reaction leading the nuclear rivals down a slippery slope to catastrophe.[31] Further, they seem to have been unaware of the risk of accidental war resulting from unforeseen events or loss of control resulting from the 'fog of war'. Possibilities include an unanticipated initiative by a military commander that might provoke a nuclear retaliation; a major terrorist attack in either country (say, on a chemical plant or a nuclear facility) that might be treated as an enemy strike; a false warning of a nuclear strike; and so on. Some portent of the first comes from the report that,

[29] Robinson, 'The Sino-Soviet Border Conflict', p. 283.

[30] Seymour M. Hersh, 'The Getaway', *The New Yorker*, 28 January 2002. See also Raja Mohan, 'Between War and Peace'.

[31] Raghavan, 'Limited War and Nuclear Escalation in South Asia'.

at the height of the December 13 crisis, the commander of an Indian strike corps was sent on leave for positioning his forces 'too close' to the border.[32]

It is impossible to quantify the risk of nuclear war in such a situation. It would be more pertinent to consider whether *any* risk is worth the potential consequences of a nuclear conflict breaking out. Any calculation of the use of force must involve a cost-benefit estimate of potential gains over potential loss. It is hard to think of a potential gain from threatening nuclear war that might outweigh the potential cost of one actually occurring. The second problem is with respect to the attainment of one's objectives. The example of the Sino-Soviet conflict is not reassuring, for it underscores the problem of reversibility. The object of a compellence strategy may appear to succumb, only to reverse its position at a time of its own choosing. Third, if the coercive action carries no deadline, it is difficult to separate it from posturing, or 'a ceremony with no consequences'.[33] That seems to be the problem with India's strategy today. But if it does carry a deadline, it imposes on the subject state the onus of action. If that action consists of military escalation and the associated risk of nuclear conflict, then it is surely likely to be difficult to initiate.

Besides projecting a direct compellent threat against Pakistan by means of its massive military build-up, India also put Pakistan under indirect pressure through the United States. The politics of nuclear weapons has generally been understood in terms of bilateral relationships between nuclear-armed adversaries or between a nuclear-armed state and a non-nuclear state. India and Pakistan, however, have gone one step further. They have engaged in a strategy of inviting outside intervention in their conflict over Kashmir. Pakistan did this in 1999 by initiating the Kargil conflict. India engaged in a similar, though not identical, exercise through the mobilization of conventional forces after the 13 December crisis. Both cases represent not so much threats to use nuclear force directly as attempts to provoke *a fear of nuclear war* in the global community, especially the United States, and thus to invite external intervention on their respective sides. In the Kargil conflict, Pakistan tried (and failed) to use the United States to force India to negotiate on Kashmir. In the 13 December crisis, India was somewhat

[32] 'Lt-Gen Vij Moved Forces "Too Close" to the Border', *The Times of India*, 22 January 2001.

[33] Schelling, *Arms and Influence*, p. 72.

more successful in getting the United States to pressurize President Musharraf to drop his support for cross-border terrorism in Kashmir.

For India, the strategy did pay dividends. Reflecting a common perception in the US, the *New York Times* on 26 December 2001 called for the Bush Administration to 'temper' the brewing crisis over Kashmir, 'one of the most dangerous flashpoints in the world'.[34] Some analysts judged that India was deliberately creating a 'sound and light show', as Stephen P. Cohen put it in an interview to *The Washington Post*.[35] But the problem, as another commentator observed, was that 'the risks are so cataclysmic that Washington must do more. . . .'[36] Here again, the threat that leaves something to chance was at work.

The United States not only found it necessary to intervene, but to put considerable pressure on Pakistan to accede to Indian demands. On 29 December, President Bush telephoned both Prime Minister Vajpayee and President Musharraf. But the tenor of his calls differed: while assuring the former of his co-operation in fighting terrorism, he urged the latter, in the words of White House spokesman Scott McClellan, 'to take additional strong and decisive measures to eliminate the extremists who seek to harm India, undermine Pakistan, provoke a war between India and Pakistan and destabilize the international coalition against terrorism'.[37] India kept up the pressure by refusing to reverse its mobilization. A week later, British Prime Minister Tony Blair, who had consulted with Bush before visiting the subcontinent, concluded his visit with a sharp statement calling on Pakistan to drop its support for terrorists fighting in Kashmir.[38] On the same day, Bush backed Blair's demand by saying, 'I think it's very important for President Musharraf to make a clear statement to the world that he intends to crack down on terror'.[39] However, as the momentum of its own war against the terrorists declined, US support for India's position inevitably became less enthusiastic. India was on several occasions asked to reduce

[34] 'South Asian Brinkmanship' (edit), *New York Times*, 26 December 2001.

[35] Peter Slevin, 'Pakistan Groups Called Terrorist Organizations', *Washington Post*, 27 December 2001.

[36] Nicholas D. Kristof, 'This is Not a Test', *New York Times*, 26 December 2001. See also Michael R. Gordon, 'As Threat Eases, U.S. Still Sees Peril in India-Pakistan Buildup', *New York Times*, 20 January 2002.

[37] 'Bush Leans on Pakistan President' (AP Report), *The Times of India*, 29 December 2001.

[38] Craig Whitlock, 'Blair Urges Pakistan to Crush Terrorists', *Washington Post*, 8 January 2002.

[39] Ibid.

its military pressure on the border.[40] The continuing US pressure on Pakistan does not appear to have been related only to India's build-up, but in significant measure to its own perceptions and interests, for instance in relation to the kidnapping and murder of Daniel Pearl, an American reporter, and the hunt for Osama bin Laden.

The Prospects for Stability

Expectations of regional nuclear stability may be assessed at two levels: the operational and the political. At the operational level, it is evident that there is a need for confidence building measures to reduce the risk of nuclear conflict.[41] That decision-makers in both India and Pakistan were aware of this is clear from the prominent place given to nuclear risk reduction measures in the Lahore Memorandum of Understanding (1999). The Kargil conflict, unfortunately, caused the issue to be relegated to the backburner. The steady move towards operationalization of nuclear weapons will bring it to the forefront again, particularly if active deployment occurs. Ironically, deployment will in itself give a fillip to arms control by raising the degree of risk. At the political level, it is imperative that a process of dialogue be set in motion to reduce the high degree of tension that has persisted between India and Pakistan. Above all, there is an urgent need to separate the risks associated with nuclear weapons from the substantive political differences between the two countries. That in itself is a not inconsiderable political task.

How might the role of the United States in the region affect nuclear stability? It is clear that the US has come to the region to stay for the foreseeable future: it has now a considerable physical presence in Central Asia, Afghanistan, and Pakistan, and an increasingly close political, economic, and military relationship with India. On the whole, since its fundamental interest as a hegemonic power is global equilibrium, the US will be inclined to play a dampening role in regional conflict, especially to prevent a nuclear war between India and Pakistan. On the other hand, it is also true that its strategic interest and physical presence appears actually to have encouraged first Pakistan and then India to indulge in rocking the nuclear boat with the aim of inducing American

[40] Atul Aneja, 'India, US Differ on De-escalation', *The Hindu*, 6 February 2002.

[41] For a detailed study, see W. P. S. Sidhu, Brian Cloughley, John H. Hawes and Teresita Schaffer, *Nuclear Risk-Reduction Measures in South Asia*, (Washington, D.C.: Henry L. Stimson Center, November 1998).

intervention on their respective behalves. There is the additional possibility that the deterioration of US-China relations and the possible emergence of a US-India nexus against China will bring instability to the region, resulting in a renewed adversarial relationship—this time with a nuclear component—between India and China. However, the prospects of a Sino-Indian nuclear confrontation are remote. The India-China border dispute is a relatively marginal one, economic and political relations between the two are on the upswing, and there is nothing in their relationship to justify recourse to a nuclear confrontation.

Considerable apprehension has also been expressed in various quarters that the American interest in building a national missile defence may have a domino effect, stimulating offensive build-ups not only in Russia, but also successively in China, India, and Pakistan. However, that seems unlikely to happen, since missile defence, in itself unlikely to be sufficiently effective to guarantee hits on all targets, can be offset by countermeasures. Besides, any Chinese response to a US missile defence will be in the form of augmented long-range capability, which has no bearing on India (and by extension on Pakistan), which falls within China's intermediate-range capability.[42]

Finally, a balanced understanding of the strategic character of nuclear weapons is essential. It is clear that Indian decision makers have had difficulty in achieving this, and that they have had an excessively political view of these weapons. While the political conception of nuclear weapons has its strengths in terms of an awareness of the direct risks associated with the potential use of nuclear weapons, it also carries serious risks. Because nuclear weapons are not really seen as usable, and because there is an inadequate appreciation of their operational aspects, notably with respect to escalation from sub-nuclear to nuclear conflict, Indian decision makers have tended to take inordinate risks under pressure. This is seen in the shift from a strategy of deterrence to a strategy of compellence in the 13 December crisis. I have argued that the compellence strategy, besides being unlikely in itself to yield the desired results, is laden with risk and undermines Indian security. A more balanced appreciation of the political and military facets of nuclear weapons is essential for the evolution of a stable nuclear doctrine and posture.

[42] For a comprehensive discussion of the issue, see Michael Krepon and Chris Gagne, (eds.), *The Impact of US Ballistic Missile Defenses on Southern Asia* (Washington, D.C.: Henry L. Stimson Center), July 2002.

6

Nuclear Safety

G. Balachandran

Introduction

Nuclear safety is not a recent issue. Ever since the incidents in the Three Mile Island (USA, 1979) and Chernobyl (Ukraine, 1986), which were the sites of the two major accidents in nuclear power industry, the international community has paid serious attention to the issue of nuclear safety. A number of international conventions, such as the Nuclear Safety Convention, were negotiated and put in place. However, while the earlier concern about nuclear safety was 'to protect individuals, society and the environment from harm by establishing and maintaining in nuclear installations effective defences against 'radiological hazards', after the terrorist attack on 11 September 2001 international concerns about nuclear safety have been expanded to include nuclear terrorism as well. As a result, a number of new safety issues need to be addressed to prevent various acts of nuclear terrorism.

While the concerns about nuclear safety are valid and need to be addressed in a responsible manner, there are disturbing signs that the new concerns about nuclear terrorism are being used to pursue agendas which have very little to do with either nuclear terrorism or nuclear safety. These include expansion of mandatory international control regimes and attempts to enter and regulate the nuclear programmes of countries that have so far resisted efforts to adhere by unequal international treaties such as the Nuclear Non-Proliferation Treaty (NPT).

This chapter describes the earlier concerns about nuclear safety in the context of various civilian programmes, the new problems in nuclear safety management arising from nuclear terrorism concerns after 11 September, the new initiatives being proposed and the potential pitfalls of such approaches for India. It also touches upon those aspects of command and control issues, that may have implications for nuclear safety, and discusses them in the context of South Asia.

Nuclear Safety Pre-September 11

Nuclear safety has been a major concern from the earliest days of the application of nuclear technology for civilian purposes. In fact, the Statute of the International Atomic Energy Agency (IAEA) explicitly requires the IAEA,

> To establish or adopt, in consultation and, where appropriate, in collaboration with the competent organs of the United Nations and with the specialized agencies concerned, standards of safety for protection of health and minimization of danger to life and property (including such standards for labour conditions), and to provide for the application of these standards to its own operation as well as to the operations making use of materials, services, equipment, facilities, and information made available by the Agency or at its request or under its control or supervision; and to provide for the application of these standards, at the request of the parties, to operations under any bilateral or multilateral arrangements, or, at the request of a State, to any of that State's activities in the field of atomic energy. [Article III (A)(6)]

In practice, this was translated to mean 'to protect individuals, society and the environment from harm by establishing and maintaining in nuclear installations effective defences against radiological hazards' (Fig. 1).

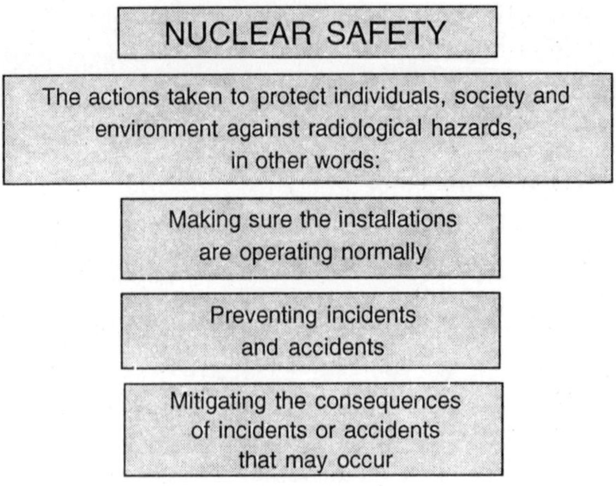

FIGURE 1

General safety objective

The general nuclear safety objective is to protect individuals, society and the environment from harm by establishing and maintaining in nuclear installations effective defences against radiological hazards.

The protection system is effective as stated in the objective if it prevents significant addition either to the risk to health or to the risk of other damage to which individuals, society and environment are exposed as a consequence of industrial activity already accepted.

Thus while nuclear safety was always of great concern to the IAEA and others, the two major accidents in the history of civilian nuclear power programmes shook the complacency of the nuclear establishment. These were the Three Mile Island incident in USA in 1979 and the far more serious Chernobyl accident in Ukraine in 1986. These two events resulted in a strengthening of the role of the IAEA on nuclear safety issues. Post Chernobyl a number of legally binding international safety agreements aimed at strengthening international co-operation in nuclear, radiation and waste management safety were developed and adopted by the international community. They are now being implemented by the parties to these agreements, with the support of the IAEA. They include:

(i) the *Convention on the Physical Protection of Nuclear Material* (which was opened for signature on 3 March 1980 and entered into force on 8 February 1987);
(ii) the *Convention on Early Notification of a Nuclear Accident* (which was opened for signature on 26 September 1986 and entered into force on 27 October 1986);
(iii) the *Convention on Assistance in the Case of a Nuclear Accident or Radiological Emergency* (which was opened for signature on 26 September 1986 and entered into force on 26 February 1987); and
(iv) the *Convention on Nuclear Safety* (which was opened for signature on 20 September 1994 and entered into force on 24 October 1996); and
(v) the *Joint Convention on the Safety of Spent Fuel Management and on the Safety of Radioactive Waste Management* (which was opened for signature on 29 September 1997 and entered into force on 18 June 2001).

In addition, the IAEA created a set of advisory bodies with harmonized terms of reference to have a uniform preparation and review process for safety standards in 1996 to assist it in preparing and reviewing all its documents, namely the *Advisory Commission for Safety Standards (ACSS), the Nuclear Safety Standards Advisory Committee (NUSSAC), the Radiation Safety Standards Advisory Committee (RASSAC), the Waste Safety Standards Advisory Committee (WASSAC), and the Transport Safety Standards Advisory Committee (TRANSSAC).* The IAEA assigned to each of these bodies a Scientific Secretary who co-ordinates the work of the body with the relevant Agency policies and programmes, and appoints a Technical Officer for the preparation of each document in accordance with the recommendations made.

A number of other initiatives were also undertaken. In 1990 the IAEA, in cooperation with the Organisation for Economic Cooperation and Development (OECD), developed the International Nuclear Event Scale (INES) to standardize the reporting of nuclear incidents/accidents. A number of criteria and indicators were defined to assure coherent reporting of nuclear events by different official authorities, as follows:

- Level 7: characterized by large off-site impact, widespread health and environmental effects. Example: Chernobyl (former USSR)—1986.
- Level 6: significant off-site release, likely to require full implementation of planned countermeasures. Example: Kishtim (former USSR)—1957.
- Level 5: limited off-site release, likely to require partial implementation of planned countermeasures. Examples: Windscale (UK)—1957, Three Mile Island (USA)—1979.

Levels 5-7 are related to severe damage of the reactor core and the radiological barriers.

- Level 4: significant damage to the reactor core or radiological barriers and/or a fatal exposure of a worker (or more), but the off-site impact is minor, resulting in public exposure within the prescribed limits. Examples: Windscale (UK)—1973, Saint-Laurent (France)—1980, Buenos Aires (Argentina)—1983.
- Level 3: characterized by very small off-site impact, although related to severe spread of contamination on-site or acute health

effects upon a worker (or more). It is a 'near accident' event, when no safety layers are remaining. Example: Vandellos (Spain)—1989.

- Level 2: an incident with no off-site impact, related to significant spread of contamination on-site or overexposure of a worker.
- Level 1: an anomaly beyond the authorized operating regime.
- Level 0: a 'below-scale event' of no safety significance.

Of the five international conventions referred to earlier, India has ratified the first three. It has signed but not ratified the Convention on Nuclear Safety and has not yet signed the Joint Convention on the Safety of Spent Fuel Management and on the Safety of Radioactive Waste Management. India's accession to the Convention on Physical Protection of Nuclear Material is an indication of India's commitment to adhere to the highest international norms and standards for the protection of such materials and to prevent them from falling into the hands of unauthorized personnel, in particular, criminal and terrorist organizations.

India's reluctance to ratify the other two conventions arises from the distinction made by these conventions between civilian and military nuclear activities. Thus, at the time of signing the Convention on Nuclear Safety, India had clearly expressed its reservations about the scope of the Convention. India argued that '(it) continues to believe that a Convention on Nuclear Safety should cover all power plants, civil and military. We note, however, that the present convention covers only civilian nuclear power plants. We hope that the safety aspects of nuclear power plants in the military domain would also be given attention, to achieve comprehensive nuclear safety worldwide'.[1]

As far as the Joint Convention on the Safety of Spent Fuel Management and safety of Radioactive Waste Management is concerned, it is well known that India has fundamental and philosophical objections to considering spent fuel as waste. India's stand is that in the closed nuclear fuel cycle, spent fuel is not waste but a valuable source of energy. In the uranium and plutonium cycles, the plutonium-239 produced and the balance uranium-235 available in the fuel are valuable fissile materials. Even the spent fuel used in Light Water Reactors contains more uranium-235 than natural uranium, and is a potential fuel for Heavy Water Reactors which use natural uranium as fuel. In the thorium cycle, in which India has a great stake, because of its vast thorium reserves, its basic rationale lies in converting or breeding uranium-233

[1] Input from the remarks of the discussant Dr Placid Rodriguez.

TABLE 6.1: NUCLEAR PLANT SAFETY RECORD

		Level 1	Level 2	Level 3	Level 4
1997	IAEA	16	13	2	0
AERB	5	1	0	0	1998
IAEA	1	13	0	0	
AERB	5	1	0	0	1999
IAEA	4	14	3	1	
AERB	2	0	0	0	

Note: Compiled by the author.

from thorium-232. India, therefore, cannot be a party to any convention that equates spent fuel to waste.

Pakistan has ratified the first four but is yet to sign the Joint Convention on Safety of Spent Fuel Management. India is a member of all the Advisory Commissions.

The Indian record on nuclear plant safety has been quite good. The majority of events have been at Level 0, characterized as comprising a deviation with no safety significance. And there has been no event of level 3 and above. Most of the events have been confined to Level 1 with couple of events at level 2 or in between. Table 6.1 provides data on the nuclear events globally as listed by the IAEA and the Indian events as given by the Atomic Energy Regulatory Board (AERB). It can be seen that the Indian record in maintaining reactor safety practices is ahead of the international practices.

The other aspect of nuclear safety is control of the level of radiation exposure experienced by individuals as a result of nuclear activities. The AERB sets the safety levels and reviews the radiation exposures of workers in various occupations at both Department of Atomic Energy (DAE) units and non-DAE institutions. The Annual Report of the AERB regularly includes the results of such reviews. From the AERB reports and the reports of such reviews in more advanced countries it appears that the instances of exposure higher than the dose limits prescribed by AERB are slightly higher in India. This is because of, as the AERB report recently pointed out, poor work practices.

ISSUES OF NUCLEAR SAFETY AFTER SEPTEMBER 11

The events of 11 September 2001 had a major impact on the problem of nuclear safety especially in the context of nuclear terrorism. Although there have been many reports suggesting that the Al Qaida organization had been seeking nuclear, chemical, and biological weapons, and also seeking to purchase stolen nuclear material from the former Soviet Union for use in nuclear explosives, no trace of any type of special nuclear material or any major cache of radioactive substance has so far been found in Afghanistan in any of the Al Qaida offices or training camps. Nevertheless, the daring attack on the World Trade Center in New York and the Pentagon in Washington, DC does not rule out that such organizations might use WMD (Weapons of Mass Destruction) in future as one of the instruments of terrorism. While there are no doubt valid reasons for why the threat of nuclear terrorism calls for a reappraisal of nuclear safety standards and procedures, there are definite political overtones to the current global, primarily Western inspired, calls for a new international regime on nuclear safety.

Nuclear Terrorism

It would be appropriate to discuss here some of the elements of nuclear terrorism that need examination. There are four categories of risk associated with nuclear terrorism. They are related to: (i) nuclear weapons; (ii) nuclear facilities; (iii) nuclear materials; and (iv) radioactive materials.

NUCLEAR WEAPONS

Complete nuclear weapons falling into the hands of terrorists are, of course, the most serious category of nuclear terrorism. The global stockpile of assembled nuclear weapons runs into thousands—more than 30,000—but are these primarily stockpiled in the two major nuclear weapon states, the US and Russia, which together account for nearly 95 per cent of the global arsenal. While the nuclear stockpile of the USA and Russia runs into tens of thousands, that of UK, France, and China are in the hundreds, while that of India and Pakistan are at most in tens. Further, the nuclear weapons in the USA, Russia, UK, France, and China are fully deployed at multiple locations, while those of India and Pakistan are not reported to be deployed and in any case are not at a multiplicity of sites. It is obvious, therefore, that the chances of nuclear weapons being lost or stolen are statistically far higher in the former five nuclear weapon states than the South Asian nuclear arsenal. Further, nuclear weapons are large and readily accountable. Therefore, they are reasonably well secured and protected in nuclear stockpiles against thefts or possession by unauthorized persons.

The chances of a readily assembled nuclear weapon falling into the hands of terrorists are even more remote. And this is more true of South Asia than elsewhere. Of course, this does not include cases where state actors collude with non-state groups in the transfer of nuclear weapons or cases of insider thefts. While such an event is also unlikely, recent concerns in the US about the safety of the Pakistani nuclear arsenal suggest that the probability of this occurring is higher in Pakistan than elsewhere.

NUCLEAR FACILITIES

From its very inception, the nuclear industry has been aware of the extremely hazardous nature of its operations and has been careful to make security at nuclear facilities (power plants, fuel fabrication, enrichment, reprocessing, and waste management plants) tight and robust. Again, because of the management and use of highly toxic and dangerous nuclear material at these facilities, their design construction requires far higher standards of safety features such as double containment of vessels, ability to withstand damage in very severe environmental disasters such as hurricanes, tornados, and earthquakes. While they may not be able to withstand organized attacks such as the crash of a fully laden jumbo aircraft into the facility, they will be able to withstand many other forms of terrorist attacks using small arms, mortars, and truck bombs. Further, countries with nuclear facilities have upgraded the security at these installations post 11 September and, therefore, the chances of a nuclear facility being destroyed with the consequent release of radioactive elements into the environment are very very slim.

NUCLEAR MATERIAL

Given that the chances of terrorists getting their hands on a ready-made nuclear bomb are very slim, what are their chances of getting hold of nuclear materials to manufacture and successfully detonate a nuclear bomb? Not very high.

First of all, the terrorists will have to obtain nuclear weapon usable material—the usual estimates being 25 kg of highly enriched uranium (HEU) or 8 kg of plutonium (Pu) to make a bomb. Such materials are not commonly available and even where available, are under national or international safeguards. According to the IAEA, there were 71 countries with significant nuclear activities at the end of 2000. Of these 71 countries, IAEA safeguards were being applied at all significant nuclear activities in 62 countries. The countries where the IAEA did not have safeguards on all the nuclear activities were the five NPT recognized nuclear weapons states (NWS), India, Israel, Pakistan, and Georgia. While a safeguards agreement has been signed with Georgia, it has not yet come into force. So, in respect of these 62 non-nuclear weapon states all their declared nuclear activities have been brought under IAEA safeguards, and all their nuclear material has also been brought under IAEA safeguards.

According to the IAEA: 'In fulfilling the safeguards obligations of the Agency in 2000, the Secretariat—having evaluated all the information acquired in implementing safeguards agreements and all other information available to the Agency—found no indication of diversion of nuclear material placed under safeguards or of misuse of facilities, equipment or non-nuclear material placed under safeguards. On this basis, the Secretariat concluded that the nuclear material and other items placed under safeguards remained in peaceful nuclear activities or were otherwise adequately accounted for.'[2]

Of the nine countries that do not have fullscope IAEA safeguards in place, one-Georgia—has already signed the safeguards agreement but only its coming into force remains to be completed. The remaining eight states have all the nuclear-weapon capable material in their control; so, potentially only these states can be the sources of such material for terrorists.

Weapon Grade Nuclear Material: Stock and Production

According to reliable estimates, the global stock of weapon-grade fissile material at the end of 1999 was 248 MT of Pu and 1665 MT of HEU.[3] Of these, the five NPT recognized nuclear weapon states had an estimated 247 MT of Pu and 1664 MT of HEU. The two South Asian nuclear weapon states had between them 0.315 MT of Pu and 0.690 MT of HEU. China is one nuclear weapon state, which still continues with the production of weapon-grade fissile material. The two South Asian states also continue with such production although

[2] See Safeguards, *International Atomic Energy Agency Annual Report 2000*, Vienna, p. 1.

[3] David Albright and Mark Gorwitz, *Tracking Civil Plutonium Inventories: End 1999* (London: ISIS, October 2000).

their annual production capacities have been estimated at 20 kg of Pu in India and 110 kg of HEU in Pakistan.[4]

Given the relative sizes of the stocks of weapon-grade fissile material in the NPT-accepted Nuclear Weapon States and South Asia, it is apparent that the material in the nuclear weapon states needs to be protected with far greater attention and care than in South. Asia. Another factor that needs to be considered is that while the material in South Asia is expressed in gross figures—that is they include such material in assembled weapons and held otherwise—the material in the NPT recognized nuclear weapon states is exclusive of the nuclear weapons already assembled. In other words, in the case of the South Asian states the data given is in respect of their *total* production of fissile material. It is obvious, therefore, that loss of weapons-grade fissile material poses a far more serious challenge to the nuclear weapon states than India and Pakistan.

Further, while the physics of manufacturing a nuclear weapon is not very complex, in practice the process of actually producing a nuclear weapon is a far from trivial exercise. It calls for a certain degree of scientific and technical expertise and access to reasonably sophisticated machinery and equipment.

For all these reasons the likelihood of South Asia being a region where terrorists would be able to deploy a nuclear weapon can be ruled out. If at all this happens it is far more likely to be the result of such groups' activities in the nuclear weapon states.

Other Nuclear Material

While the chances of a nuclear weapon falling into the hands of terrorists are small, there are greater chances of their being able to make use of non-weapon grade fissile materials—such as power reactor fuel elements, spent fuel, and radiation sources used in many civilian applications. Such materials could be used for making a 'dirty bomb' i.e., a radioactive source material surrounded by conventional explosives. Detonation of such a device in a public place would cause the spread of radiation particles. Such devices are known as Radiological Dispersion Devices (RDD). These devices will not have the effect of a nuclear bomb. Neither will they have any of the media reported effects of

[4] ISIS Estimates 1998. Fact Sheet: India and Pakistan—Current and Potential Nuclear Arsenals.

either large casualties or widespread dissemination of radioactivity.[5] However, even if the RDD do not cause any major casualties or property damage, they would certainly have a major psychological impact on the general population. To that extent this issue needs to be addressed in a more realistic fashion.

What are the radioactive materials that could be used in a RDD? We will separately discuss nuclear materials and radiological materials used in civilian applications such as Cesium 137, Cobalt 60, and Polonium 210. All these materials are commonly used in medical and industrial procedures and activities.

The civilian nuclear power industry requires a large amount of nuclear materials for its working. According to the World Nuclear Association, the 438 nuclear power reactors with an installed capacity of 3,53,416 megawatts-electric (Mwe) would require an estimated 64,956 MT of uranium (U) or 76,603 MT of natural uranium ore concentrates (U_3O_8).[6] Here again the requirements arising from South Asia are very small. The power reactors in India and Pakistan are expected to generate a demand for only 368 MT of Uranium. The demand from the NPT NWS is estimated to be 37,531 MT of Uranium.

The spent fuel discharged by these power reactors contains plutonium, which can be extracted from the spent fuel by reprocessing. The spent fuel discharged from power reactors in countries that have IAEA safeguards will come under safeguards and, as mentioned earlier, the IAEA has been certifying every year that the nuclear material under its supervision is fully accounted for and no diversions or losses have taken place. Roughly 50 per cent of the annual discharge of spent fuel from nuclear facilities comes under the IAEA while the rest remains outside its supervision. The only countries where all power plants are not covered by IAEA safeguards are the five nuclear weapon states and India. Pakistan has no power reactor which is not under IAEA safeguards. Of those covered by the IAEA, the nuclear weapon states account for over 95 per cent of the fissile material stocks, with India accounting for the rest.

[5] Explosive dispersal of either several kilograms of plutonium or several kilograms of spent fuel, even in a heavily populated area would not be expected to cause any near-term deaths; hundreds of long-term deaths could occur if weather conditions were right, though these would be difficult to detect against the substantial background rate of cancer. See Steve Fetter and Frank von Hippel, 'The Hazard from Plutonium Dispersal by Nuclear-warhead Accidents', *Science and Global Security*, Vol. 2, No. 1, 1990, pp. 21-41.

[6] World Nuclear Power Reactors 2000-1 and Uranium Requirements, World Nuclear Association, London, March 2002.

The plutonium in the spent fuel is roughly of the order of 1 per cent of the spent fuel. The 70,000+ MT of spent fuel discharged every year therefore contains approximately 70 MT of Pu.[7] In US, for example, the annual discharge of spent fuel is of the order of 2000+ MT while the amount of Pu contained in them is roughly 18-20 MT.[8] The amount of Pu in the spent fuel discharged annually in India, which is not under IAEA safeguards, is well below 1 MT.

Thus, in respect of nuclear materials of non-weapon grade as well, the South Asian stockpile and annual production of such material is far less than, and insignificant compared to, that in the nuclear weapon states.

RADIOACTIVE MATERIALS

Radioactive sources (isotopes) are widely used in a variety of civil applications in the agricultural, industrial, medical, and research areas. They vary widely in physical size and properties and the amount of radioactivity they generate, depending on the application for which they are intended. Unlike in the case of nuclear materials, source material, fuel assemblies, and spent fuel, the security measures applied to such other radioactive materials are very lax and require tightening with the aim being to prevent accidental access to such materials or petty thefts. There is thus a possibility of such materials falling into the hands of anti-social and terrorist elements. Although their use in RDD would not cause any serious physical destruction or heavy casualties, it would certainly have a psychological impact.

According to a study, 'the theft of (such) sources has not traditionally come from malevolent criminal intent. Rather, the sources were stolen more for economic benefit or simply out of curiosity. In fact, there is no record of radioactive source being stolen for sabotage or terrorist activities—except for a number of reported cases related to the Republic of Chechnya in the Russian federation. (According to Russian press reports, six years ago, Chechens used a canister containing the radioactive element Caesium to scare shoppers in a Moscow marketplace,

[7] Tracking Civil Plutonium Inventories: End 1999. David Albright and Mark Gorwitz, *ISIS*, October 2000.

[8] US Spent fuel data from 'US Spent Fuel Update: Year 2000 in Review', NAC Worldwide Consultants, Winter 2001. Plutonium content of spent fuel from various INFCIRC/549 (Information Circular) reports submitted by USA to the IAEA.

and in 1998 officials in the Republic defused a booby-trapped explosive attached to a container of radioactive material).'[9]

The IAEA has been maintaining the Illicit Trafficking Database Programme since 1993 and some 70 states have joined it. According to the IAEA, 'for the period 1 January 1993 to 1 April 2001, the database recorded more than 550 incidents of which about two-thirds have been confirmed by States. Of these confirmed incidents, about half involved nuclear materials and the rest radioactive sources. . . . Of the confirmed incidents with nuclear material, one-third involved low-enriched uranium (LEU) and 17 cases, or 10 per cent, involved highly enriched uranium (HEU) or plutonium. In most cases the quantity of HEU or Pu encountered was small compared to the amounts required for a nuclear explosive. The majority of confirmed incidents involving nuclear material occurred in Europe.'[10]

The Indian regulations and experience with the handling of radioactive materials is dealt with in detail in the AERB annual reports, and in a recent paper at an international conference.[11] The AERB is the competent authority in India to issue codes and guides on regulatory procedures relating to specific applications of radioactive material. There are about 400 institutions which are engaged in industrial gamma radiography. There are about 1000 radiography sources which are being used in about 500 radiography sites. About 800 radiography devices are annually transported for replacement.[12] There have been incidents of theft of radiography sources, although these have been minor. During the period 1986-99, there were 25 cases of missing radiography sources out of which 13 could not be traced.[13] The AERB has been constantly upgrading its training facilities for personnel involved in these activities since in most cases of missing sources the main reason for such loss has been improper storage or transport and carelessness on the part of the radiography personnel.

[9] Abel J. Gonzalez, 'Security of radioactive sources: The evolving new international dimensions', *IAEA Bulletin*, Vol. 43, No. 4, 2001, pp. 39-48.

[10] 'IAEA Illicit trafficking database Programme', *IAEA Bulletin*, Vol. 43, No. 4, 2001, p. 15.

[11] A. Kumar et al., 'Safety and Security of Radioactive Materials: The Indian Scenario', IAEA-CN-86-30, International Conference on Security of Nuclear Material and Radioactive Sources, Stockholm, 7 May 2001.

[12] Op. cit., pp. 52.

[13] Op. cit., pp. 52.

The Political Dimensions of Concerns about Nuclear Safety

While the concerns about nuclear terrorism and nuclear safety are valid and need to be addressed, the current campaign being waged for nuclear safety by the US and its allies have a number of negative features, intentional or otherwise, which need to be studied by India in some depth. What are these?

The first is the intention to use the current hysteria about nuclear terrorism to push an agenda for even more restrictive control regimes. In the immediate aftermath of the 1990-1 Gulf War and the attendant concerns about the Iraqi nuclear programme, the US forced the Nuclear Suppliers Group (NSG) to broaden and tighten its safeguards requirements with the result that India, too, was adversely affected. Following that initiative, members of the NSG have denied India all nuclear transfers. Even the recent Russian contract for sale of fuel for Tarapur was objected to by the US and its allies in the NSG, although in the past three countries—US, France and China—had supplied fuel for Tarapur. Now there is a similar call to further tighten the control regimes.[14]

The second is to bring into force, under the auspices of the IAEA, mandatory reporting regimes to monitor the nuclear activities of states which do not currently accept such requirements. In the wake of the Gulf War, because of proliferation concerns about the Iraqi nuclear programme, the US and its allies tightened the fullscope requirements of the NPT by proposing Additional Protocols to agreements already in place between the non-nuclear weapons states party to the NPT. Although in the initial discussions many non-NWS parties to the NPT signed the Additional Protocol, very few have ratified it. As one analyst recently wrote, 'On the negative side, the rate of accession has been slower than anticipated and disappointing. Whether as a result of inertia, bureaucratic impediments, concerns about intrusion on national sovereignty or for other reasons, only 22 of the 187 parties to the NPT (not yet including any of the five nuclear weapon states, all of whom have voluntary safeguards agreements with the IAEA under the NPT

[14] 'The Nuclear Suppliers Group (a body external to the IAEA) should adopt more stringent requirements prohibiting exports to countries that do not provide levels of security comparable to those called for in the INFCIRC/225/rev.4. Matthew Bunn and George Bunn,'Nuclear Theft and Sabotage: Priorities for Reducing New Threats', *IAEA Bulletin*, Vol. 43, No. 4, 2001, p. 25.

regime) have ratified the Protocol and entered it into force. Only two of these are states with significant nuclear activity.'[15]

The third is to erode national sovereignty under the excuse of international concerns. As a recent analyst wrote, 'To begin with, we need to think beyond the boundaries between national sovereignty and the international state system within which we have lived from the outset of the nuclear age; in particular to balance the traditional demands of sovereignty and the legitimate demands of the international community.'[16]

The fourth is to posit a state of high instability in South Asia, conjure up an apocalyptic vision of a nuclear holocaust in South Asia, and use all these to bring India's entire nuclear programme under international safeguards, which it has refused to do so far. As Lawrence Scheinman has suggested, 'with respect to safeguards that each of the non-NPT states, i.e. India, Pakistan, Israel and Cuba, but 'primarily India, have nuclear facilities and locations, not related to their weapons programmes, that are outside of international safeguards. Voluntarily submitting these facilities to IAEA safeguards (similar to the concept of voluntary offers of the nuclear weapon-states which themselves vary) would send a positive message that they value safeguards, and would help to reinforce the importance of the principle of having effective means of inspection to ensure compliance with undertakings. In so far as export controls are concerned, they could be strongly urged to adopt the practices of the vast majority of nuclear exporters with respect to supply conditions and restraints even to the extent of notifications of exports to the IAEA to increase knowledge of nuclear profiles wherever the Agency conducts safeguards.'[17]

As shown earlier, the primary source of nuclear weapons and nuclear materials, which could be used by terrorists, are all concentrated in the NWS. Most of the illicit trafficking in nuclear materials and other radiological materials has been confined to Europe. South Asia does not figure as a major depository of such materials and does not appear in the UN databank on Illicit Trafficking. Therefore, South Asia is not an issue of major concern as far as safety of nuclear materials goes. It is true that in recent months concerns have been expressed about the links between the Pakistani nuclear establishment and the Al Qaida,

[15] Lawrence Scheinman, 'Transcending Sovereignty in the Management & Control of Nuclear Material', *IAEA Bulletin*, Vol. 43, No. 4, 2001, p. 34.

[16] Op. cit., p. 34.

[17] Op. cit., p. 35.

but that is a matter between the international community and Pakistan. Such concerns must be evaluated on their own merits and the attempts to enmesh India into a system of international controls merely to bring the Pakistani programme under control will not be of much help in curbing the possibility of illicit diversion from Pakistan.

As for the linkage between nuclear safety and stability in South Asia, no convincing case has been made out so far to indicate that there is any such relationship. All indicators show that there are none.

7

Nuclear Doctrine in South Asia

Raja Menon

Nuclear Doctrine

Owing to the casual way in which the words doctrine and strategy have been interposed, particularly in nuclear weapons literature, it is necessary to go into what doctrine actually implies. To compose a broad definition it is also necessary to go into the history of warfare. Doctrine became important when the local commander needed guidance on the principles that guided his superior on how force was to be used. Some well established and unambiguous examples are Genghis Khan, who emphasized speed of action when in doubt, and Admiral Nelson who advocated close action to captains also afflicted with doubt. Hence the word doctrine contains a strong element of 'use' of a particular arsenal or force. Doctrines are invariably written at the level of a service although the 'use' of the doctrine may reach into the grand strategic, the strategic, the operational, and the tactical levels.[1] Not surprisingly, doctrines have been developed over time, reflecting the experience of that service in fighting past wars. Many of the early doctrines that the superpowers developed during the Cold War would, in retrospect, look like unintelligent madness. During all the years that Curtis LeMay led the Strategic Air Command, he obstinately held the view that American nuclear weapons were meant to be used by dropping them during his lifetime on the Soviet Union to achieve 'victory'.[2] That was LeMay's 'doctrine', and obviously arose from the only such

[1] '*The Fundamentals of British Maritime Doctrine*', Her Majesty's Stationery Office, 1995, p. 42.

[2] Curtis LeMay, *America is in Danger* (New York: Funk & Wagnals, 1968), pp. 82-3.

experience the world had had till then in Hiroshima and Nagasaki to force the surrender of a fanatically motivated fighting force.

In Sept 1957 LeMay briefed Robert C. Sprague a member of Eisenhower's Gaither Committee 'I will know from own intelligence whether or not the Russians are massing their planes . . . for a massive attack against the United States.' And he said 'if I come to that conclusion, I'm going to knock the shit out of them before they get off the ground'. 'General, that isn't national policy', Sprague remembers saying. 'You know that'. LeMay, he says, replied, 'No, it's not national policy, but it's my policy'.[3]

LeMay was a strong, opinionated man who controlled the destiny of the SAC (Strategic Air Command) for many years and imprinted on that organization his own views, as has been seen by the statements that his successors made after he retired. It is clear that the SAC 'believed' in a pre-emptive first strike, which was definitely at variance with President Eisenhower's own version of US nuclear doctrine. Eisenhower's personal belief was that nuclear forces should be 'saved' for a retaliatory second strike, and that it would be the size of the second strike that would deter. In 1960, 15 years after Hiroshima, the US nuclear 'doctrine' ran on many parallel tracks, and was out of the control of the President with 10,000 tactical warheads deployed in twenty different systems[4] in Europe. These facts are necessary to understand that great nuclear instability was caused by both sides in the Cold War before a saner philosophy was developed, which attempted to define some of the rules for achieving deterrence and stability. Even after the President attempted to bring the entire system under his control, a false 'missile gap' bogey was created in the media and the American strategic community, leading to the creation of even larger missile forces. In retrospect, it can be conjectured that Robert McNamara's, former Secretary of Defense in the Kennedy Administration, initial attempts to logically structure the American arsenal were designed to control the US armed forces rather than to deter the Soviets.

The Russians were equally culpable in assuming extremely illogical public postures. Writing under the pressure of communist ideology, Marshal Sokolovskiy produced his infamous *Soviet Military Strategy*, which described how troops would fight 'through' a nuclear war to

[3] John Newhouse, *The Nuclear Age* (London: Michael Joseph, 1989), p. 280. Quoting Robert Sprague's interview with LeMay.

[4] McGeorge Bundy, *Danger and Survival* (New Delhi: Rekha, 1988), p. 339.

achieve 'victory' on the battlefield.[5] It often spoke of the victory of socialism which could not be defeated by military technology such as with nuclear weapons. The author of this chapter was present at a seminar where a retired Russian diplomat spoke of a 30-day campaign to take the Soviet Army through Germany, France, and Spain to the Atlantic, although he was adamant that this plan would not be embarked upon as a conquest, but only as active defence.[6]

What the entire Cold War narrative reveals is the immutability of very major forces at work once weaponization has taken place that often bypass or submerge government procedures and institutions. These forces seek new arsenals, new capabilities eliminate old assumptions, perceive new threats where none existed before, and make entirely fresh calculations on what is minimum and what is credible. South Asia is admittedly a different cultural region from Europe or the USA, and a case could be made that high level political decisions in South Asia are made 'differently' from those in the West. Such claims are often made in conferences or seminars, but it takes a giant leap in faith to believe that being different is the same as being wiser, better, or more intelligent. McNamara pushed Washington into declaring a nuclear doctrine 15 years after Hiroshima; Washington could well have delayed doing so by another ten years but for the pressure created by one individual. The declaration was an accident of history, and the normal processes of government may not have moved the nuclear world into understanding the necessity for transparency in doctrine.

How dangerous even well meaning analysts can be is illustrated by Wohlstetter's historic article 'The Delicate Balance of Terror'.[7] This article is considered today as the first clearly articulated belief in deterrence and the value of the second strike. At that time, the article was used to lambast the US government for its 'sleepy' attitude towards deterrence by possessing the wrong kind of weapon systems and not enough of the right kind. So, while it rightly led to the withdrawal of the vulnerable SAC bases all over the world, Wohlstetter's arguments did lead to an increase in the US arsenal. But in the subcontinent, as we shall see later, many of the technical analyses made by Wohlstetter have not made any impact even 43 years later, and that is a cause of

[5] V.D. Sokolovskiy, *Soviet Military Strategy* (Bristol: Crane Russak, 1984).

[6] Wilton Park Conference on 'Confidence and Security Building Measures in Europe and South Asia', June 2001.

[7] A. Wohlstetter, 'The Delicate Balance of Terror', *Foreign Affairs*, Vol. 28, June 1959, pp. 211-34.

alarm. Besides providing compelling arguments for withdrawing vulnerable airbases from all over the world, Wohlstetter also argued about the futility of fielding intermediate range ballistic missiles (IRBMs) like the Thor and Jupiter (both army controlled missiles). He argued about the necessity for independent analyses to distinguish bad systems from good ones and the ability of the political class to be 'aware' of the implications of technological change and communications. At first glance, what is of concern is the inability to incorporate even those lessons learnt by the United States in Wohlstetter's time, on the grounds that South Asia is 'different', or that South Asia needs to learn nothing from the superpowers since the latter got so many things wrong.

Non-Weaponized Deterrence

Prior to 1998, the feeling of separateness was manifested in the belief that a non-weaponized nuclear state could provide deterrence in South Asia. It is quite possible that in theory this may be the case, but it was never argued, simulated, or analysed. With the bomb known to have been ready by 1990 or 1991, the Government of India got cold feet about striking out against the Comprehensive Test Ban Treaty (CTBT) and the Nuclear Non-Proliferation Treaty (NPT) and passed up a golden opportunity to test, along with China and France, in the fall of 1995. This failure was sought to be explained by government funded agencies as being informed by a deliberate strategy called Recessed Deterrence or Non-Weaponized Deterrence (NWD); it marked the first attempt at evolving a doctrine but was manifestly a failure. The nearest attempt to define what NWD could have been comes in the monumental work written by Ashley Tellis[8] many years after the second tests at Pokhran. Tellis believes that if all the discrete elements of the entire nuclear weapons system chain, like the command, control, communication, computing, intelligence and information (C4I2) centre, the dual use rocket systems, the national command posts and authorities, the hardened and dispersed sites, etc., had been made and incorporated, but without overtly testing nuclear weapons, then deterrence may have been achieved. I have not much objection to this, but an Indian stamp of approval on this variant of NWD would have depended on how this complex idea was received in Islamabad or Beijing. Whether the

[8] Ashley Tellis, *India's Nuclear Posture* (Santa Monica: RAND, 2002), pp. 221-9.

Indian government could have put together all the 'other' pieces of the jigsaw referred to as an ideational system by Tellis is a moot point, as attempts to test proclaimed dual use missiles and technology demonstrators produced violent international reactions almost equivalent to those occurring upon testing of atomic weapons.

On the ground, the strongest unspoken support to an Indian NWD doctrine came through a similar Pakistani belief in its own NWD. Islamabad's security management was manifestly different from that of India with Islamabad's nuclear ambition solely linked to combating India. As long as India did not test, or go through steps indicating the creation of nuclear delivery systems and a command and control system, Pakistan was content with NWD. The man who steered the Pakistani bomb programme through the turbulence of frequent political changes, General Aslam Beg, has this to say about NWD[9]: 'In the case of weapons of mass destruction, it is not the numbers that matter, but the destruction that can be caused by even a few. The strategy of terror starts working from the first notion that there is retaliation. The fear of retaliation lessens the likelihood of war between India and Pakistan. I can assure you that if there was no such fear, we would probably have gone to war in 1990.' Commenting on the General's remarks, Perkovich concludes with the statement that if Beg had sent any nuclear signals in 1990 they were not received in Delhi. This is an understatement. In Indian military circles, the idea that the subcontinent came close to war in 1990 is looked upon as being ridiculous. These dysfunctional views between the two capitals is a classic example of how NWD can only create misunderstandings, leading to nuclear instability in a crisis. In the absence of National Command Posts and Authorities and clearly defined nuclear alert status, one side can only guess what the other side is up to. In the absence of clearer information, a worst case scenario has to be assumed and acted upon. This is normal military doctrine. The fact that Delhi was coolly unconcerned with what General Beg thought amounted to nuclear signalling is a telling instance of the confusion that jury rigged doctrines can create.

From the American and Pakistani point of view, the incident that triggered off the Gates mission is also illustrative of the dangers of

[9] Interview given by General Beg to George Perkovich October, 1992 as quoted in Perkovich, *India's Nuclear Bomb* (Los Angeles, University of California Press, 1999), p. 312.

NWD.[10] The US intercepted a message sent internally[11] by Islamabad to the Pakistan Atomic Energy Commission (PAEC) to prepare one nuclear weapon. Without revealing what it was that had set them off, the Gates mission visited Islamabad and Delhi and concluded that they had either prevented war or nuclear war—although foreign military attachés were taken around the peacetime locations of India's strike corps to see that no mobilization had taken place. This incident resembles the 1984 incident when US satellite surveillance 'noticed' two squadrons of Jaguars missing in Ambala and concluded that they had been forward deployed, when, in fact, they had been parked under some trees.[12] There is simply not enough literature on NWD to treat it as doctrine. If it was the South Asian intention to pursue NWD as a reliable doctrine it should have been subjected to the rigorous analyses and questioning that nuclear doctrine has been subjected to for over four decades. In proceeding from NWD to weaponization, South Asia moved away from a most destabilizing regime to a more conventional form of danger.

Why NWD would have been more dangerous can best be studied by war gaming or simulation. This would have been pertinent to a region, which has seen three conventional wars in the space of half a century, with near continuous firing across the LoC in the intervening years. It is clear, therefore, that unlike the US and USSR situated across the globe from each other, a nuclear war in South Asia would, most likely, escalate out of a conventional war. It is interesting to note that in the USA, nuclear DEFCON 2 is assumed when shooting begins, a condition that never stops in South Asia.[13] If the political intention is to create nuclear stability through deterrence in India and Pakistan, deterrence would have to be extremely 'strong' to withstand the shock of a conventional war. It is, therefore, necessary to look at the 'strength' of deterrence and rely on that strength, rather than resort to postures

[10] In May 1990, US Deputy National Security Advisor Robert Gates came to New Delhi, ostensibly to avert a nuclear war between India and Pakistan.

[11] Michael Krepon and Mishi Faruqee (eds.), 'Conflict Prevention and Confidence-Building Measures in South Asia: The 1990 Crisis.' The Henry L. Stimson Center, Occasional Paper 17, April 1994, pp. 30-1.

[12] Interview with a retired Vice Chief of Air Staff. October 2000.

[13] 'Defense readiness conditions (DEFCONs) describe progressive alert postures primarily for use between the Joint Chiefs of Staff and the commanders of unified commands.' As explained in http://www.fas.org/nuke/guide/usa/c3i/defcon.htm, accessed on 15 March 2003.

like Launch on Warning and Launch under Attack, alternatives that were popular in Washington. Non-Weaponized Deterrence implies that when an armed conflict is about to begin, the scientists on both sides would begin a flurry of activity to collect the fissile material, place them into warheads, mate the warheads to the delivery vectors, move these vectors around and take all the action necessary for planning a nuclear pre-emptive first strike. These activities would feed the fear and insecurities on both sides, when war is already being fought and passions and jingoism are at their zenith. Of all the dangerous actions whose occurrence could trigger a nuclear war, I have come across none more fraught with calamitous consequences than imposing NWD in a region where shooting wars are common.

Weaponization without Doctrine

The overt nuclear tests in May 1998 conducted by India did not reduce the dangers of NWD, since they were undertaken in haste, without the development of delivery systems, a command authority, a command centre, doctrine, or communications. All that the tests achieved in the subcontinent was to remove some doubts about the technological capabilities of both countries, while creating some new ones. The tests of May 1998 represented a pact between the politicians and the scientific community in India. None of the other bureaucracies were involved. Not surprisingly, at that time the future course of India's nuclear arsenal was most unclear. The scientific community was at pains to show that they were not Dr Strangeloves, and described the future arsenal as a modest one that could 'do the job'. Questions regarding accuracies of delivery systems, yields, the weight of a second strike response, method of disposal and camouflage, the location and type of command and control all lay in the future.[14] It may be remembered that the literature preceding the tests indicated a vague non-technical and declaratory kind of debate. The bomb was called the nuclear 'option'. Asking for having a doctrine meant that one was dubbed a hawk. Its necessity was substantiated on the grounds that India could then 'stand up' to the bigger powers. Not having a doctrine meant succumbing to nuclear apartheid. Not surprisingly, South Asia began to be known in Washington as the home of 'declaratory' policies,

[14] Limited audience briefing at United Services Institution (USI), New Delhi and Centre for Policy Research (CPR), New Delhi, June and August 1998.

lacking background or substance. However, if May 1998 showed New Delhi to be in an unprepared state to answer any questions on nuclear doctrine, February 1999 saw what can only be described as dramatic progress towards stabilizing the nuclear situation in South Asia.

THE LAHORE MEMORANDUM

When one sees the 15 to 17 years that the US took to attempt articulating a transparent nuclear doctrine that could be read by Moscow,[15] the lapse of just nine months between May 1998 and the Lahore summit is a remarkable achievement by the Indian Prime Minister. It is also a damning indictment of the poor statesmanship of General Musharraf who was planning the conflict in Kargil at that time without comprehending what would be lost if the Lahore summit was allowed to fail—which it did. If India and Pakistan had moved to put nuclear Confidence-Building Measures (CBMs) in place immediately after the Lahore meeting, South Asia could indeed have shown that it was not only culturally different, but also possessed of a greater sensitivity towards dealing with Weapons of Mass Destruction. Unfortunately, the Memorandum of Understanding signed between the two Foreign Secretaries was never translated into agreements before the Kargil conflict took place. There were eight clauses in the memorandum that visualized:[16]

- Bilateral consultations on security concepts and nuclear doctrines;
- Advance notification of ballistic missile tests;
- National measures to prevent accidental or unauthorized use; notification in case of such use; measures to prevent misinterpretation by the other side;
- Memorandum on foregoing further testing;
- Measures to prevent incidents at sea;
- Mechanism to review implementation of CBMs;
- Enhanced communication between the two sides;
- Bilateral consultations on security and disarmament in international fora.

Of these eight measures, five of them are taken from the slew of understandings arrived at between the US and USSR in the early 1970s,

[15] Robert McNamara's speech at Ann Arbor Spring 1962, McGeorge Bundy, *Danger and Survival* (New Delhi: East West Press, 1989), p. 484.

[16] Memorandum of Understanding 21 February 1999, *The Hindu*, 22 February 1999.

preceding and following SALT I, and hence embody well-tested and proven agreements. But, undoubtedly, the most statesman- like of these measures and not replicated in the US-USSR context was the first one—bilateral consultations on security concepts and nuclear doctrines. If doctrines had been exchanged and discussed it would have meant the early establishment of a transparent nuclear relationship. Great benefits could have followed, like an early commencement of nuclear arms control negotiations, banning of Tactical Nuclear Weapons, and capping of delivery systems. Indeed, the field was wide open and optimists in India were preparing a position on nuclear arms control, when Musharraf struck at Kargil. Incidentally, the concluding paragraph of the Memorandum of Understanding required that the technical details would be worked out by experts before mid-1999 with a view to reaching bilateral agreements.

The Draft Indian Nuclear Doctrine

If the two countries needed to consult each other on nuclear doctrines, as required in the Lahore Memorandum, someone had to write a draft doctrine. This task was given to the National Security Advisory Board (NSAB), which completed the task by August 1999. The draft report was published on 17 August.[17] The NSAB quite rightly concluded that the Kargil conflict should not be permitted to interfere with the long and complex process of achieving nuclear stability in South Asia. Now that more than four years have elapsed since the doctrine was written, how do its objectives look in retrospect? It would be best to deal with this document under the same headings which its drafters had used.

OBJECTIVES

This section attempts to place the doctrine against the larger backdrop of international relations by declaring a no-first-use (NFU) policy and aggregating it with the resolve to maintain a minimum credible deterrent posture. States have often chosen to use nuclear weapons to deter conventional war, but India's doctrine clearly defines the role of its arsenal to deter nuclear use by another state. Although survivability is dealt with separately later, the doctrine claims to have looked at the technological factors that will influence survivability, although there is

[17] Draft Report of the NSAB on Indian Nuclear Doctrine, available at http://www.fas.org/nuke/guide/india/doctrine/990817-indnucld.htm.

no literature of any kind, either official or unofficial, to suggest that the survivability issue has been reckoned with by Indian strategic circles.

ACHIEVING DETERRENCE

This paragraph rightly emphasizes survivable forces, a robust command and control system, and the will to use nuclear weapons. The emphasis on early warning and intelligence conflicts with the geography of South Asia and the earlier emphasis on maintaining a survivable second strike which is presumably necessary due to the short aircraft and missile flight times in South Asia.

NUCLEAR FORCES

It is difficult for anyone with any knowledge of nuclear strategy to reconcile this paragraph. For a nuclear force to be effective, enduring and flexible, there can be no place for aircraft delivered bombs, since the country has abjured No-first-use and also placed emphasis on survivable second strike forces. Even more disturbing are the possible reasons why a triad has been envisaged, with its seemingly unexplained beneficial connotations regarding the word 'triad'. The triad in the USA was a relic of inter-service rivalry, which had gone on unchecked for 18 years before McNamara reined it in. The fact that the same inter-service rivalry has surfaced in India within a year of weaponizing to skew the country's nuclear weapon choices in favour of any particular service is depressing. It is a sign of the same forces being at work in India as those in the US that had taken its arsenal sizes to absurd levels. The only aircraft deliverable nuclear bomb in the US inventory is the variable yield B-61 runway denial bomb, which is still deployed in Europe as a first use weapon to incapacitate enemy airfields. The entire survivable second strike concept collapses if it is linked with the most fragile of nuclear weapon systems. This paragraph leaves one with the feeling that for each service it is business as usual despite the NSAB's rhetoric on putting in place a minimum credible deterrent.

COMMAND AND CONTROL

Most people believe that command and control (C2) only entails establishing the mechanism of nuclear use. This is unfortunate. If the C2 organization is properly set up, nuclear use will not occur, but in the long years of nuclear peace, the C2 organization would have played a major role. What should that role be? It involves the creation of deterrence and deterrence signalling from one country to another. The primary task of the NSAB should have been to look at the national legislation regarding nuclear weapons and nuclear matters. The Atomic Energy Act (1962) is a law that has little relevance to India today. Written at a time when the State wished to arrogate to itself the right to all matters relating to atomic energy, this act is nothing but a relic of a socialist economic past. It has no clause dealing with nuclear weapons, the national command authority, the care and custody of nuclear weapons and fissile material, and the prevention of their theft and loss. C2 in a country begins with legislation which allocates responsibilities to various organs of the government, a process that is difficult to enforce in India, where government seemingly has only rights but few responsibilities. Legislation must also separate the competing bureaucracies of defence, external affairs, and science administration into clearly demarcated areas. Only legislation can prevent situations where the scientific community makes bombs or rockets which were never asked for by the user in the first place.

SECURITY AND SAFETY

It is inconceivable how the security of nuclear material can be ensured without the involvement of the defence services. The narrative of how the bomb cores were transported from the Bhabha Atomic Research Centre (BARC) to Pokhran in May 1998 under the escort of an army company without the escort commander being told what was being escorted is surely not the best manner for transporting nuclear material. These aberrations can only be corrected by legislation, but the draft doctrine is silent on the subject.

SUMMARY

The most remarkable thing about the draft doctrine was that it was ever written at all in a country notorious for opaque policies and declaratory rhetoric. The draft was to have been studied and implemented by the National Security Council (NSC), which got cold feet in the light of the intense public debate on the subject. This was unnecessary, but two factors undid all the good that this attempt at transparency achieved. The first was the Kargil conflict, and the second the aggressive posturing by members of the Indian strategic community to embarrass Pakistan on its inability to declare an NFU regime. Some people in India believe that Pakistan's unwritten doctrine of maintaining a nuclear arsenal for redress its conventional arms asymmetry will be a source of embarrassment for Pakistan's External Affairs Ministry. This is quite unlikely since NATO, comprising so many member nations, had precisely such a doctrine for 45 years. It appears that once again India's declaratory policies are getting ahead of reasoned action on the ground.

The Kargil War and Pakistan's Nuclear Doctrine

Since 1988, there has been a belief in Indian Services Headquarters that the Pakistani bomb, which probably materialized a couple of years earlier than in India, was meant to be used if India crossed the 'nuclear threshold'. The belief in Indian Services Headquarters was that it was a geographical threshold. In this manner, over the years, Indian planners have had to try and piece together what the Pakistani nuclear doctrine could be, though all writers are clear that Pakistan will try and get out of an unfavourable conventional situation by threats of nuclear use. Most Indian military thinkers are also clear that Pakistan's attempts to 'lower' the nuclear threshold will not be believed by India, which is certain that the threshold remains at a robust level. How will these calculations mature in the course of time? The Pakistanis believe that their nuclear strategy is no different from that of NATO, and therefore the doctrine is well tested. I have shown, however, that this Pakistani belief is seriously flawed because, in Europe, NATO was the status quo power and threatened nuclear use very early if the Warsaw pact upset that status quo.[18] In South Asia, Pakistan is the revisionist power and would start the conflict to upset the status quo. As an Indian response and escalation is expected and Pakistan would try its best to smother that escalation; it is only if the situation worsens considerably that nuclear use would be threatened.

But India does not know really where this mythical line called the nuclear threshold is situated and would disbelieve any 'early' attempt by Pakistan to declare that the threshold has been reached. This is exactly what happened during the Kargil crisis, when junior ministers in Pakistan were obviously primed to say that the threshold had been reached.[19] Both the Indian Prime Minister and National Security Adviser dismissed these threats out of hand.[20] In fact, Kargil has con-

[18] Raja Menon, *A Nuclear Strategy for India* (Delhi: Sage, 2001), pp.195-8.

[19] Shamshad Ahmed's statement reported in *The Hindu*, 1 June 1999.

[20] *Hindustan Times*, 5 July 1999, and *Times of India*, 1 July 1999.

vinced Delhi that Pakistan's first cry of alarm at approaching the 'threshold' will always be a bluff, since they had cried wolf during this war when the Indian troops were on their own side of the LoC. The nuclear signalling during the Kargil conflict led to one of the first cogent pronouncements on India's nuclear doctrine, devoid of declaratory rhetoric, when the Indian Chief of Army Staff General V.P. Malik stated that India believed that there was space for conventional warfare.[21] This statement was picked up by a large number of commentators in Pakistan, and this author has heard it repeated at many seminars with Pakistanis. Unfortunately, the Indian General's remark was given a twist to mean that India intends to use its conventional superiority to strike against Pakistan so that Delhi can go on denying the Kashmiris their 'freedom'.

This narrative is necessary to explain how the development of nuclear stability between India and Pakistan has been handicapped by the full stop at Lahore. Any progress now is reminiscent of the pre-McNamara years of the Cold War when each side was dependent on press statements coming from the other side, often of dubious authenticity and value. In that sense, the value of the first clause in the Lahore Memorandum on consultations on doctrine is apparent despite the fact that it never got off the ground. Apart from the diplomatically important clause of NFU, the nuclear doctrines of the two countries are fundamentally different. Pakistan's doctrine has embedded in it the belief that nuclear weapons can help Pakistan get out of a deteriorating conventional war situation against a superior conventional power, which is also nuclear armed. It is interesting that the first act of nuclear signalling, referred to earlier, was by Pakistan on 1 June 1999, when it was known that India had deployed fully all along its border with Pakistan, particularly along the Rajasthan border, as a possible prelude to widening the war. From the Indian side there were calculated attempts to signal to Pakistan, after the Kargil War had ended, that India did not believe nuclear weapons deterred conventional war. This signalling was done by Defence Minister George Fernandes at an Institute of Defence Studies and Analyses (IDSA) seminar[22] when he stated that: 'Conventional war remained feasible, though with definite limitations, if escalation across the nuclear threshold is to be avoided.'

Whilst Fernandes' speech did make the point that conventional war

[21] IDSA Seminar on *Asian Security*, New Delhi, 5 January 2000.
[22] Ibid.

is possible, he unfortunately confirmed Pakistan's nuclear doctrine that there is such a nuclear threshold and India's conventional superiority could only go up to that mythical line. One would think that the Pakistanis would have been overjoyed at a confirmation from someone no less than the Defence Minister of India that their nuclear doctrine had been understood and validated by the Indians. But at a conference in Bangkok, a Pakistani Brigadier who did the staff work in the Pakistani Nuclear Planning Division (NPD) expressed dissatisfaction at the Indian Defence Minister's concession that conventional war cannot go beyond a certain point because of the threat of nuclear war. He felt that the Defence Minister should have said that, since the scope and intensity of a conventional war is uncertain, and that its momentum may be un-controllable, India should concede that conventional war cannot be *begun* in South Asia.[23] Here again we have another example of vague nuclear signalling going all wrong, being misunderstood and positions being taken which can be dangerous. Perhaps the error on India's part lay in the government's refusal to either ignore or accept the draft nuclear doctrine, and partly perhaps it does not address this question directly. In fact, the draft nuclear doctrine is unequivocal in its intention to punish a nuclear strike on this country, but translating this resolve to mean that a Pakistani nuclear threat would be disbelieved during the course of a conventional war is a signal that India has not sent so far.

Accidental Nuclear War

If the Lahore Memorandum is dead for all practical purposes, both India and Pakistan continue to see its benefits and have unilaterally moved to implement those measures that are plainly beneficial to themselves. Just as India has moved expeditiously on writing a draft doctrine, Pakistan has moved towards strengthening national control over its arsenal. The National Command Authority (NCA) has an operational and developmental division in which the Head of State presides.[24] While the defence services control one division at the intermediate level, the Foreign Minister controls the other. They have also moved towards creating a Nuclear Regulatory Authority. In all these

[23] Brig. Naeem Salik, Centre for International Security and Cooperation (CISAC) Conference, Bangkok, 6 August 2001.

[24] The organizational tree was explained in detail by Brig. Naeem Salik, the Representative of Pakistan's NPD at the CISAC Conference, Bangkok, 6 August 2001.

respects, the objective of the drafters of the Lahore Memorandum has been achieved in one area in Pakistan, namely moving towards reducing the risks of accidental nuclear war and preventing unauthorized use. With the number of fundamentalist organizations operating in Pakistan, anxiety in other countries has persuaded the Pakistani government into strengthening their C2 organization. The pervasive influence of the army in all areas of the NCA does remain a source of worry, as competing advice from other bureaucracies may be ignored. Nevertheless, they have moved ahead of India in this regard. What is more disconcerting in the Indian case is the extreme secrecy that pervades a subject that should be transparent. The slow and ponderous steps to establishing a National Command Post (NCP), designating a line of succession to the Prime Minister, establishing an alternative NCP, and so on are cloaked in unnecessary secrecy, which is disturbing because the overarching imperatives of transparency do not appear to have been understood.

Doctrine and Nuclear War through Misperception

Probably at the apex of the necessity to exchange transparent doctrines is the need to prevent nuclear war through misperception. Political misperception combined with doctrinal misperceptions compounds the dangers that could become calamitous. Here again, the lessons of Central Europe need to be studied. Politically the West had no doubt that they were the status quo power, and was unhappy with Poland, Czechoslovakia, and Hungary being behind the Iron Curtain. Apart from making propaganda, they were unwilling to fight a war to liberate Eastern Europe. But they also feared the Soviet Union's intentions, which they read as an ideological urge to conquer Western Europe. Declassified documents from Moscow now convey the impression that Moscow never had any political objective of invading Western Europe although military plans existed for such a campaign. As mentioned earlier a former Soviet diplomat revealed this during a conference on confidence and security building measures in June 2001.[25] So what in fact did happen in Western Europe, was that unknown to both sides, two status quo powers existed in their own fashion. If this assumption is valid, then the doctrinal merits of NATO and Warsaw Pact strategies come into doubt.

[25] See footnote 6.

Was it the NATO nuclear doctrine that deterred the Warsaw Pact countries? Perhaps it did, but in the absence of any political motive to go to war, we will never know. Nevertheless, the Nuclear Planning Group, formed by NATO in the mid-1960s did simulate the Central European scenario very closely and repetitively; the results were explained quite succinctly by Michael Quinlan in his lectures at the United Services Institution (USI).[26] The results have been adequately promulgated but the most important one is that if a weaker conventional power attempts to exit from a deteriorating conventional war situation by using nuclear weapons against a stronger conventional power also armed with nuclear weapons, the weaker power would considerably worsen its situation. This position has also been graphically demonstrated by this author,[27] and this is the reason why NATO, as the weaker conventional power, had enunciated nuclear first-use and very early use as its nuclear doctrine. Moreover, since the Germans protested that early use to stop a land invasion would necessarily mean the use of many weapons on German soil, NATO then planned deep strikes into Eastern Europe as its defence strategy and boldly proclaimed such a policy to assuage the feelings of the Germans. If this dangerous move could have been considered a deterrent, it is only because NATO has no political intention to invade Eastern Europe and this nuclear strategy was purely defensive.

In South Asia, there is little doubt in the mind of Indian thinkers that India is the status quo power, while Pakistan, the weaker conventional power, is the revisionist power. This assumption does not quite obtain across the border as we shall see. The Indians view cross-border terrorism and the Pakistan army's encouragement to it as the first act of a revisionist power, which really means that a sub-conventional war has begun. In Pakistan the view so far is deceptive. Privately, the Pakistani's have been fully aware of what they have been doing, but publicly assume the position that Kashmir is an indigenous uprising, and that Indian escalation would mark the beginning of a conventional war. Here lie the first seeds of misperception. While Pakistan takes a public posture that India will initiate a conventional war with the objective of dismembering Pakistan, India holds the view that Pakistani cross-border terrorism is a low intensity conventional war and the

[26] Talk by Michael Quinlan on 'The Development of NATO Nuclear Doctrine' at the USI on 16 February 2000, published in *USI Journal*, Vol. 130, pp. 276-86.

[27] Menon, *A Nuclear Strategy for India*, pp. 195-7.

Indian riposte represents only a counter-attack. The statements of George Fernandes and General Malik must be seen in this context.

At the grand strategic level, there is no doubt that if Indian conventional superiority cannot be exploited, because of the fear of crossing the nuclear threshold, Pakistan, a state with 19 per cent of India's Gross Domestic Product (GDP) would have effectively neutralized India's military superiority. The question must then be asked whether India needs to maintain and augment its conventional superiority against Pakistan which is unusable. It also raises basic questions about the efficacy of Indian nuclear doctrine. If the ultimate test of the Indian doctrine is to ensure that an enemy state will not use nuclear weapons against India in the most likely scenario, then India must adopt a public position of questioning the nuclear threshold theory of Pakistan. So far, Indian thinkers have adopted two variants of what is essentially a defeatist attitude. One theory holds that limited wars are possible against Pakistan, but eventually the limit of the war reaches up against Pakistan's nuclear threshold. The second theory holds that even limited wars will not comprise a ground war but only include an air bombing campaign that will inflict some punishment, without approaching Pakistan's geographical threshold. What Indian strategists have to ensure is that within the short span of time since 1998, we do not box ourselves into a calamitously disadvantageous position.

Whenever public pronouncements of this nature are made what we are undertaking is a form of deterrence signalling to Islamabad that their doctrine is working and that ours is not. A further nail in the coffin of the Indian doctrine may well be the messages brought across from Islamabad by two Italian researchers who got someone in Pakistan's NPD to elaborate further on their nuclear threshold.[28] This time the Pakistanis articulated four thresholds—a geographical one, a military threshold, a political cohesion limit and an economic loss line. What we are seeing here is a fishing expedition mounted on a perception of Indian pusillanimity. In Islamabad's position, I would be tempted to do the same. If my theory of a geographical threshold has been swallowed, why not put out three more baits?

To go back to the original idea of exchanging doctrines, we can see how far we have travelled in just five years in the absence of the Lahore Memorandum. We in India should not discard the NSAB's draft doc-

[28] Author's interview of Prof. Maurizio Martellini and Paolo Cotta Ramasumo, New Delhi, 13 February 2002.

trine, but make it a living doctrine, to be modified in the light of experience of the real world. The first modification is overdue because, as can be seen, the Pakistani doctrine essentially attempts to codify the Indian ability to deter nuclear war during the course of a conventional war. The threat of nuclear superiority and the threat of a primitive second strike capability has not dissuaded it from threatening first use. This dysfunction could be either doctrinal, or arise from the fact that the Indian doctrine is not supported by the forces necessary to execute that doctrine. I can believe that the latter case may be true, and that when India demonstrates its technological maturity to possess a truly survivable second strike, the Indian doctrine may become more credible. In the meanwhile, my contention that Pakistan's attempt to get out of a bad conventional situation by resorting to nuclear use would make Pakistan's condition infinitely worse, is getting a hearing in Pakistan, at least as evident by Ayesha Agha's article in the *Friday Times*.[29]

THE INDIA-CHINA CO-RELATION

The ideal solution to achieve nuclear stability in South Asia would be to lock China, India, and Pakistan into a triangular nuclear agreement. The reality on the ground, however, is still far from this ideal. Most foreign observers refuse to believe that for many years India's primary and long-term concern was China's nuclear arsenal, an anxiety fuelled by China's ongoing modernization of its nuclear arsenal. Although there is no 'hot' dispute between India and China, the fear in Delhi of being overwhelmed by a superior nuclear China is greater than the fear of nuclear instability with Pakistan. The Pakistani nuclear arsenal is a Chinese creation. The extreme irrationality of Beijing in passing on nuclear secrets to Pakistan has still not found any credible explanation in either Delhi or Beijing. This act gives rise to the growing Indian fears of Chinese nuclear threats in the future, particularly after China arms itself with a modern nuclear arsenal. Indian fears derive from the fact that with a very small arsenal, China could destroy most of India's nuclear arsenal and yet retain enough weapons to deter its possible second strike. Thus there would be no deterrence available to India.

It is in India's interest to keep the nuclear competition with China at a low level. However, steps to discuss the nuclear question with China

[29] Ayesha Agha, 'Credibility of Pakistani Doctrine', *Friday Times*, 1-8 March 2002.

were continuously rebuffed until 1999 on the grounds that India was not a nuclear power. India is prepared to live in nuclear asymmetry with China because Beijing's concerns go beyond India. At the unofficial level, the Pakistanis have expressed willingness to live in nuclear asymmetry with India,[30] but have questioned how this asymmetry could be limited and verified. With the Indo-China dialogue remaining at only very basic levels on security concerns, it will take many years before the dialogue matures to include the nuclear deterrent. In the meanwhile it makes sense to de-limit the Indo-Pakistan arsenals at manageable levels.

Any discussion on limiting nuclear weapons during the years 1999-2002 was upset by the uncertainties created by the American declaration to deploy its National Missile Defence (NMD). While the Western powers and Russia were obviously unconcerned, China's arsenal has become vulnerable. Beijing's reaction to the NMD was, therefore, reactively leading to cascading uncertainties in India and Pakistan. It seems clear at the time of this writing that whatever Chinese objections to the NMD in the diplomatic arena, its leadership has decided to consider the NMD as a reality, and develop their arsenal accordingly. This is no surprise to India which had foreseen a Chinese nuclear modernization in any case. If China is secure in its security perceptions *vis-à-vis* the US, it would be less constrained in coming to an agreement with India. However, it is unlikely that a nuclear dialogue with China can begin except at Beijing's initiative.

[30] Track-II Meeting in Honolulu in July 1999 under the auspices of 'Second Chance', arranged by Asia Pacific Center for Strategic Studies.

8

Nuclear Stability, Deterrence, and Terrorism

Karl-Heinz Kamp

With the end of the Cold War the relevance of nuclear weapons and public attention on the pros and cons of nuclear deterrence had decreased significantly—at least in the East-West context. With the step by step 'rapprochement' of Russia and NATO culminating in the inclusion of Russia in NATO's new decision making forum 'At 20', which was agreed on at the Summit Meeting in Rome in May 2002, even the rationale of nuclear deterrence as an insurance policy against a residual threat posed by a potentially 're-imperialist' Russia has further dwindled.

In recent times, however, deliberations on nuclear forces have made their way back on the political agenda, albeit in various and sometimes opposite directions. The terrorist attacks of 11 September 2001 particularly have highlighted two contradictory developments. On the one hand, Moscow's shift to the West, vigorously pushed by President Vladimir Putin, and a fundamental redefinition of Russian-American relations has opened the window of opportunity for significant reductions in the nuclear arsenals available to both sides. The deep nuclear cuts at the US-Russian level, which might also lead to reductions in the nuclear stockpiles of France and the United Kingdom, could further reduce the relevance of nuclear weapons in the Euro-Atlantic strategic relationship. At the same time, though, the tragedy of 11 September seems to have seduced significant parts of the US strategic community to regard nuclear strikes as one possible option to cope with the threat posed by international terrorism. Should these trends crystallize, it could lead to a major transformation of US nuclear strategy from deterrence into the direction of nuclear warfare. Further down the road, this could lead to new nuclear doctrines and new kinds of nuclear weapons—in sum, to some kind of a 'second coming of the nuclear age'.

Radical developments in other regions of the world have further contributed to bring the nuclear question back on the agenda again. At the beginning of the US campaign against the Taliban regime in Afghanistan, serious concerns were expressed particularly with regard to the security of the Pakistani nuclear arsenal in case of a possible destabilization of the government under President Musharraf. International concern about a potential nuclear escalation were further fuelled by rising tensions between India and Pakistan in Spring 2002.

The reappearance of the nuclear question on the international agenda in various forms and contexts requires careful analysis. This article intends to examine the question of nuclear stability, especially with regard to the lessons learned from the Cold War, and the problems of deterrence after 11 September.

Roots of Nuclear Instability

From the perspective of international stability, the problem is not that certain states simply *possess* nuclear weapons. The real danger is that they might *abuse* their nuclear capabilities to underpin aggressive policies *vis-à-vis* their neighbours or perceived enemies. Countries with irresponsible governments, that have managed to achieve nuclear status might even detonate a nuclear weapon, either intentionally or accidentally as a result of mishandling or lacking control. To illustrate this point: hardly anyone can seriously regard the nuclear status of France or Great Britain as a source of instability. In both cases, the dependability of the political leadership is taken for granted. Thus, the use of nuclear weapons by either of these governments is an extremely remote scenario, only imaginable in the case of a truly vital threat to their survival. If, however, Saddam Hussein, did have nuclear weapons, things would look quite different as he is likely to recklessly use nuclear weapons either against a neighbouring state or against forces from other countries engaged in a crisis management operation in the region.

Thus, it is predominantly the issue of political reliability that determines nuclear stability. From that perspective, the problem of nuclear stability in the Indo-Pakistani relationship seems not to be as dangerous as commonly assumed. Notwithstanding the concerns of many observers who regarded the nuclear tests of India and Pakistan in May 1998 as the ultimate security challenge to global security, there seems to exist a fairly significant level of nuclear stability in South Asia. Despite existing tensions and sometimes belligerent rhetoric on both sides, a true nuclear crisis between the two countries has not taken place yet. India and Pakistan have even fought the Kargil War in 1999 with each other, without its leading on to nuclear escalation. Even after 11 September, when the collapse of the Pakistani leadership appeared to be a realistic possibility, President Musharraf (presumably supported by the United States) acted responsibly to increase the security of Pakistan's nuclear posture. China, the largest nuclear power in Southern Asia did not take any steps either to weaken nuclear stability.

However, the fact that political actors on all sides have acted responsibly so far—at least in regard to nuclear escalation—does not provide an 'all clear' signal for the stability of the region. Another war over Kashmir is always looming large and the domestic situation in Pakistan is hard to predict. What is more, further military action by the United States, be it in the Gulf region or elsewhere, might have far-reaching consequences for stability on the Indian subcontinent. It is worth noting, however, that international concerns regarding South Asia becoming the future nuclear trouble spot after India's and Pakistan's nuclear tests have not been substantiated yet.

'Nuclear Learning' as a Precondition for Nuclear Stability

The evolution of nuclear strategy throughout the antagonistic East-West relationship of the Cold War was driven by a constant process of nuclear learning on both sides. In the early days of the nuclear age, nuclear warheads were regarded as 'just another weapon'—much more destructive than conventional explosives but not qualitatively different. That explains the broad support for the build-up of nuclear forces in the Soviet Union and by NATO. Nuclear weapons were regarded as a cost efficient option for the defence requirements of both sides, since they allegedly provided 'more bang for the buck' or 'more rubble for the Rouble'.

This pro-nuclear trend was supported by the fact that nuclear energy in general had a positive connotation for the societies of the 1950s and early 1960s. In fact, radio commercials and newspaper advertisements drew the picture of a bright nuclear future with atomic vacuum cleaners and cars driven by tiny reactors. As a result, the ecological or medical dangers of nuclear explosions were grossly underestimated. Military personnel were allowed to watch nuclear tests close to 'ground zero' in almost every nuclear state, not at least to analyse the long-term effects of radiation on the human body.

It took the East and the West a number of severe nuclear crises—especially the Cuban Missile Crisis—to make decision makers understand that the detonation of a nuclear weapon would profoundly change the international system and would open a Pandora's box with hardly any chance to close it again. Military exercises and nuclear war games displayed the enormous levels of destruction that could be caused by nuclear exchanges. The prospect of coming close to the abyss of total devastation helped to correct the sanguine views about nuclear warfare. This broad understanding revealed that nuclear war would have a fundamentally different quality as compared to a conventional exchange, not only with respect to the number of casualties but also with regard to the danger of global annihilation.

In retrospective, decision makers on both sides have learned the lessons of potential nuclear escalation and probable nuclear instability very well. As a result, in almost every East-West confrontation since the late 1960s, Moscow and Washington acted extremely cautiously so as to not escalate the situation. However, this did not prevent the superpowers from acting militarily in their own backyards, but whenever the other superpower was involved and whenever a nuclear crisis was imaginable, then political and military de-escalation gained utmost priority.

This can be illustrated by the following example. When the Soviet Union invaded Czechoslovakia in 1968, NATO demonstratively reduced the number of reconnaissance flights along the East-West demarcation line. Normally, in a military crisis, the political leadership intends to increase its intelligence efforts to gain a clearer picture of what is going on. In this case, however, NATO wished to convey the signal of not exacerbating the already highly sensitive situation. This, of course, did not inhibit declaratory policy from sharply condemning the attack on a sovereign country. But the hidden message that NATO did not want to pour oil into the fire, since this could make the crisis get out of control, with potential nuclear implications, was clear. Historical evidence shows that this message was understood correctly by the Soviet side.

STABILITY, TECHNOLOGY AND DETERRENCE

Throughout the East-West conflict, both superpowers regarded strict control of their nuclear weapons as their utmost priority. This is particularly true of the Cold War experience of Germany as the most heavily nuclear armed non-nuclear country in the world. The first US nuclear weapons were deployed in Germany in 1953—actually without the knowledge of the German government. Even today, the United States keeps an undisclosed (at least, not to the public) number of nuclear weapons in special US ammunition sites in Germany, Belgium, Greece, Italy, The Netherlands, United Kingdom, and Turkey.

The major decision making authority for these weapons is the American President. He has the ultimate authority to decide on the use of any US nuclear weapon. However, the public belief, that the President could pick up the phone and kill 70 million people or just to 'push a button' is mistaken, not only in legal, but also in practical terms. Legally, American laws and the NATO Treaty explicitly define the criteria for the use of military force, such as an attack on NATO territory. In addition, if a President would decide to use nuclear weapons, it would require the co-operation of a number of people, simply because no President is fully aware of all the details of nuclear release procedures. For instance, the President cannot physically open the so called 'football', that is the suitcase with the nuclear codes that is always kept close to the President. He would need the help of the officer carrying the suitcase.

With regard to US nuclear weapons on German soil there is another limitation upon the presidential authority in place, namely the so-called 'dual key arrangement'. This term indicates a regulation by which the nuclear bombs remain under the operational control of the United States, whereas the delivery means, namely the Tornado aircraft, belong to the Bundeswehr, and the pilots continue to operate under German command. The details of how to put these two components together in a crisis are codified in the so-called 'Programs of Cooperation' (POC), which have been negotiated between the United States and all its allies with US nuclear weapons on their territory. Under these regulations, the nuclear weapons in Germany cannot be employed without the consent of the German government to use German fighter planes as delivery means. Vice versa, German military personnel cannot employ the nuclear weapons independently either. In fact, US custodial teams guarding the warheads have strict orders to shoot down

German individuals who try to acquire unauthorized access to the weapons.

Another critical aspect of nuclear command and control is the question of nuclear warhead safety. Here, all nuclear states are confronted with the so-called 'always/never problem'. To preserve their deterrent value, nuclear weapons have to be always functional and operational. On the other hand, for the sake of stability, they must never detonate in case of an accident or an unauthorized use. Stability, in turn, is a precondition for deterrence, since only a political decision maker who is confident regarding escalation control (bolstered by safe and stable nuclear procedures) will be able and willing to convey a credible deterrence message.

The United States have solved that problem technically with the so-called 'Permissive Action Links' (PAL) installed on every nuclear weapon. These electronic devices and sophisticated code systems can lock the weapons to guarantee the presidential authority. They can also limit the time span on the functionality of the weapon, which means that a military commander, who has got the presidential authority to use a nuclear weapon, has this authority for only a fixed period of time. This excludes the danger that military officers might fool around with the weapons after the presidential order has expired. To further increase the physical security of US nuclear weapons in Europe, all American warhead depots host special 'destruction teams'. These weapon specialists will render nuclear weapons technically inoperable in case of an attack by terrorist groups or opposing forces.

To an extent, the combination of nuclear learning, technology, and control procedures has led to a very high margin of nuclear stability, not only in NATO but also in the erstwhile Warsaw Pact Countries. At the same time, the value of the nuclear posture for deterrence purposes could be maintained, since the ultimate control of the political authorities could evidently be guaranteed in peacetime as also under combat conditions.

Deterrence and Terrorism

The catastrophe of 11 September 2001 has not only fundamentally changed important parameters of international security, it has also raised the question of the relevance of deterrence—be it with conventional or nuclear weapons—against the spectre of international terrorism. It is worth noting that apocalyptic fears with regard to major terrorist attacks are not merely a result of the high number of casualties in New York city and Washington, D.C., these anxieties are mostly due to the fact that the destruction of the Twin Towers in New York demonstrated the incredible efficiency of asymmetrical warfare. The readiness of some fanatics to sacrifice their lives for the success of the operation proved to be the major 'equalizer' to counter the huge military capabilities of the Western industrial powers. The attacks on the United States displayed that it takes terrorists only minimal organizational skills, a few personnel, and limited financial resources to bring the United States to its knees and to obtain for the terrorists—at least, for a limited time—eye level contact with the most powerful military force in the world.

Notwithstanding these tragic memories, one can argue that the West has achieved a victory against international terrorism. Notwithstanding the still evolving situation in Afghanistan, it is no exaggeration to describe the fight against the Taliban as resulting in a huge success. Apparently, the achievement of the United States is not confined only to the military level. Actually, in spite of the failure of the Soviet Union in Afghanistan, a victory for the US as the largest military power in the world against one of the poorest countries in the world was not much of a miracle. Instead, the true accomplishment following the tragedy of 11 September is the fact that there were no further terrorist attacks against the United States after 7 October 2001 when the air strikes against Afghanistan began. This was really surprising given all the dire warnings issued by the Al Qaida representatives that they would definitely carry the war into the United States, should American forces get engaged in Afghanistan. It was all the more astonishing given that the 'New York model' of terrorist attacks can quite easily be repeated almost anywhere in the world. Modern industrial societies in general and civil air traffic in particular remain highly vulnerable; an event similar to the destruction of the World Trade Center cannot be prevented with any great assurance.

One can argue that the absence of further terrorist action of such a magnitude was not an accident, but a result of the American deterrence message. Immediately after 11 September, the United States has concentrated its vast military capability either in Central Asia or earmarked it for deployment in the region to send an unmistakable sign of determination. In addition, President Bush and the entire US administration has obviously deliberately chosen an aggressive rhetoric and intentionally used elements of simplification. All this had doubtlessly sent a strong signal of resoluteness, which had its effects not only in Afghanistan itself, but almost on a worldwide scale. It is most likely that these signs have been interpreted in an unambiguous way, to imply that if the Al Qaida network commits another major assault on the United States, Afghanistan would simply cease to exist. The message sent out is that, like in the 11 September case, a group can be identified as the culprits and a government identified as the sponsors of terrorism, then the host region or country would have to face complete devastation by the US conventional forces. It is not by accident that some American newspapers came out with cartoons showing a map of the region with Afghanistan being depicted by a huge lake.

The consequences of that message were twofold. On the one hand, no country can further afford to openly support terrorist activities against the United States and can show off as being proud of such operations. And second, even the so-called states of concern have remarkably shifted sides quickly and demonstratively joined the US-led anti-terror coalition—even if some like Sudan had suffered from American military assaults earlier.

Meanwhile, the United States has put more meat on the bones of its deterrence message and has declared its preparedness to carry on their fight against terrorism, even if a significant number of American casualties would be entailed. Thus, the overt declaration of the US to take military action against Iraq does not merely aim to get rid of the Saddam dictatorship but also intends to support the general deterrence message issued by the United States.

These developments permit a number of conclusions being reached with regard to the relationship between deterrence and terrorism. Assuming that key representatives of the Al Qaida network would take stock of their actions on 11 September and the subsequent war in Afghanistan, they would need to draw two conclusions (provided that they would act in a rational way). The first judgement would be that modern industrial societies are extremely vulnerable and thus it is quite simple to cause severe damage to the detested 'Western way of life'. The second conclusion, however, would be that any fundamentalist organization will put its own existence at risk if it undertakes a major attack against the United States. Evidently, an American counter-strike would not be limited, neither geographically, nor in its duration. Instead, it would aim at the total destruction of the terrorist structure.

This fundamental dilemma for the terrorists has been reinforced by the 9 November tragedy. Any future terrorist attack would have to be even more devastating to top the September event and acquire sufficient international attention—just to blow up a building in the Midwest or a US military barrack in Europe would not be enough to gain its way into the international limelight. This, however, would raise the danger of self-annihilation.

One may doubt whether terrorists will realistically undertake such a cost-benefit analysis, since many of them are regarded as 'undeterrable'. This argument might certainly hold true for individual assassins like the suicide attackers in the Middle East, ready to blow themselves up at an Israeli bus stop. The leadership of terrorist groups, however, are likely to behave differently. Terrorist actions almost always have an 'idea' or a 'mission', however bizarre this idea might appear. Those who are in charge of these groups must rate the survival of their organizations (and thereby their own survival) very high, this being a precondition for the survival of the mission. Thus, this can be the one point towards which deterrence can be directed.

As an analogy (with all the admitted analytical weaknesses of comparison), one could refer to the example of Saddam Hussein during the Gulf War. He is widely regarded as undeterrable and absolutely ruthless. However, there is strong evidence to urge that explicit deterrence threats from Washington and Tel Aviv against his life and against the physical existence of his family kept him from using chemical and biological weapons against Israel during the Gulf War.

This is not to argue that every form of terrorism can be deterred by the resolute use of force. The rising violence in the Israeli-Palestinian conflict reveals almost every day that military operations are not the most suitable means to stop regional terrorism. Thus, the current success against the Taliban cannot be regarded as a total solution for the fight against terrorism. Indeed, it has been only successful against a special form of terrorism—certainly against its very apocalyptic form.

Nevertheless, the success achieved so far indicates that the international community does not necessarily have to face Armageddon in the years to come. Instead, deterrence in its various forms will remain one option in the fight against international terrorism. However, the question of which form of deterrence—conventional or nuclear—is suitable against which kind of terrorist threats will require further consideration. Furthermore, whether and how deterrence can be utilized if a terrorist organization cannot be linked to a country or a government, which can become the target of the deterrence message needs to be scrutinized. For the time being, the available data on these issues is very limited. However, it is likely and to be feared that this database will grow in the years to come.

9

Nuclear Stability in Southern Asia: An Indian Perspective

P.R. Chari

Introduction

The phrase 'nuclear stability in Southern Asia' can be parsed into its constituent elements. Thus 'Southern Asia', 'stability', and 'nuclear', liberally used in the preceding chapters, must be decomposed to understand their import despite knowing that this would be entering contested territory.

'Southern Asia' requires initial attention; it is clearly designed to capture the looming presence of China upon the subcontinent. Is this real? South Asia, comprising the seven SAARC nations is a recognizable geographical entity, distinguished by its history, cultural and civilizational links. An argument can be made that excluding Afghanistan and Myanmar from South Asia is anomalous; they impinge on its stability by the smuggling of arms and drugs and terrorists into the region. Extending the limits of South Asia to include Central Asia, Gulf region, Thailand, Malaysia, and Indonesia, however, is excessive,[1] since they share minimal economic, political or strategic commonalities with South Asia to justify this enforced grouping.

Southern Asia, however, can be aggregated in strategic (political-military-nuclear) terms to include China, since it constitutes part of the nuclear threat perceived by India's strategic elite, despite considerable scepticism in the West. Prime Minister Vajpayee's controversial letter to President Clinton immediately after the nuclear tests con-

[1] See the definition of Southern Asia adopted by Jasjit Singh in Chapter 3.

ducted by India on 11 and 13 May 1998 identified India's 'nuclear environment' to comprise 'an overt nuclear weapon state on our borders, a state which committed armed aggression against India in 1962 . . . that country has materially helped another neighbour of ours to become a covert nuclear weapon state. At the hands of this bitter neighbour we have suffered three aggressions in the last 50 years. And for the last 10 years we have been the victims of unremitting terrorism and militancy. . . .'[2] This convoluted language recognizes India's nuclear threat to include apart from Pakistan, China, which developed strategic linkages with Pakistan after 1965.[3] The nuclear danger that India perceives from China had its roots in three events that closely followed each other in the 1960s, viz., India's humiliating defeat in the India-China border conflict (1962); explosion of China's first nuclear device (1964); and China's ultimatum to India during the Indo-Pak war of 1965. Collectively, these events inspired India's militarization of its civilian atomic energy programme.[4] The nuclear threat from China could heighten in future if it accelerates its nuclear programme to counter the US deployment of its missile defence systems; this could also seriously affect India's national security.[5] Strategically envisaged, South Asia includes China to establish the larger entity of 'Southern Asia'.

The term 'stability' is associated with its synonyms—solidity, substantiality, strength, and firmness. Ideally, stability must exist between nuclear-armed adversaries in the interests of their survival and regional peace; hence danger arises from nuclear weapon powers being changeable, irresolute, and unsteady in their relations with adversaries, since this could trigger nuclear confrontations and crises. The empirical

[2] 'Text of Vajpayee's letter to Clinton', *The Hindu*, 14 May 1998.

[3] More recently, this includes the transfer by China of both nuclear (design information of its fourth nuclear explosive device) and missile (M-11 missiles) technology to Pakistan, apart from conventional arms transfers.

[4] Its roots can be traced to Prime Minister Lal Bahadur Shastri's authorization of the Subterranean Nuclear Explosive Programme in 1965 that sanctioned research being undertaken by the Atomic Energy Commission to conduct nuclear tests for peaceful purposes. A detailed description of this shift in India's nuclear policy is available in George Perkovich, *India's Nuclear Bomb: The Impact on Global Proliferation* (New Delhi: Oxford University Press, 2000), esp. Chapter 2, 'The First Compromise Shift towards a Peaceful Nuclear Explosive', pp. 60-85.

[5] Two likely countermeasures that China might adopt is MIRVing its missiles and/or enlarging its intercontinental-range and intermediate/medium-range missile inventory to penetrate the national and theatre missile defences protecting the United States and its East Asian allies, viz., Taiwan and Japan.

evidence, indeed, reveals that, 'nuclear equations are most unsettled and tension-producing at the outset of any such pairing',[6] as the earliest interactions between the United States and Soviet Union in the late 1940s and early 1950s inform us.

The requirements of 'nuclear' stability can now be analysed. Two nuclear dyads obtain in Southern Asia—India-Pakistan and India-China. Do they constitute a tripolar nuclear structure? The international system has experience of dyadic but not tripolar nuclear structures. In the conventional sphere, the possibility of fighting a two-front war has always been configured into planning exercises by the Indian armed forces. Theoretically, a two-against-one nuclear crisis involving Pakistan and China in confrontation with India is conceivable. Theoretically, it is also possible to visualize missile trajectories emanating from the Northern Territories/Sinkiang, which could make it difficult for India to be certain of the identity of the attacker. Therefore, India would need to war-game scenarios involving a two-front nuclear crisis despite its complexities.

This chapter will focus on different aspects of nuclear stability in Southern Asia within this framework. Whether the Indo-Pak nuclear tests conducted in May 1998 have added or detracted from their security will be initially discussed. International concerns regarding the nuclear instability engendered in South Asia by the Kargil conflict and long-enduring border confrontation can be exaggerated, but cannot be ignored. Why? The Indo-Pak border stand-off, despite its serious implications for nuclear stability, was initiated by India to resolve its problem with cross-border terrorism into Kashmir. Did it work? Is the limited war thesis urged by India feasible? Negotiating nuclear confidence-building measures in the region would be stabilizing, but is this feasible in the vitiated atmosphere obtaining? Finally, what conclusions can be drawn to achieve nuclear stability in the region?

May 1998 and Subcontinental Stability/Instability

It is obvious that the reciprocal nuclear tests conducted by India and Pakistan in May 1998, followed by their claims to have become *de facto* nuclear weapon powers, cannot be reversed. Equally, their nuclear

[6] Michael Krepon, 'South Asia: A Time of Trouble, A Time of Need', in Jill R. Junnola and Michael Krepon (eds.), *Regional Confidence Building in 1995: South Asia, the Middle East and Latin America,* The Henry L. Stimson Centre, Report No. 20, December 1995, p. 5.

capabilities could be 'capped', but their 'rollback' or 'elimination'[7] is not realistically possible. Whether the nuclear tests added to or subtracted from the stability of Southern Asia and the security of India and Pakistan is a moot question, but the answers heard in India are on predictable lines: For the proposition, it is argued that the nuclear tests made overt what was long suspected, viz., both countries could exercise their nuclear option at will; that a nuclear posture based on 'non-weaponized' or 'recessed' deterrence was inherently unstable;[8] that the nuclear tests made India's progression along the ladder of nuclear capabilities to weaponization and deployment easier; and that the international community takes India more seriously now—witness the steady procession of high officials to New Delhi from the United States and its allies, apart from Russia, to urge India to exercise restraint during the Kargil and border confrontation crises.

Against the proposition, it is urged that India's adversarial relations with Pakistan and uneasy relations with China reached their nadir after the tests; that India became the object of economic sanctions which, though not crippling, carried a strong message of disapproval; that Indo-Pak crises are now under close international scrutiny arising out of concerns that they could escalate beyond the nuclear threshold; that India's nuclear tests provided Pakistan with the perfect rationale to conduct its own tests and proceed more confidently with its border intrusions into Kargil. Paradoxically, 'the unintended consequence of India's nuclear tests was to propel Pakistan's nuclear tests forward, after which India found itself deterred in crossing the Line of Control (LoC) to attack Pakistan's operational bases in Skardu [during the Kargil conflict]'.[9]

This much is clear: the nuclear tests did not extinguish the military threats afflicting Indian security. In fact, sub-conventional warfare—variously described as proxy war, low intensity conflict, and cross-border terrorism—continues in Kashmir, exhibiting an admixture of external encouragement and internal dissidence. Nor has there been

[7] It would be recollected that the essence of the Clinton Administration's non-proliferation policy was encapsulated in the intention 'to cap, then over time, reduce, and finally eliminate the possession of weapons of mass destruction and their means of delivery' in South Asia.

[8] This argument is elaborated in Raja Menon's essay in this volume.

[9] P.R. Chari, 'Conclusion, Indo-Pak Relations: Uncertain Future', in Maj. Gen. Ashok Krishna, AVSM (Retd.) and P.R. Chari (eds.), *Kargil: The Tables Turned* (New Delhi: Manohar, 2001), p. 261.

any abatement of the recurrent crisis afflicting Indo-Pak relations. The Kargil conflict (1999) and the Indo-Pak border confrontation (2001-2) proved exceptions to the empirical rule that nuclear weapons engender caution between adversarial states. Indeed, the post-nuclear tests history in South Asia has demolished the belief that a stable peace, premised on a 'balance of terror', would be ushered into the region. Instead, the Kargil conflict proved the exception to two theses governing the nuclear age, that democracies do not war against each other,[10] and that nuclear weapon powers do not conflict directly with each other.[11]

From the Pakistani perspective, the nuclear tests placed it 'in a better position to challenge India through low intensity conflict. . . . This meant that India could now be denied the luxury of expanding the conflict and capitalizing on the [sic] conventional symmetries.'[12] This calculation did not, however, appreciate the limitations of mutual deterrence, in that nuclear weapons cannot acquire political advantage since international pressure would deny their use for achieving strategic ends. The Kargil conflict and the Indo-Pak border confrontation in 2001-2 emphasized the reality that India and Pakistan could not launch a conventional offensive, but the danger of conflict erupting, not from design, but by accident or misperception remained ever-present. Conflict was avoided partly due to good fortune, but also the result of American pressure guided by its interests to pursue the war against terrorism in Afghanistan without being distracted by an Indo-Pak conflict.

India's dependence on the United States to achieve its political objectives is evident from the naïve belief that 'the presence of [the] US fleet in the Arabian Sea is the guarantor that nuclear weapons would not be used by Pakistan. If and when Pakistan takes out its weapons and starts readying them for firing, the US can never be sure that some of them may not be aimed at the US carriers. . . . In these circumstances, the US, which is keeping Pakistan under close surveillance,

[10] Nawaz Sharif then headed a civilian government in Pakistan, although its Kashmir, defence and nuclear policies were firmly within the span of control of the armed forces. Nawaz Sharif was deposed shortly after the Kargil conflict ended in an army coup led by General (now President) Musharraf.

[11] The only exception to this empirical rule is the Ussuri (Damansky island) clashes between China and the erstwhile Soviet Union that occurred in the spring of 1969; they are comparable to the Kargil conflict.

[12] Ejaz Haidar, 'Stable Deterrence and Flawed Pakistani Nuclear Strategy', *The Friday Times,* 2 February 2002.

will destroy the Pakistani nuclear weapons through accurate non-nuclear strikes.'[13] This dependence on the United States to ensure the elimination of the nuclear threat from Pakistan is dangerous and could lead to grave miscalculations. However, this assessment, made at the height of the Indo-Pak border confrontation, reveals the perplexity among votaries of India's nuclearization. Their hope that it would enhance stability in Indo-Pak relations has been belied by the continuance of serious Indo-Pak crises; it is arguable, on the contrary, that the nuclear tests have engendered greater instability in South Asia.

India-China relations, on the other hand, are on the upswing following a brief freeze after Defence Minister George Fernandes identified China as the major threat justifying India's nuclear tests. Their bilateral talks on resolving their long-standing border dispute and negotiating confidence-building measures are being held regularly, although their pace is glacial. A new context for India-China cooperation has arisen from their mutual concern with cross-border terrorism emanating from Afghanistan. China is aware of Pakistan's involvement in these activities, but has not identified it due to political considerations. Neither has it stopped providing Pakistan with nuclear and missile technology, despite stout denials whenever they come to light. Sino-Pak military and nuclear cooperation comprises the substance of India's security concerns. The nuclear tests have not reduced this aspect of the Chinese threat to India's national security or the basic tensions and instabilities underlying their relationship.

Destabilizing Factors in South Asia

THE EXAGGERATIONS

Analysts have overstated the nuclear dangers in South Asia during the Kargil and Indo-Pak border crises; the belief that a nuclear exchange between India and Pakistan was imminent, and would encourage other nuclear aspirants to develop nuclear weapons was rife. Robert Einhorn, former US Assistant Secretary of State for Non-proliferation, stated that: 'The mere fact of the first use of nuclear weapons since Hiroshima and Nagasaki could have the effect of lowering the threshold for nuclear

[13] K. Subrahmanyam, 'Indo-Pak Nuclear Conflict Unlikely', *The Times of India*, 2 January 2002. The author was the Convenor of India's National Security Advisory Board, which counsels the National Security Council.

engagements in the future. This would establish a very damaging precedent.'[14] Adding to this alarm the weekly *India Today* published a lead story dramatically entitled 'If Pakistan Nukes India . . .', it speculated on the damage to life and property that would occur in enlarging concentric circles within discrete time-frames from 'ground zero' if Delhi or Mumbai were targeted by a nuclear weapon. The weekly cited an anonymous Indian official ominously declaring that India would respond with a 'massive nuclear force that will ensure that Pakistan as we know it now does not exist'.[15] Not to be outdone, a rival weekly, *Outlook,* published a story under the banner 'Small is Scary' informing that Pakistan possessed tactical nuclear weapons (TNWs) that could be used against advancing tank columns. The Indian armed forces had factored this possibility into planning exercises. A senior defence ministry official also stated that, 'It is right to presume that Pakistan has TNWs, although we can counter it with a strategic nuclear strike.'[16] India's adherence to its declared no-first use policy was ignored here!

INCENDIARY STATEMENTS

These exaggerations were indubitably informed by the constant reiteration of threats after the nuclear tests by high-ranking leaders and officials in both countries. Immediately after India's tests, Home Minister (now Deputy Prime Minister) Advani declared that this 'decisive step to become a nuclear weapon state has brought a qualitatively new stage in Indo-Pak relations, particularly in finding a lasting solution to the Kashmir problem',[17] implying that India could resolve its Kashmir problem now behind its nuclear shield. The Chagai tests conducted by Pakistan, of course, dampened the finding of this 'lasting solution'. Then, again, during the Kargil conflict, Pakistan's Foreign Secretary warned that Islamabad could use 'any weapon' in its armoury to defend the country's territorial integrity.[18] The long-drawn out Indo-Pak border confrontation witnessed a surfeit of aggressive statements being issued by the two leaderships, interspersed with bland disclaimers that they would not initiate a nuclear conflict. For example, India's

[14] Michael Richardson, 'Fears spread that Other Asian Nations will Seek Nuclear Arms', *International Herald Tribune,* 6 June 2002.

[15] *India Today,* 10 June 2002.

[16] *Outlook,* 10 June 2002, p. 44.

[17] *The Hindu,* 19 May 1998.

[18] 'Any Weapon Will Be Used, Threatens Pak', *The Hindu,* 1 June 1999.

Defence Minister, George Fernandes, declared that, 'Everyone is raring to go—from the ordinary jawan to the mid-level officer to the men at the top. . . . In fact, something that actually bothers them is that things might now reach a point where one says there is no war.'[19] A former Chief of the Air Staff rubbished Pakistan's threat of a nuclear response, holding that, 'A nuclear capability pitted against another can act as a deterrent only for nuclear warfare, not against conventional warfare. I do believe aerial assaults can chisel out many chinks in Pakistan's defences in PoK [Pakistan occupied Kashmir]. We have to gnaw away to push back the LoC further.'[20]

Pakistan was not remiss in making similar belligerent statements. Munir Akram, Pakistan's envoy to the United Nations, declared that Pakistan relied on the 'means it possessed to deter Indian aggression', and would not 'neutralize' its deterrent by a doctrine of no-first-use. He added that any action by India across the border, any aerial attack on Pakistani territory and its assets, and any action to economically strangle it would be viewed as aggression and would be 'responded to by Pakistan'.[21] President Musharraf was also quoted saying, 'the possession of nuclear weapons by any state obviously implies that they will be used under some circumstances', when asked why Pakistan did not renounce the first use of nuclear weapons against India.[22]

Conceivably, there were three different audiences being addressed by these belligerent assertions and threats—domestic, India/Pakistan, and the international community. Taken in their totality the impression conveyed was one of extraordinary naiveté obtaining, and lack of understanding that nuclear weapons are not conventional arms with greater destructive powers, but constitute qualitatively different armaments that shift the dangers of conflict onto an entirely different and extraordinary plane.

PROVOCATIVE ACTIONS

Confrontational statements and declarations were accompanied by feckless actions during the Kargil and border confrontation crises. The full truth may never be known, but it is clear that the availability of

[19] 'We could take a Strike and Survive, Pakistan won't: Fernandes', Interview with *Hindustan Times*, 30 December 2001.

[20] 'Air Strike a Must to Fix Pak: Tipnis', *The Indian Express*, 22 June 2002.

[21] 'We'll use Nukes Even In Conventional War: Pak', *The Times of India*, 30 May 2002.

[22] 'N-arms Possession Implies Usage: Musharraf', *The Hindu*, 5 June 2002.

nuclear weapons informed both countries, despite a loud debate in India on the merits of fighting a nuclear war. One account reveals that India, during the Kargil conflict, activated all its three types of nuclear delivery vehicles and kept them on what is known as Readiness State 3—meaning that some nuclear bombs would be ready to be mated with the delivery vehicles at short notice. The air force was asked to keep its Mirage fighters on stand-by. DRDO [Defence Research and Development Organization] scientists headed to where the *Prithvi* missiles were deployed and at least four of them were readied for a possible nuclear strike. Even an *Agni* missile capable of launching a nuclear warhead was moved to a western Indian state and kept in a state of readiness . . . . [P]akistan too is learnt to have kept its nuclear weapons in an advanced state of readiness.[23]

The authenticity of this account is uncertain, but the absence of any official denial is hardly reassuring about the durability of crisis stability in South Asia.

Bruce O. Riedel, a former member of the Clinton Administration's National Security Council, has also revealed that during the Kargil conflict US intelligence had uncovered 'disturbing evidence that the Pakistanis were preparing their nuclear arsenals for possible deployment'.[24] Another former official has confirmed that the United States had learnt that Pakistan was moving its intermediate-range *Ghauri* missiles, intended to carry nuclear warheads, out of storage to new locations. It was assessed that this movement was either offensive in nature or intended to disperse them in anticipation of a pre-emptive Indian strike.[25] According to Riedel, 'Clinton asked Sharif if he knew how advanced the threat of nuclear war really was? Did Sharif know his military was preparing their nuclear tipped missiles? Sharif seemed taken aback and only said that India was probably doing the same.'[26]

[23] Raj Chengappa, *Weapons of Peace: The Secret Story of India's Quest to be a Nuclear Power* (New Delhi: Harper Collins Publishers India, 2000), p. 437. The author says that he 'had conducted close to two hundred interviews with a range of the key people involved that included former prime ministers, presidents, ministers, generals, secretaries to government, diplomats, strategists and the scores of scientists both known and unknown'.

[24] Alan Sipress and Thomas E. Ricks, 'Clinton Aide Says Pakistan Prepared Missiles for Launching', *Washington Post,* 15 May 2002.

[25] Ibid.

[26] 'Clinton to Nawaz: You set U.S. up to fail, I won't let it happen', *The Indian Express,* 18 May 2002. Cited from Bruce Riedel's, *American Diplomacy and the 1999 Kargil Summit at Blair House,* Centre for the Advanced Study of India, University of Pennsylvania. Riedel was present during the Clinton-Nawaz Sharif meeting.

This account emphasizes the fragility of crisis stability in South Asia. The fact that the Kargil conflict did not escalate to the nuclear level must again be attributed to good fortune and US intervention.

We are too near the Indo-Pak border confrontation for its different aspects to become clear. The passage of time will, no doubt, clarify its nuclear aspects, adding to what is currently in the public domain. However, the *Outlook* magazine quoted officials in Pakistan's Atomic Energy Commission informing that the warheads they possessed were in place, and that tactical nuclear weapons had been moved closer to the Indo-Pak border.[27] George Fernandes, when asked about India's missile deployment, said, 'missile systems are in position', adding that, 'At the moment, we are concentrating on *Agni* II missiles with a range of 2500 km.'[28]

Most disconcertingly, this period of high crisis was used by India and Pakistan to test their nuclear-capable missiles. Inevitably these launches raised the temperature further in a surcharged atmosphere. Thus, India's test-firing of its *Agni* II missile drew adverse comment from Pakistan, which noted that, 'the Indian test has regional implications. We hope the international community will take note of this Indian behaviour, which is prejudicial to the pursuit of stability in our region, especially during the current situation. . . . We also have the means to defend ourselves.'[29] Further concern was expressed after India tested its *Brahmos* supersonic cruise missile, developed along with Russia: 'Introduction of this new weapon system will aggravate the existing balance in the region and further encourage India's hegemonic designs . . . this cooperation is clearly in violation of the international obligations of Russia as a member of the Missile Treaty Control Regime (MTCR).'[30] Later, Pakistan test-fired its nuclear capable *Ghauri* missile. This was explained as being 'part of the research and development of Pakistan's indigenous missile programme, which is an essential element of Pakistan's policy of maintaining minimum deterrence in the interest of our security'.[31] India's Foreign Ministry spokesperson opined that India was 'not particularly impressed by these missile antics, clearly targeted at the domestic audience of Pakistan'.[32]

[27] *Outlook,* 10 June, 2002, p. 44.
[28] 'India's Missile System "in Position": Fernandes', *The Hindu,* 27 December 2001.
[29] 'Unwise Behaviour, says Pak', *The Hindu,* 26 January 2002.
[30] 'Pakistan concerned over Indian Missile Test', *The News,* 30 April 2002.
[31] 'Pakistan Test Fires Nnuclear-capable Missile', *Hindustan Times,* 25 May 2002.
[32] 'Pakistan to Test Missiles', *The Dawn,* 25 May 2002.

Quite apart from the domestic constituencies being addressed by *both countries* via these missile tests, two other reasons were operating. First, the Other was being addressed to appreciate that its armed forces and territory would be devastated by a nuclear attack. Second, these missile tests were also addressed to the international community, particularly the United States, to restrain the Other, lest tensions and instabilities lead to conflict, and the conflict turns nuclear. Their major effect, however, was to destabilize the situation further. The incongruity of this posture is that, even whilst flexing their muscles and inching towards a conflict, the secret hope in both countries was that the United States would intervene and broker a compromise solution. Consequently, it is arguable that this brinkmanship policy, informed by the US presence in the background, might not have reached the proportions it did had the US announced at the very outset that it had no intention of intervening in the crisis. China, incidentally, was neutral during the Kargil and Indo-Pak border crises, contending itself with making equivocal statements urging both nations to resolve their disputes peacefully, but without seeking either an interventionary or mediatory role.

Doctrinal Differences and Instability

Apart from incendiary statements and provocative statements the mismatch between their nuclear doctrines aggravates the inherent instabilities in the Indo-Pak adversarial relationship. Four areas of inconsistency have manifested themselves.

First, stated nuclear doctrine. India had published its nuclear doctrine for eliciting public opinion.[33] Although its exact status is unclear, the nuclear doctrine consolidated several pledges made earlier by the government, like adherence to a no-first use policy, establishment of a credible minimum deterrent, and placing a moratorium on further nuclear testing.[34] Pakistan has not declared its nuclear doctrine, but its contours are available from the writings and declarations by important non-officials.[35] The absence of a dialogue to understand each other's

[33] Text of the Indian Nuclear Doctrine, released on 17 August 1999, may be seen at www.meadev.gov.in/govt/indnucld.htm

[34] These commitments were declared in Prime Minister Vajpayee's Statement in Parliament, 'Bilateral Talks with the United States', 15 December 1998, available at www.meadev.gov.in

[35] As, for instance, Agha Shahi, Zulfiqar Ali Khan, and Abdul Sattar, 'Securing Nuclear Peace', *The News*, 5 October 1999. These three authors are influential in Pakistan. In fact, Abdul Sattar became the Foreign Minister, shortly after this article was published.

perceptions regarding nuclear weapons is hardly conducive to nuclear stability. This general proposition could be illustrated by noting their difficulty in recognizing each other's 'red lines', identifying a nuclear posture, and declaring the circumstances in which nuclear weapons could be used.

Second, it is arguable that the belligerent statements made and provocative actions undertaken during the Kargil and border confrontation crises illustrate a signalling exercise by India and Pakistan. The problem here is the opacity regarding their 'red lines' and knowing what impermissible actions could trigger a nuclear response. Is it only a line in the sand? Pakistan's vulnerability as the weaker conventional power indicates that its nuclear threshold might be lower than that of India. But, where exactly are those 'red lines'? Different answers have emanated from Pakistan. An influential view holds that 'the assumption has been that if the enemy launches a general war and undertakes a piercing attack threatening to occupy large territory or communication functions, the "weapon of last resort" would have to be invoked'.[36] President Musharraf warned that if the pressure on Pakistan becomes intolerable; then 'as a last resort, the atom bomb is also possible'.[37] It was later clarified that 'last resort', meant, 'all of Pakistan was under threat of disappearing from the map'.[38] General Kidwai, head of Pakistan's Strategic Planning Division, has also stated that nuclear weapons could be used 'if the very existence of Pakistan as a state is at stake'. This was elaborated to mean a situation being created where India 'conquers a large part of its [Pakistani] territory' or 'destroys a large part either of its land or air forces' or 'proceeds to the economic strangling of Pakistan' or 'creates a large scale internal subversion in Pakistan'.[39]

India has not clarified where its 'red lines' lie. But its circumspection in countering the Kargil intrusions—its army and air force had strict orders not to cross the Line of Control and the conflict zone was not enlarged beyond the Kargil-Drass sector—suggests its self-imposition of limitations on retaliatory action. Earlier, India had eschewed cross-border excursions into Pakistan in the 'hot pursuit' of militants. This suggests that India's 'red lines' could resemble those defined by

[36] Ibid, p. 3.

[37] 'Atom Bomb against India a Possibility: Musharraf', *Hindustan Times,* 6 April 2002.

[38] 'Nukes Last Option, Clarifies Pak', *The Asian Age,* 12 April 2002.

[39] Paolo Cotta-Ramusino and Maurizio Martellini, *Nuclear Safety, Nuclear Stability and Nuclear Strategy in Pakistan,* Landau Network Centro Volta, http://www.mi.infn.it/-landnet. See also Appendix 6.

Pakistan. In the absence, however, of any bilateral dialogue, an area of uncertainty persists; hence the international community was rightly concerned with the dangers inherent in the Kargil conflict and the Indo-Pak border confrontation. Rhetorical statements threatening the use of nuclear weapons were very counter-productive in this milieu.

Third, India's draft nuclear doctrine had recommended its acquiring a capability to shift from 'peacetime deployment to fully employable forces in the shortest possible time' [Clause 3.2]. The time frame for their deployment would therefore need to be reduced. Does India then favour a 'launch-on-attack' nuclear posture as distinguished from a 'launch-on-warning' stance that is inherently unstable? And, especially when command and control arrangements are immature. Nothing suggests that Pakistan has adopted a similar relaxed posture, since it does not subscribe to a no-first-use policy; indeed, it might wish to economize on its command and control requirements by adopting a 'launch-on-warning' nuclear posture. This mismatch in nuclear posture between the two adversaries adds to potential instabilities, and portends the danger of nuclear weapons being used by accident.

Fourth, the dichotomy in views between India and Pakistan on a no-first-use declaration is total. India adheres unequivocally by this policy, but Pakistan shuns it equally unambiguously. The belief that the stronger conventional power can make this declaration, but its weaker adversary cannot due to fears of being overwhelmed in a conventional conflict, parallels the situation obtaining in Europe during the Cold War. The Warsaw Pact had declared a no-first-use policy, but NATO did not reciprocate on the grounds that it was the weaker alliance, and needed the additional security of nuclear weapons to defend Western Europe. A similar argument is being used by Pakistan to eschew a no-first-use policy.

Further, India perceives nuclear weapons 'only as strategic weapons, whose role is to deter their use by an adversary'.[40] But, Pakistan seems determined to take advantage of its non-adherence to a no-first-use policy to lower the nuclear threshold for repulsing an Indian cross-border attack and 'make space for low intensity conflict without the fear of having to fight a large-scale conventional conflict'.[41] In fact, Pakistan's support to cross-border terrorism in Kashmir is being con-

[40] See Jaswant Singh's interview with C. Raja Mohan, 'India Not to Engage in an N-Arms Race', *The Hindu,* 29 November 1999.

[41] Ejaz Haider, 'Stable Deterrence and Flawed Pakistan Nuclear Strategy'.

ducted under the nuclear shadow. For its part, India is self-deterred from attacking Pakistan by its subscription to a no-first-use policy. The traumatic events of 11 September have completely altered the context in which India's no-first-use policy was framed. This will become clear from a discussion of India's limited war thesis, to which attention is drawn below.

Limited War under the Nuclear Shadow

India's Defence Minister, George Fernandes, developed a plausible scenario for fighting a conventional conflict in a nuclear environment by stating:

> . . . the issue was not that war had been made obsolete by nuclear weapons, and that covert war by proxy was the only option, but that conventional war remained feasible though with definite limitations if escalation across the nuclear threshold was to be avoided . . . India has demonstrated in Kargil that its forces can fight and win a limited war, at a time and place chosen by the aggressor.[42]

On another occasion, he declared that, 'Pakistan can't think of using nuclear weapons despite the fact that they are not committed to the doctrine of no first use like we are. We could take a strike, survive and then hit back. Pakistan would be finished.'[43] To what extent India's destruction was survivable—one-fourth, one-third, one-half—was not clarified; that Pakistan would be annihilated informed the minister's belief that it would not launch a first strike. Proceeding further, limited wars, in theory, can be restricted in terms of space or time or weapons employed, as illustrated by the Kargil conflict. But there is no convincing answer to the conundrum whether war, an extended process of extreme violence between inimical states, can be fought under predetermined rules, discounting the danger of escalation. The question whether limited war can be controlled and its escalation prevented is basically unanswerable. I have argued elsewhere that: 'In truth, India's security has worsened after it became an overt nuclear power; how-

[42] Jasjit Singh, *Asia's New Dawn: The Challenges to Peace and Security* (New Delhi: Knowledge World, 2000), pp. xvii-xviii. This statement was made in the Opening Address by the Minister at the Second International Conference on 'Asian Security in the 21st Century' organized by the Institute of Defence Studies and Analyses, New Delhi, in January 2000.

[43] 'We could Take a Strike and Survive, Pakistan won't: Fernandes', *Hindustan Times,* 30 December 2001.

ever, the concerned official and non-official communities find this verity hard to accept. Hence their urging of new and risky modalities to affirm India's strategic 'superiority' over Pakistan by asserting that a limited war against Pakistan could be victoriously fought'.[44]

A context for India's limited war thesis was created by Pakistan when it began using its nuclear capabilities, demonstrated at Chagai in May 1998, to enlarge its proxy war in Kashmir, occupy territory across the LoC triggering the Kargil conflict, and accelerating cross-border terrorism to instigate *fidayeen* suicide attacks upon the Indian security forces in Kashmir. Admittedly, the primary causes for disaffection in Kashmir lie in several grievous mistakes committed by past Indian governments like rigging the elections, ignoring the Islamic militancy mushrooming in Kashmir over the last two decades, and the poor quality of governance, which allowed Pakistan to take advantage of the fertile ground provided by these local dissatisfactions.

In this milieu, the terrorist attacks on the Jammu & Kashmir Legislative Assembly in Srinagar on 1 October 2001 and the Indian Parliament on 13 December 2001 forced the Indian government to deploy its armed forces along the LoC and the international border, which led Pakistan to react by moving its own forces, precipitating the Indo-Pak border confrontation crisis.[45] India's reasons for this deployment was ostensibly to coerce Pakistan into ceasing its support for cross-border terrorism and handing over some twenty named fugitives who had been provided sanctuary in Pakistan. The danger of this confrontation escalating or conflict being initiated by misperception or accident was accepted. In other words, this controlled crisis was precipitated by India to achieve its strategic objectives of stopping cross-border terrorism, despite its potent dangers of spinning out of control. As perceptively noted, 'There is a delicate balance between nuclear capability acting as a deterrent and it being the cause for breakdown of deterrence. The appropriate diplomatic response lies in adopting the stance of nuclear brinkmanship: threaten to cross the brink and hope your enemy gives in first.'[46] This manoeuvre obviously required good fortune to succeed without falling into the nuclear abyss. American

[44] P.R. Chari, 'Limited War Against the Nuclear Backdrop', *Peace and Conflict* (An IPCS Bulletin), Vol. 5, No. 6, 2002, p. 6.

[45] This crisis has partly abated with both countries deciding (October 2002) to pull back their forces from the international border, though not the Line of Control.

[46] Arpit Rajain, 'Coercive Diplomacy or Nuclear Brinkmanship?', http://www.ipcs.org/issues/00/96-ndi-arpit.htm. 15 July 2002.

intervention was also effective to ensure that the crisis did not escalate and was ultimately defused.

Several reasons can explain India's pursuit of coercive diplomacy by this contrived crisis—it needed to be seen as 'doing something' for local consumption; it took advantage of the US-led coalition's war against terrorism which had indicted Pakistan; it capitalized on Pakistan's isolation in the world and its parlous financial situation; and it calculated on US intervention ensuring that a possible Indo-Pak conflict did not reach general war levels.[47] A school of thought in India holds that this policy, compounding coercive diplomacy and nuclear brinkmanship, did work. The argument proceeds that Pakistan had to concede that it would not support cross-border terrorism into Kashmir, and that it would dismantle its indigenous Islamic fundamentalist and *jihadi* organizations. It is another matter that President Musharraf may not deliver on these pledges. But his admission that Pakistan was supporting the Kashmir insurgency—this was strenuously denied earlier—has greatly eroded Pakistan's credibility, and it would find it difficult to continue this activity in future. An interesting analysis claims that India indulged in pyschological war by its nuclear brinkmanship, which comprised 'nuclear signalling, conventional mobilization, border posturing, possible covert operations, political rhetoric and a diplomatic offensive'.[48] However, India's use of coercive diplomacy via the limited war option has succeeded in reducing the extent of cross-border terrorism emanating from Pakistan, although it would be optimistic to hold that it would ever be fully halted.

Several arguments can now be made to interrogate this happy conclusion. First, the limited war theory remains untested. Neither the Kargil conflict nor the Indo-Pak border stand-off led India to undertake an offensive across the border. India carefully skirted this modality in defiance of military logic in the Kargil conflict. Despite its need to relieve pressure on its troops struggling to clear the intrusions in mountainous territory, and the consequent need to accept higher casualties, it did not permit them to cross the Line of Control. Ironically, the Kargil conflict established the viability of Pakistan's 'salami slicing' tactics against India. This procured some tactical gains initially, but

[47] These possibilities are discussed in Gaurav Kampani, 'India's Compellence Strategy: Calling Pakistan's Nuclear Bluff', CNS Research Story of the Week, 10 June 2002, available at http://cns.miis.edu/pubs/week/020610.htm, accessed on 15 June 2002.

[48] Atypically, Firdaus Ahmed, 'A Smoke Screen Called Limited War', http://www.ipcs.org/issues/800/832-ndi-firdaus.htm, accessed on 15 August 2002.

ended in a strategic disaster for Pakistan, since its general staff had not anticipated India's massive response, or the inevitability of international pressure being mounted upon it to withdraw its forces from across the Line of Control.

Second, whether and when a limited war might escalate to the general war level and cross the nuclear threshold is a highly speculative issue. As noticed above, India is vague about where its nuclear threshold lies, whilst Pakistan speaks with many voices on this vital question. When a limited war would escalate across the nuclear threshold, therefore, is essentially unknowable. A senior Indian official has conceded that, should there be another Pakistan-engineered attack upon military or civilian establishments, 'surgical strikes are the realistic option. But we also know that there will be retaliation on other parts of the border from Pakistan. It'll escalate and will not be confined to one region.'[49] Such blasé thinking presages uncertainty and an unstable situation obtaining.

Third, the success of the Indian strategy in obtaining assurances from Pakistan about checking cross-border terrorism and dismantling its *jihadi* infrastructure—yet to be credibly demonstrated—was largely premised on a set of fortuitous circumstances, viz., the international atmosphere turned hostile to terrorism after 11 September and the American physical presence in Pakistan. There is nothing to suggest that these fortuitous circumstances are replicable, or that this happy turn of events endorses a limited war thesis as being valid in a nuclear environment.

Apropos, Pakistan's Kashmir policy of bleeding India by inflicting a thousand cuts is flawed for at least three reasons: First, it was irrational for Pakistan to believe that India would relinquish its hold over Kashmir on which it has expended so much blood and treasure. In truth, India can afford the financial and military costs involved almost indefinitely. The continuance of Pakistan's Kashmir policy has, instead, led to the *jihadis* acquiring a place of prominence for themselves in Pakistan—this was displayed in the recently held elections which has brought the Islamic parties into power in Baluchistan and the North West Frontier Province (NWFP) and added to their significance in national politics. Ironically, Pakistan has become the victim of its own feckless strategy. The irrationality of Pakistan's Kashmir policy becomes further apparent since 'allowing the practice of cross-border terrorism to dictate

[49] Interview with Yogendra Narain, Defence Secretary, in *Outlook*, 10 June 2002.

policy effectively legitimizes the behaviour . . . that if applied within Pakistan's borders would threaten the integrity of the state'.[50] This can now happen.

Second, the irrationality of supporting cross-border terrorism in Kashmir as state policy was underscored by the dramatic events of 11 September 2001. Transnational terrorism came into sharp focus, and the global war against terrorism has gathered momentum. Pakistan's support to the US-led coalition's war against terrorism in Afghanistan, and its simultaneous support to cross-border terrorism in Kashmir are logically inconsistent. It is now recognized that: 'The Taliban were a millstone round our neck, *jihad* in Kashmir a concept which had outlived its utility. On our own we wouldn't have had the sense to reverse these policies. It was the post-September 11 world, which knocked the stuffing from our most cherished illusions. We were left with no choice except to quickly get in step with the new realities.'[51]

Third, the United States and its coalition partners have made it plain to Pakistan that it cannot continue its feckless policy of state support to terrorism in Kashmir; neither are they willing to accept the *jihadis* as 'freedom fighters'. China, too, has not countenanced Pakistan's Kashmir policy, since the instability engendered could spill over into its neighbouring Muslim-minority provinces. The US presence in South and South-Western Asia—Pakistan, Afghanistan, Uzbekistan, apart from Bahrain and Saudi Arabia—has physically encrusted; this will make it difficult for Pakistan to evade US surveillance. Realism requires India to appreciate that cross-border terrorism will continue, perhaps at reduced levels, until the internal problem in Kashmir is resolved. It can also be hoped that Pakistan would, in time, discontinue its feckless Kashmir policy, but a more enduring elimination of militancy in Kashmir requires India to deal more purposively with the issues causing disaffection in the state.

It is clear that limited war in the present state of Indo-Pak nuclear relations cannot be pursued as a national strategy. Suggesting that limited war is feasible and planning for it is fraught with dangerous consequences for nuclear stability. What can be done instead to heighten nuclear stability in Southern Asia is discussed below.

[50] Neil Joeck, 'Nuclear Relations in South Asia', in Joseph Cirincione (ed.), *Repairing the Regime: Preventing the Spread of Weapons of Mass Destruction* (Washington, D.C.: Carnegie Endowment for International Peace, 2000), p. 8.

[51] Ayaz Amir, 'Creative anarchy Pakistani style', *Dawn Internet Edition,* 9 August 2002.

The CBM Route to Nuclear Stability

The knee-jerk proposition made to enhance nuclear stability in asymmetric situations is to enlarge confidence-building measures (CBMs) between the adversaries. A wide range of military and non-military CBMs have been established between India and Pakistan. These CBMs were generally difficult to negotiate but, thereafter, to sustain. Pious commitments in declaratory CBMs to cease hostile propaganda, for instance, have never been observed. Not unexpectedly, this casual approach towards the sanctity of bilateral treaties and agreements destroys the mutual trust on which CBMs must rest.

Turning to nuclear CBMs between India and Pakistan, the Agreement on the Prohibition of Attack against Nuclear Installations and Facilities is subsisting, which envisages both countries annually exchanging information regarding 'the latitude and longitude of its nuclear installations and facilities and whenever there is any change'.[52] An entire range of nuclear CBMs for negotiation were included in the Memorandum of Association attached to the Lahore Declaration (February 1999).[53] These included 'an agreement on prevention of incidents at sea', setting up 'appropriate consultative mechanisms to monitor and ensure effective implementation of these [negotiated] CBMs', engaging in 'bilateral consultations on security, disarmament and non-proliferation issues', and enjoining both countries 'to provide each other with advance notification in respect of ballistic missile flight tests', 'abide by their respective unilateral moratorium on conducting further nuclear test explosions', 'undertake a review of the existing communications . . . with a view to upgrading and improving these links and to provide for fail-safe and secure communications', and to 'undertake national measures to reduce the risks of accidental or unauthorized use of nuclear weapons under their respective control'. Many of these measures have, quite obviously, drawn on agreements reached by the United States and the erstwhile Soviet Union during the Cold War years; hence they are tried and tested means to stabilize adversarial nuclear relationships.

There are several other nuclear CBMs that could be suggested for negotiation between India and Pakistan such as:

[52] Text of this Agreement may be seen in Michael Krepon and Amit Sevak, *Crisis Prevention, Confidence Building, and Reconciliation in South Asia* (New Delhi: Manohar, 1996), pp. 254-5.

[53] Text of the Lahore Declaration and the Memorandum of Understanding, 21 February 1999, available on http://www, ipcs.org/ documents/ 1999/1-jan-mar.htm, accessed on 20 April 1999.

- The need for a common language to understand each other's signalling, and recognizing different states of alert in an emergency; this is of supreme importance to defusing future crises and avoiding conflict.
- Mutual acceptance of nuclear asymmetry to avoid arms racing. Thus Pakistan should accept that India's nuclear capability has to include China, just as India would have to accept that China's nuclear capability would need to configure the United States within its ambit.
- Bilateral agreement on declaring a 'no-first-use' pledge with China. There is some confusion regarding China's general no-first-use declaration, since it makes an exception about areas that it considers part of China, like Arunachal Pradesh. This needs to be clarified in a separate agreement between the two countries.
- Harmonizing nuclear doctrines to locate 'red lines', the posture for deploying nuclear weapons, and their use in a countercity or counterforce mode, developing tactical (battlefield) nuclear weapons.

However, two problems intrude in pursuing the CBM modality in the Indo-Pak context. First, past history informs us that the CBMs established only function effectively during normal times, but fail during emergencies. For instance, 'hotlines' between the Military Operations Directorates become the first casualty in times of crisis, when the need for them is greatest. Past history shows that hotlines become dysfunctional or are manned by junior officers unable to take any decisions during crises or, even worse, are used to convey disinformation.[54] Second, the most plausible scenario for a nuclear exchange between India and Pakistan arises from a sub-conventional conflict—proxy war, low intensity conflict, cross-border-terrorism—leading to a high-profile attack on a public figure or institution. This could trigger a cross-border attack, leading to an expanding conventional war, which could, in turn, lead to a nuclear clash, either by accident or due to misperception or, again, a pre-emptive strike by one of the adversaries. A continuum obtains between sub-conventional and nuclear conflict, suggesting a gamut of CBMs being emplaced to prevent conventional conflict and the first rungs of the escalatory ladder being ascended. Nuclear CBMs, therefore, must be addressed within this holistic framework to address the roots of sub-conventional and conventional conflict.

[54] P.R. Chari, *Indo-Pak Nuclear Standoff: The Role of the United States* (New Delhi: Manohar, 1995), p. 165.

Turning to the Sino-Indian context, a specific provision exists in the Sino-Indian Agreement (November 1996) on Confidence-Building Measures in the Military Field along the Line of Actual Control in the India-China Border Areas committing both countries not to 'use or threaten to use force against the other by any means or seek unilateral military superiority', which includes nuclear threats and the use of nuclear weapons. Both countries have committed to a no-first-use policy; so it could be urged that a fair stabilization of Sino-Indian relations has occurred. A cautionary note is appropriate here. Whilst these agreements are encouraging and provide some confidence that a direct conflict will be avoided, there is little assurance that China will refrain from assisting Pakistan to confront India and confine it within the geographical limits of South Asia. Apart from coming to 'Pakistan's defence if the latter's very existence as a nation-state is threatened by India . . . Beijing's response to the next India-Pakistan war will be shaped by its desire to protect Chinese national interests, no matter what the cost. And, geo-strategic concerns require China to covertly side with Pakistan, whilst publicly calling for restraint by both sides to appear even-handed.'[55] Sino-Indian relations could, in fact, deteriorate, especially if the rivalry between China and the United States increases, placing India in the difficult position of having to balance its relations between these two contestants. In this scenario, Pakistan's strategic significance for China would be further enhanced, affecting Indian interests adversely.

Some Concluding Thoughts

Four issues bearing on the quest for nuclear stability in Southern Asia must finally engage our attention. First, India and Pakistan must be assumed to be continuing to sophisticate their nuclear warheads, and proceeding with R&D into the modification of existing warheads and new warhead designs to, for instance, improve their yield-to-weight ratios. In fact, a CIA report informs that 'India continues its nuclear weapons development program'; and that Pakistan 'continued to acquire nuclear-related and dual-use equipment and materials from various sources—principally in Western Europe'.[56] They could abro-

[55] J. Mohan Malik, 'China's southern discomfort', *Asia Times Online,* 11 July 2002, pp. 9-10.

[56] Official Text, *New CIA Report Documents Global Weapons Proliferation Trends,* Public Affairs Office of the U.S. Embassy, New Delhi, 1 February 2002.

gate their moratorium at any stage to test these new warhead designs. This is by no means a fanciful scenario, since the US non-ratification of the Comprehensive Test Ban Treaty (CTBT) has eviscerated the treaty of all meaning. Following their testing, the weaponization and deployment of these qualitatively improved nuclear warheads is also possible. So far as missiles are concerned, their testing is proceeding steadily to improve their range and accuracy. China, too, is testing a new range of solid-fuelled missiles to ensure their greater survivability, and MIRVing them to ensure greater penetrability of adversary defences. This ongoing sophistication of nuclear arsenals in Southern Asia forebodes greater tensions and instabilities in future.

Second, technological developments, too, are proceeding in directions that foreshadow greater instability in Southern Asia. It is axiomatic that new weapons technologies will emerge as the nuclear sciences progress; already 'the possibility of intense energy release from a non-fission, non-fusion, transformation of the nucleus'[57] is being investigated. Other areas of interest include devices based on the accelerator, which could substitute for advanced reactor systems; nuclear isomers that can store extremely large amounts of energy; and stable, heavy density elements like Pu-239 but possessing very small critical masses.[58] The basic conclusion to be drawn here is that future developments in the nuclear sciences could make redundant arms control and disarmament agreements like the Nuclear Non-Proliferation Treaty (NPT), which provides the bedrock for the nuclear non-proliferation regime. This would diminish nuclear stability in Southern Asia.

Third, it is arguable that 11 September effected a radical change in the international system and shifted the focus on international terrorism, including terrorism based on Weapons of Mass Destruction (WMD), as the most potent threat to global security. Undoubtedly, the need for greater international cooperation has become imperative. But, the current US penchant for unilateralism is calculated to add to the threat from WMD proliferation and nuclear instability. The US record of unilateral decisions is impressive: it includes opposition to 'the creation of the International Criminal Court (ICC), the Kyoto Protocol on climate change, the ban on anti-personnel land mines, the biodiversity treaty, and a verification mechanism for the Biological

[57] P.K. Iyengar, 'Non-proliferation and Advances in Nuclear Science', *Current Science,* Vol. 68, No. 3, 10 February 1995, p. 253.

[58] Ibid.

Weapons Control Treaty [*sic*]'.[59] Furthermore, the US has abrogated the Anti-Ballistic Missile (ABM) Treaty, refused to ratify the CTBT, or join a UN brokered non-binding treaty limiting exports of small arms. The US abrogation of the ABM Treaty has global implications. It downgrades the sanctity of international agreements and treaties. Besides, a fresh round of missile development and deployment in Southern Asia could be expected if the US deploys its missile defences (National Missile Defence and Theatre Missile Defence) leading to a cascading effect on China, India, and Pakistan, diminishing nuclear stability in the region.

Finally, the vexed problem of Kashmir bedevils nuclear instability in Southern Asia, constituting a 'nuclear flashpoint'. This is hotly denied by New Delhi and Islamabad, but history informs us that Kashmir was the motivating factor and/or the chief theatre of operations in all the Indo-Pak conflicts that have occurred—1947-8, 1965, 1971, and 1999. Since 1989, an insurgency movement promoted by Pakistan has wracked Kashmir, interacting with internal dissidence in the state. That the Kashmir issue contributes to nuclear instability is undeniable. Over the last five decades and more, various solutions have been suggested to resolve the Kashmir problem, but it must be accepted that it involves the Kashmiris, apart from India and Pakistan.

A five-point agenda can be suggested to address the Kashmir problem premised on Pakistan halting cross-border terrorism on a permanent basis: Pakistan credibly proceeding to dismantle its socio-religious structures that promote cross-border terrorism; India commencing negotiations with Srinagar on the Autonomy Report adopted by the J&K Assembly that was summarily rejected by New Delhi; an Indo-Pak dialogue started outside South Asia; and acceptance by India and Pakistan that the geopolitical partition of Kashmir along the Line of Control, with marginal adjustments and with a provision for maintaining 'soft' borders between the two parts of Kashmir, is the only feasible solution to this long-enduring problem. Should a *modus vivendi* be discovered to the Kashmir imbroglio on these or any modified lines, it would add greatly to nuclear stability in South Asia, Southern Asia, and the world.

The issue of nuclear stability in Southern Asia encapsulates great systemic complexities: it comprises three asymmetrically situated count-

[59] Jessica Mathews, 'Estranged Partners', *Foreign Policy*, November/December 2001, p. 48.

ries in a two-against-one (China and Pakistan versus India) configuration, which has remained intact over the years. Most likely, the United States would play a mediatory role to stabilize the relationship between India and Pakistan, but would also progress its ongoing rapport with India to develop a counterweight against China and manage the Asian balance of power. It is obvious that nuclear weapons have not stabilized these triangular interactions; the post May 1998 situation provides an unrelieved picture of tensions and instabilities in Southern Asia, punctuated by two major crises. Dialogue between India and Pakistan has only taken place fitfully and in a serendipitous manner; more disconcertingly, the belief is entrenched within the Indian establishment that Pakistan seeks dialogue only to impress the international community, as the failure of the Lahore and Agra initiatives taken by India highlights. Mistrust, in short, comes in the way of dispelling mistrust and restoring confidence between India and Pakistan. The inexorable reality persists that nuclear deterrence requires dialogue and communication between adversaries that are twinned and must seek nuclear stability in a joint enterprise; the alternative is conflict that could precipitate their mutual annihilation. The issue, therefore, of establishing nuclear stability in Southern Asia cannot be ignored by the international community, no less than by the protagonists.

10

Interview with General V.P. Malik, PVSM, AVSM (Retd) Former Chief of the Army Staff

Sonika Gupta and Arpit Rajain

Overview of South Asian Nuclear Tests by Gen. V.P. Malik

India conducted the nuclear tests in 1998 due to a number of reasons.

Major among these were the pressure put on India to sign various discriminatory nuclear related treaties, namely, the Non-Proliferation Treaty (NPT) and the Comprehensive Test Ban Treaty (CTBT), and the strategic alliance between China and Pakistan.

There was widespread criticism of the decisions taken by India and Pakistan to go nuclear, especially by the nuclear weapon states. For a change, India and Pakistan were on the same side of the fence, defending their decisions to go overtly nuclear. A few months later, they signed the Lahore Declaration. The Memorandum of Understanding on Nuclear Confidence Building Measures signed by the Foreign Secretaries of the two countries, along with the Lahore Declaration, was a significant document. This Memorandum of Understanding (MoU) aimed at cooperation for nuclear stability and safety between India and Pakistan. Unfortunately, Pakistan buried the Lahore Declaration on the Kargil heights!

Before the nuclear tests, several strategists believed that if India and Pakistan were to become nuclear states, strategic stability would obtain in the subcontinent. The threshold for a conflict would be raised and a war between the two countries would not be possible. These strategists did not realize that, after achieving nuclear parity with India, Pakistan would be able to conduct its proxy war in Kashmir with a greater sense of adventurism. In fact, this began happening soon after the tests, even before the MoU was signed, and Pakistani support to militancy in Kashmir increased. This factor made the Pakistani Army bolder and more confident about their Kargil invasion.

An analysis of the Kargil War and the Indo-Pakistan security environment shows that the spectrum of conflict now includes the proxy war for which Pakistan is responsible. A strategic space exists between a proxy war and an all-out armed conflict, in that there could be a calibrated use of military force below the level of an all out armed conflict. This has led to some thought being given to the idea of limited war.

On Pakistan

Q: Would you agree that dependence on the East-West experience in drawing up India's nuclear doctrine made Indian strategists ignore the problem of cross-border terrorism and its impact on nuclear deterrence?

A: While developing the nuclear strategy and doctrine, Indian strategists did not take into account the proxy war or sub-conventional conflict on the subcontinent. But then, till recently, terrorism was not part of the spectrum of conflict for the military. In the 1990s, when I met the military leaders of several countries, including the UK, France, and the USA, they were of the view that terrorism was more of a law and order problem. The military should not get involved in it. I maintained that terrorism had invaded the developing world and sooner or later it would spread to the developed world. The military would have to get involved.

Q: Do you think this change in thinking that terrorism has to be tackled militarily has been brought about due to 11 September?

A: Yes! After 11 September, the involvement of the military in counter-terrorism has been universally accepted. The US is altering its security policies to face this new challenge. Its military is fully engaged in counter-terrorism. People are now conjuring up different scenarios of threats from terrorism. Nuclear terrorism is also being talked about.

Q. Why is deterrence not working on the subcontinent?

A. The problem is that the theory of deterrence is based on the 'rational actor' model. This stands defeated against terrorists and states with terrorists' tendencies, which are 'irrational'. In dictatorial regimes, you cannot ensure rational decision-making. When one person holds all the strings, as is the case in Pakistan today, it can have a problem in rational decision-making.

Q: What would you say to the statement that nuclear weapons deter only nuclear weapons?

A: Nuclear weapons do deter nuclear weapons. This too depends on the mindset. Between two rational actors, this deterrence will work. But can one call a man like Osama bin Laden rational?

Q: What about nuclear deterrence between two countries?

A: As I mentioned earlier, in the case of rational actors, deterrence should work. But it operates in a dynamic environment with an element of rationality in decision-making or the command and control set-up.

In India, we have a democratically elected government and a civil-military command and control system, as has been explained in the draft nuclear doctrine. A considerable amount of two-way civil and military 'filtration' takes place before an important decision can be made. The final decision rests with the Cabinet Committee on Security (CCS) headed by the Prime Minister and is 'collegial'. In Pakistan, this kind of 'filtration' does not take place. Institutionally, there is a single decision maker.

Q: Do you mean the top military leadership?

A: Yes, it is basically the President, who is also the Chief of Army Staff (COAS). The others do not count. If there were to be a democratic set-up in Pakistan, it would make a difference. There would be better chances of deterrence working between India and Pakistan.

Q: Are nuclear stability levels different when a military regime is in power?

A. It is well known that democratic countries seldom go to war with each other. Yes, there will be different levels of nuclear stability under a military and a democratic government.

Q. Coming back to limited wars; won't 'a calibrated use of conventional force' by India be perceived as a violation of the adversary's sovereignty?

A. I think the international community has come to appreciate India's security concerns *vis-à-vis* cross-border terrorism. Look at the events: to start with, there has been a decade-long proxy war. The 'attack' on Parliament in December 2001 was a serious incident, which has been followed by several others. Many people have felt that India should have crossed the Line of Control (LoC) and smashed some terrorist camps on the other side.

Q. The attack on the Parliament raised India's threshold to a very high level. The Indian response included everything short of an armed conflict. What is the next level after this? What is the benchmark in a dynamic security environment?

A. These 'grey' threshold lines can move up and down. There is no definite benchmark. There should be a reasonable justification of the decision to cross the LoC. Today, the country is divided with people on both sides of the issue. But the important point is what is our politico-military objective and what would be the final outcome of such an action. Political leaders need to act responsibly and not make rhetorical statements during a crisis.

Q. Does that mean that space exists for an armed action across the LoC?

A. Yes! There is space for such an armed action. But the politico-military objective must be very clear.

Q. In a hypothetical scenario, India could initiate a limited war and move its troops across the LoC/International Border (IB) to achieve a specific objective such as the destruction of terrorist training camps but not to occupy territory. Suppose Pakistan issues, either plainly or in ambiguous terms, a nuclear threat. What options would India have: (a) does it call off the operation and pull its troops back, and face adverse public opinion or (b) does it continue with these operations in the hope that Pakistan does not proceed with its threatened course of action?

A: I do not believe that Pakistan would trigger a nuclear war and face the consequences of Indian nuclear retaliation over this counter-terrorism issue. But that notwithstanding, the political objectives of any such conventional operation must be clear. We are talking of camps that are not permanent, where groups of 50-60 terrorists are being trained by Pakistan's Inter-Services Intelligence (ISI) and ex-servicemen. Depending upon the kind of intelligence available, one would be able to eliminate some camps and terrorists. But these camps can be re-established or shifted to another location. Even if we do manage to destroy a few of these camps, what kind of dent will that make and for how long? It would not lead to the end of cross-border terrorism. If the military is asked to strike at those camps, it will be done, but we should not expect that this act alone would solve the problem of Pakistani sponsored terrorism.

Q. In another hypothetical scenario, India launches a limited operation across the LoC or the IB, and Pakistan responds with a strike on either a counter-value target (city) or uses tactical nukes on the advancing Indian special forces/troops. Would India respond with a proportional nuclear strike or a full-fledged conventional attack?

A. A nuclear strike must be met with 'a more serious retaliation'. There is no other choice. But Pakistan choosing your hypothetically suggested course is neither logical nor likely unless India goes for a clearly 'beyond threshold' objective.

Q. But isn't escalation in a limited war scenario likely?

A. A war is dynamic and risky, and escalation is always possible. In a limited war, the question is whether you are able to control the escalation or not. I believe that is possible. I do not rule out some escalation but it can be checked. I think the Pakistani military understands this. There may be a difference of opinion but we do not reach a point where the use of Weapons of Mass Destruction (WMD) is envisaged.

Another aspect to be borne in mind is overall conventional superiority. During the Kargil war, we adopted a political strategy of self-restraint but we also made it clear to Pakistan that the intrusion was unacceptable. We brought our Naval Fleet from the East to the West Coast and tailed some Pakistani ships, including their one and only tanker. We went close to Karachi. The Armed Forces were ready for any escalation. I visited our Corps Headquarters in Rajasthan, Punjab, Gujarat and other places frequently. The message was clear that we were prepared for everything.

Q. So the conventional deterrence can also work.

A. Yes! It does.

Q. Does it work at a few levels up and down as well?

A. Depends on the situation. It is a dynamic strategic environment.

Q: In another hypothetical scenario, if India launches an attack across the border and a covert or overt nuclear 'threat' is made by Pakistan, would the Indian operation be called off or continue in the hope that Pakistan will not execute the threat?

A: The credibility of the threat will need to be verified. The Pakistan military is known for its 'bluff and bluster'. Just because it 'brandishes' such a threat, the operations will not come to a halt.

Q: If one were to launch an operation across the LoC or the IB, which is the preferred option: an air strike or a ground offensive?

A: The use of ground troops, attack helicopters, and fighter jets are linked to each other. The escalation will be much faster when the Air Force is employed; one should be prepared for it. In a limited war, an important aspect is monitoring the escalation. The enemy must not seize the initiative. All this would have to be considered.

Q: Can any mechanisms to monitor escalation be evolved? Or does this apply only to the ground situation?

A: Monitoring is possible provided there is some political commitment towards achieving stability. If you have Confidence-Building Measures (CBMs) on the ground, as many as possible, it will help to achieve stability, both in nuclear and conventional terms.

Q: Critics of CBMs say that they do not work in crisis situations between India and Pakistan.

A: To say that they do not work at all is not correct. Some of them are working today, for example, advance notification of holding military exercises and of conducting missile tests.

Q. Do you think that during the Kargil War, at any time, there was an implicit or explicit nuclear threat from either side?

A. We got reports of some missile sites being readied. Other than that, and some political rhetoric, there were no reports. I think Bruce Reidel's statement in this regard is exaggerated.[1] If the US President had any such information, he would have communicated that to the Indian Prime Minister and we would have known about this.

Q. There were other reports about the Pakistan Air Force moving some F-16s from one base to the other, and some of them being wired. . .

A. I think these are exaggerated reports. Pakistan had started the Kargil War with a deception plan of terrorists' activities. The plan had not been shared with many. Its Armed Forces were not ready for a full-scale war.

Q. What about the use of tactical nuclear weapons?

A. I don't think Pakistan has them. But that does not mean that they may not have them tomorrow.

Q. What about the use of chemical and biological weapons? There were reports that some gas masks had been found in the bunkers vacated by the Mujahideen.

A. Let me correct you first. There were no so-called Mujahideen. All those people in bunkers during the Kargil War were regular Pakistan Army personnel.

[1] Bruce Reidel's paper titled American Diplomacy and the 1999 Kargil Summit at Blair House suggesting that India and Pakistan came close to a nuclear conflict in 1999 is available at http://www.sas.upenn.edu/casi/reports/RiedelPaper051302.htm

Yes, some masks were found. But no threat was perceived from the use of chemical-biological weapons. In 1997, the Pakistan Army made a false accusation, as they often do, that India had used chemical weapons. A protest was lodged with the United Nations (UN) and some investigations were done. The 'smoke' they were referring to was of regular smoke bombs of 81 mm mortars.

As regards biological weapons, to the best of my knowledge, neither country has the intention or the capability to use these weapons. Moreover, biological weapons cannot be used in a short war.

Q. Do you think we frittered away our conventional advantage after our nuclear tests?

A. That would not be totally correct. We are geographical neighbours and will remain so. I think that in the long run, it is better to have transparency than to have a covert nuclear capability. The risk of misperception, and consequently making wrong assessments, is much higher in the latter. It is true that before these tests, we did not take into account proxy war. But then you have also to accept that today it has become more difficult for them (Pakistanis) to pursue this policy [terrorism] than it was some months ago. I may also add that in its own interests, Pakistan needs to eliminate militancy. Militancy is a double-edged weapon. On the subcontinent, those who have promoted it have subsequently suffered at its hands. Already what Pakistan did in Afghanistan has come to haunt them.

Q Do you think we can put other issues aside for a while with Pakistan and talk only about mutual confidence building measures or at least on some kind of a basic framework through which we can evolve mechanisms for nuclear risk reduction.

A. Yes, it is possible. But it cannot be done today because our condition is that they stop terrorism—that is the root cause of the current security problem—and then we will talk. If this is achieved, we should agree to a dialogue. It would then be possible to do substantial work on CBMs.

Q: What about the proposal for joint patrolling? There have been proposals for joint patrolling earlier as well.

A: In 1988, during the Punjab problem, there was a proposal for joint patrolling between the Border Security Force and the Pakistan Rangers. It did not work. It cannot work today and may even be counter-productive.

Q: What is your opinion on the use of sensors to monitor the LoC?

A: When we talk of sensors in this context, we are talking of a co-operative monitoring mechanism. The decision on the use of sensors has to come through the CCS. If there is no dialogue or co-operation, how will monitoring work? Even the technologists from Sandia National Laboratories (Albuquerque, USA) are of the opinion that, in the absence of any political understanding, sensors cannot achieve anything. In this proposal, there are certain aspects that need to be made clear. Both countries should agree that there would be no infiltration. Pakistan should dismantle its terrorists' camps, not allow terrorists to come close to the LoC, and eliminate their radio networks that exists on either side of the LoC. It should not provide them with weapons and equipment from the Pakistan Occupied Kashmir. This is the first step. The second step would be to have a dialogue at the level of border posts and units/formations and establish communication to keep each other informed about the sensors being installed. This will be part of CBMs at military levels. The third step would be actual installation. Another question is who will monitor? We have ruled out third party intervention, including the UN, on this issue. So we will have to monitor ourselves. The US and others can provide equipment and training but the actual monitoring has to be done by us.

Q. Doesn't the first step outlined by you qualify more as a precondition?

A: The idea behind the first step is to introduce political commitment. In the absence of any political commitment, these measures cannot work.

Q: There is a time lag between the political commitment being made and these things working on the ground. Do you suggest that we wait for step one to be completed before we proceed to step 2 and 3 or can these things be done simultaneously?

A: The first step must take place. Its monitoring can be done by interlocutors. But the first step is essential to introduce political commitment for making monitoring successful.

Q: Do you think military-to-military CBMs between India and Pakistan can contribute to creating political commitment to peace or do you think that first a political commitment has to be made?

A: Basic political go ahead has to be there even for military CBMs to be initiated. Thereafter, military-to-military CBMs can make a major contribution to the overall situation.

Q: It is perceived by some sections in India that Pakistan has at its core the themes of Kashmir, nuclear weapons, Islam, and the military. The country is united by these four themes. What future do you foresee for Indo-Pakistan relations in the light of these enduring themes in Pakistani identity?

A: In the short and medium term scenario, I agree. But these factors cannot stay forever. For example, if you have serious economic trouble in Pakistan, starvation taking place, then who will remember Kashmir? The situation between India and Pakistan is grim today but I do not believe that it will remain unstable forever. There is bound to be a change sometime.

Q: There is a deliberate nurturing of the anti-India feeling by having models of Pakistani missiles in public places.

A: This is not a rational act! I blame the Pak military, and the *jihadis* promoted by it, for these things. They encourage anti-India sentiments in their self-interest. It serves their objective to stay in power.

Q: Do you see the return of democracy in Pakistan as necessary for improved Indo-Pak relations?

A: A democratic government in Pakistan would be definitely better for Indo-Pakistan relations. When General Pervez Musharraf came into power, some people felt that it was an opportunity to engage with the Pakistani military directly because the military has always played a major role in formulating Pakistan's foreign policy towards India. I feel that the Pakistan military will look after its own interests first. You may recall that Nawaz Sharif did not talk about Kashmir, or India-Pakistan, during his election campaign in 1997, and yet he won hands down. Benazir Bhutto raised the Kashmir issue to a high pitch in 1989. She has different views today. I believe that democracy in Pakistan would be more conducive for stable Indo-Pakistan relations.

Q. What is your view about the current deployment?

A. Political objectives of any such military deployment must be clear. The purpose of deployment outside Jammu & Kashmir is not clear today.

Q. Do you think there is enough synchronized decision-making in India?

A. Synergy between military and political establishments needs to be further improved.

Q: Is there need for greater interaction between the media and the military in India?

A: Yes! A certain amount of interaction is necessary. If the media were briefed properly, there would be a better understanding of security matters in the country. The media does have commercial interests, but it is not anti-national.

ON CHINA

Q: Should we initiate nuclear CBMs with China?

A: We can rule out a high-intensity conventional war between India and China because of nuclear asymmetry. In an asymmetrical situation, initiation of nuclear CBMs is not advisable.

Q: Don't you think symmetry is still at least a decade away, if not more?

A: We need to develop and make *Agni* II and *Agni* III operational as early as possible.

Q: Many people in the foreign policy community are of the view that we do not perceive a threat from China: it wants to have friendly relations with India but because of the 1962 war hangover, we are not able to proceed on that?

A: If that were so, why would China have a strategic alliance with Pakistan, and continue to pursue that policy despite Pakistan having been a home for terrorism due to which China too has suffered?

Q: Would you agree that the threat from China is an indirect threat and not a direct threat across the border?

A: I am for substantial engagement with China. But the chances of a direct threat remain so long as we have a disputed border. Although we have mechanisms in place to resolve the border issue now, there is very slow movement on this issue. Even the CBMs of the 1996 Agreement (The Agreement on the Maintenance of Peace and Tranquillity Along the Line of Actual Control in the India-China Border Areas, 1996) have not been fully implemented. The indirect threat is primarily due to the Sino-Pakistani strategic alliance.

Q: What is your view of our threat perception along the Sino-Indian border?

A: The direct threat will reduce substantially once the Line of Actual Control (LAC), and then the border, is delineated. Till then this threat has to be considered.

Q: Why is China helping Pakistan militarily, when it forces India to upgrade its nuclear capability?

A: It is a 'containment' measure to keep India militarily engaged with Pakistan. India's ability to develop faster and its influence in the international arena get limited due to this reason.

Q: During the Kargil War, there were reports of China moving some 'strategic assets' to Pakistan? There also have been reports of China using the Karakoram Highway to move military help to Pakistan during the current deployment.

A: I am not aware of it. During the Kargil War, China's attitude towards India was sober; not very supportive, but it did not have an anti-India colour. There was a slight shift in Chinese foreign policy towards India after the Kargil War.

Q: What role does the 1962 Sino-Indian war play in our relations with China? Is it a hangover we should get over or should we treat it as a lesson?

A: Whether you win or lose a war, the lessons of a war must always be remembered. It takes a very long time to get over the emotions attached with a war.

Q: Do you think that a more transparent government policy on the 1962 war would help us get over the trauma?

A: Definitely. During my time as COAS, we considered de-classification of the Henderson Brooks Report. But we did not get the right opportunity. I had directed that all senior officers posted to Army Headquarters should study that Report.

Q: What do you think will be China's military strategy towards India in the years to come?

A: Both countries are focusing on economic development. Along with economic development, China takes good care of its overall strength. Economic and security strength are complimentary. Coercive diplomacy works more effectively when a country has greater economic and security strength!

Q: Do you think we could make some kind of common cause on the anti-terrorism front with China? Do you think it will be effective enough to have an impact on the ground situation in Kashmir?

A: The Chinese are concerned about Xinjiang and Tibet. They understand our problem in J&K due to *jihadi* terrorism. I think they want to have a dialogue on terrorism and to activate the joint working group formed for this purpose, but their strategic alliance with Pakistan is a constraint.

Q: What about our concerns regarding Chinese activities in the Bay of Bengal?

A: We should be alert, but need not consider every speculative report that is published in the media to be true.

APPENDICES

APPENDIX 1

Paper Tabled in Indian Parliament on Evolution of India's Nuclear Policy, 27 May 1998

On 11 May a statement was issued by Government announcing that India had successfully carried out three underground nuclear tests at the Pokhran range. Two days later, after carrying out two more underground sub-kiloton tests, the Government announced the completion of the planned series of tests. The three underground nuclear tests carried out at 1545 hours on 11 May were with three different devices—a fission device, a low-yield sub-kiloton device and a thermonuclear device. The two tests carried out at 1221 hours on 13 May were also low-yield devices in the sub-kiloton range. The results from these tests have been in accordance with the expectations of our scientists.

In 1947, when India emerged as a free country to take its rightful place in the comity of nations, the nuclear age had already dawned. Our leaders then took the crucial decision to opt for self-reliance, and freedom of thought and action. We rejected the Cold War paradigm whose shadows were already appearing on the horizon and instead of aligning ourselves with either bloc, chose the more difficult path of non-alignment. This has required the building up of national strength through our own resources, our skills and creativity and the dedication of the people. Among the earliest initiatives taken by our first Prime Minister Pt. Jawaharlal Nehru, was the development of science and inculcation of the scientific spirit. It is this initiative that laid the foundation for the achievement of 11 and 13 May, made possible by exemplary cooperation among the scientists from Department of Atomic Energy and Defence Research & Development Organisation. Disarmament was then and continues to be a major plank in our foreign policy now. It was, in essence, and remains still, the natural course for a country that had waged a unique struggle for independence on the basis of 'ahimsa' and satyagraha'.

Development of nuclear technology transformed the nature of global secu-

[1] Available at http://meadev.nic.in/, accessed on 15 July 1998.

rity. Our leaders reasoned that nuclear weapons were not weapons of war, these were weapons of mass destruction. A nuclear-weapon-free-world would, therefore, enhance not only India's security but also the security of all nations. This is the principle plank of our nuclear policy. In the absence of universal and non-discriminatory disarmament, we cannot accept a regime that creates an arbitrary division between nuclear haves and have-nots. India believes that it is the sovereign right of every nation to make a judgement regarding its supreme national interests and exercise its sovereign choice. We subscribe to the principle of equal and legitimate security interests of nations and consider it a sovereign right. At the same time, our leaders recognized early that nuclear technology offers tremendous potential for economic development, especially for developing countries who are endeavouring to leap across the technology gaps created by long years of colonial exploitation. This thinking was reflected in the enactment of the Atomic Energy Act of 1948, within a year of our independence. All the numerous initiatives taken by us since, in the field of nuclear disarmament have been in harmony and in continuation of those early enunciations.

In the 50s, nuclear weapons testing took place above ground and the characteristic mushroom cloud became the visible symbol of the nuclear age. India then took the lead in calling for an end to all nuclear weapon testing as the first step for ending the nuclear arms race. Addressing the Lok Sabha on 2 April 1954, shortly after a major hydrogen bomb test had been conducted, Pt. Jawaharlal Nehru stated that 'nuclear, chemical and biological energy and power should not be used to forge weapons of mass destruction'. He called for negotiations for prohibition and elimination of nuclear weapons and in the interim, a standstill agreement to halt nuclear testing. The world had by then witnessed less than 65 tests. Our call was not heeded. In 1963, an agreement was concluded to ban atmospheric testing but by this time, countries had developed the technologies for conducting underground nuclear tests and the nuclear arms race continued unabated. More than three decades passed and after over 2000 tests had been conducted, a Comprehensive Test Ban Treaty was opened for signature in 1996, following two and a half years of negotiations in which India had participated actively. In its final shape, this Treaty left much to be desired. It was neither comprehensive nor was it related to disarmament.

In 1965, along with a small group of non-aligned countries, India had put forward the idea of an international non-proliferation agreement under which the nuclear weapon states would agree to give up their arsenals provided other countries refrained from developing or acquiring such weapons. This balance of rights and obligations was absent when the Nuclear Non-Proliferation Treaty (NPT) emerged in 1968, almost 30 years ago. In the 60s our security concerns deepened. But such was our abhorrence of nuclear weapons and such our desire to avoid acquiring them that we sought instead security guarantees from major nuclear powers of the world. The countries we turned to for support and understanding felt unable to extend to us the assurances that we then sought. That is when and why India made clear its inability to sign the NPT.

The Lok Sabha debated the NPT on 5 April 1968. The then Prime Minister, late Smt. Indira Gandhi assured the House that 'we shall be guided entirely by our self-enlightenment and the considerations of national security'. She highlighted the shortcomings of the NPT whilst re-emphasizing the country's commitment to nuclear disarmament. She warned the House and the country 'that not signing the Treaty may bring the nation many difficulties. It may mean the stoppage of aid and stoppage of help. Since we are taking this decision together, we must all be together in facing its consequences.' That was a turning point. This House then strengthened the decision of the Government by reflecting a national consensus.

Our decision not to sign the NPT was in keeping with the basic objective of maintaining freedom of thought and action. In 1974, we demonstrated our nuclear capability. Successive Governments thereafter have continued to take all necessary steps in keeping with that resolve and national will, to safeguard India's nuclear option. This was also the primary reason underlying the 1996 decision in the country not subscribing to the Comprehensive Test Ban Treaty (CTBT); a decision that met the unanimous approval of the House yet again. Our perception then was that subscribing to the CTBT would severely limit India's nuclear potential at an unacceptably low level. Our reservations deepened as the CTBT did not also carry forward the nuclear disarmament process. On both counts, therefore, yet again our security concerns remained unaddressed. The then Minister for External Affairs, Shri I.K. Gujral had made clear the Government's reasoning to this House during the discussions on this subject in 1996.

The decades of the 1980s and 1990s meanwhile witnessed the gradual deterioration of our security environment as a result of nuclear and missile proliferation. In our neighbourhood, nuclear weapons increased and more sophisticated delivery systems were inducted. Further, in our region there has come into existence a pattern about clandestine acquisition of nuclear materials, missiles and related technologies. India, in this period, became the victim of externally aided and abetted terrorism, militancy and clandestine war through hired mercenaries.

The end of the Cold War marks a watershed in the history of the twentieth century. While it has transformed the political landscape of Europe, it has done little to address India's security concerns. The relative order that was arrived at in Europe was not replicated in other parts of the globe.

At the global level, there is no evidence yet on the part of the nuclear weapon states to take decisive and irreversible steps in moving towards a nuclear-weapon-free-world. Instead, the NPT has been extended indefinitely and unconditionally, perpetuating the existence of nuclear weapons in the hands of the five countries who are also permanent members of the UN Security Council. Some of these countries have doctrines that permit the first use of nuclear weapons; these countries are also engaged in programmes for modernization of their nuclear arsenals.

Under such circumstances, India was left with little choice. It had to take necessary steps to ensure that the country's nuclear option, developed and safeguarded over decades not be permitted to erode by a voluntary self-imposed restraint. Indeed, such an erosion would have had an irremediably adverse impact on our security. The Government was thus faced with a difficult decision. The only touchstone that guided it was national security. Tests conducted on 11 and 13 May are a continuation of the policies set into motion that put this country on the path of self-reliance and independence of thought and action. Nevertheless, there are certain moments when the chosen path reaches a fork and a decision has to be made. 1968 was one such moment in our nuclear chapter as were 1974 and 1996. At each of these moments, we took the right decision guided by national interest and supported by national consensus. 1998 was borne in the crucible of earlier decisions and made possible only because those decisions had been taken correctly in the past and in time.

At a time when developments in the area of advanced technologies are taking place at a breathtaking pace, new parameters need to be identified, tested and validated in order to ensure that skills remain contemporary and succeeding generations of scientists and engineers are able to build on the work done by their predecessors. The limited series of five tests undertaken by India was precisely such an exercise. It has achieved its stated objective. The data provided by these tests is critical to validate our capabilities in the design of nuclear weapons of different yields for different applications and different delivery systems. Further, these tests have significantly enhanced the capabilities of our scientists and engineers in computer simulation of new designs and enabled them to undertake sub-critical experiments in future, if considered necessary. In terms of technical capability, our scientists and engineers have the requisite resources to ensure a credible deterrent.

Our policies towards our neighbours and other countries too have not changed; India remains fully committed to the promotion of peace with stability, and resolution of all outstanding issues through bilateral dialogue and negotiations. These tests were not directed against any country; these were intended to reassure the people of India about their security and convey determination that this Government, like previous Governments, has the capability and resolve to safeguard their national security interests. The Government will continue to remain engaged in substantive dialogue with our neighbours to improve relations and to expand the scope of our interactions in a mutually advantageous manner. Confidence building is a continuous process; we remain committed to it. Consequent upon the tests and arising from an insufficient appreciation of our security concerns, some countries have been persuaded to take steps that sadden us. We value our bilateral relations. We remain committed to dialogue and reaffirm that preservation of India's security create no conflict of interest with these countries.

India is a nuclear weapon state. This is a reality that cannot be denied. It is not a conferment that we seek; nor is it a status for others to grant. It is an endowment to the nation by our scientists and engineers. It is India's due, the right of one-sixth of humankind. Our strengthened capability adds to our sense of responsibility; the responsibility and obligation of power. India, mindful of its international obligations, shall not use these weapons to commit aggression or to mount threats against any country; these are weapons of self-defence and to ensure that in turn, India is also not subjected to nuclear threats or coercion. In 1994, we had proposed that India and Pakistan jointly undertake not to be the first to use their nuclear capability against each other. The Government on this occasion, reiterates its readiness to discuss a 'no-first-use' agreement with that country, as also with other countries bilaterally, or in a collective forum. India shall not engage in an arms race. India shall also not subscribe or reinvent the doctrines of the Cold War. India remains committed to the basic tenet of our foreign policy—a conviction that global elimination of nuclear weapons will enhance its security as well as that of the rest of the world. It will continue to urge countries, particularly other nuclear weapon states to adopt measures that would contribute meaningfully to such an objective.

A number of initiatives have been taken in the past. In 1978, India proposed negotiations for an international convention that would prohibit the use or threat of use of nuclear weapons. This was followed by another initiative in 1982 calling for a 'nuclear freeze'—a prohibition on production of fissile materials for weapons, on production of nuclear weapons and related delivery systems. In 1988, we put forward an Action Plan for phased elimination of all nuclear weapons within a specified time frame. It is our regret that these proposals did not receive a positive response from other nuclear weapon states. Had their response been positive, India need not have gone for the current tests. This is where our approach to nuclear weapons is different from others. This difference is the cornerstone of our nuclear doctrine. It is marked by restraint and striving for the total elimination of all weapons of mass destruction.

We will continue to support such initiatives, taken individually or collectively by the Non-Aligned Movement which has continued to attach the highest priority to nuclear disarmament. This was reaffirmed most recently, last week, at the NAM Ministerial meeting held at Cartagena which has 'reiterated their call on the Conference on Disarmament to establish, as the highest priority', an ad hoc committee to start in 1998 negotiations on a phased programme for the complete elimination of nuclear weapons with a specified framework of time, including a Nuclear Weapons Convention. The collective voice of 113 NAM countries reflects an approach to global nuclear disarmament to which India has remained committed. One of the NAM member initiatives to which we attach great importance was the reference to the International Court of Justice resulting in the unanimous declaration from the ICJ, as part of the Advisory Opinion handed down on 8 July 1996, that 'there exists an obligation to pursue in good faith and bring to a conclusion negotiations leading to nuclear disarmament in all its aspects under strict and effective international control'. India was one of the countries that appealed to the ICJ on this issue. No other nuclear weapon state has supported this judgement; in fact, they have sought to decry its value. We have been and will continue to be in the forefront of the calls for opening negotiations for a Nuclear Weapons Convention, so that this challenge can be dealt with in the same manner that we have dealt with the scourge of two other weapons of mass destruction—through the Biological Weapons Convention and the Chemical Weapons Convention. In keeping with our commitment to comprehensive, universal and non-discriminatory approaches to disarmament, India is an original State Party to both these Conventions. Accordingly, India will shortly submit the plan of destruction of its chemical weapons to the international authority—Organisation for the Prohibition of Chemical Weapons. We fulfil our obligations whenever we undertake them.

Traditionally, India has been an outward looking country. Our strong commitment to multilateralism is reflected in our active participation in organizations like the United Nations. In recent years, in keeping with the new challenges, we have actively promoted regional cooperation, in SAARC, in the Indian Ocean Rim, Association for Regional Cooperation and as a member of the ASEAN Regional Forum. This engagement will also continue. The policies of economic liberalization introduced in recent years have increased our regional and global linkages and the Government shall deepen and strengthen these ties.

Our nuclear policy has been marked by restraint and openness. It has not violated any international agreements either in 1974 or now, in 1998. Our concerns have been made known to our interlocutors in recent years. The restraint exercised for 24 years, after having demonstrated our capability in 1974 is in itself a unique example. Restraint, however, has to arise from strength. It cannot be based upon indecision or doubt. Restraint is valid only when doubts are removed. The series of tests undertaken by India have led to the removal of doubts. The action involved was balanced in that it was the minimum necessary to maintain what is an irreducible component of our national security calculus. This Government's decision has, therefore, to be seen as part of a tradition of restraint that has characterized our policy in the past 50 years.

Subsequent to the tests Government has already stated that India will now observe a voluntary moratorium and refrain from conducting underground nuclear test explosions. It has also indicated willingness to move towards a de-jure formalization of this declaration. The basic obligations of the CTBT are thus met: to refrain from undertaking nuclear test explosions. This voluntary declaration is intended to convey to the international community the seriousness of our intent for meaningful engagement. Subsequent decisions will be taken after assuring ourselves of the security needs of the country.

India has also indicated readiness to participate in negotiations in the Conference on Disarmament in Geneva on a Fissile Material Cut-off Treaty. The basic objective of this treaty is to prohibit future production of fissile materials for use in nuclear weapons or nuclear explosive devices. India's approach in these negotiations will be to ensure that this treaty emerges as a universal and non-discriminatory treaty, backed by an effective verification mechanism. When we embark on these negotiations, it shall be in the full confidence of the adequacy and credibility of the nation's weaponized nuclear deterrent.

India has maintained effective export controls on nuclear materials as well as related technologies even though we are neither a party to the NPT nor a member of the Nuclear Suppliers' Group. None the less, India is committed to non-proliferation and the maintaining of stringent export controls to ensure that there is no leakage of our indigenously developed know-how and technologies. In fact, India's conduct in this regard has been better than some countries party to the NPT.

India has in the past conveyed our concerns on the inadequacies of the international nuclear non-proliferation regime. It has explained that the country was not in a position to join because the regime did not address our country's security concerns. These could have been addressed by moving towards global nuclear disarmament, our preferred approach. As this did not take place, India was obliged to stand aside from the emerging regime so that its freedom of action was not constrained. This is the precise path that has continued to be followed unwaveringly for the last three decades. That same constructive approach will underlie India's dialogue with countries that need to be persuaded of our serious intent and willingness to engage so that mutual concerns are satisfactorily addressed. The challenge to Indian statecraft is balancing and reconciling India's security imperatives with valid international concerns in the regard.

The House is aware of the different reactions that have emanated from the people of India and from different parts of the world. The overwhelming support of the citizens of India is a source of strength for the Government. It not only tells that this decision was right but also that the country wants a focused leadership, which attends to national security needs. This the Government pledges to do as a sacred duty. The Government have also been greatly heartened by the outpouring of support from Indians abroad. They have, with one voice, spoken in favour of the Government's action. The Government conveys its profound gratitude to the citizens of India and to Indians abroad, and looks to them for support in the difficult period ahead.

In this, the fiftieth year of our independence, India stands at a defining moment in our history. The rationale for the Government's decision is based on the same policy tenets that have guided the country for five decades. These policies were sustained successfully because of the underlying national consensus. The present decision and future actions will continue to reflect a commitment to sensibilities and obligations of an ancient civilization, a sense of responsibility and restraint, but a restraint born of the assurance of action, not of doubts or apprehension. The *Gita* explains (Chapter VI-3) as none other can: *Action is a process to reach a goal; action may reflect tumult but when measured and focused, will yield its objective of stability and peace.*

APPENDIX 2

Indian PM's Statement in Parliament, 15 December 1998

Sir,

Since the 11 and 13 May tests, the Government has, from time to time, taken the House into confidence and sought views of the Hon'ble Members. This was done through statements and discussions in the House on 27-9 May, 8 June and on 3-4 August. Nevertheless, I wish to re-emphasize some salients of our policy.

I take this opportunity to reiterate that India's commitment to global nuclear disarmament remains undiluted. As Hon'ble Members are no doubt aware, India has consistently maintained that a nuclear-weapon-free-world would enhance not only our security but the security of all nations. That is why numerous initiatives in this direction were taken during the last fifty years; such steps as would encourage decisive and irreversible measures for the attainment of this objective. Regrettably, the international community, particularly countries that have based their security on nuclear weapons or a nuclear umbrella, have been reluctant to embrace this objective. Keeping open our nuclear option, therefore, became a national security imperative three decades ago, an imperative equally valid for India in the post-Cold War period. The option that was exercised in May 1998 was thus a continuation of a decision taken near 25 years earlier; during which period India had demonstrated an exemplary nuclear restraint, given the exceptional security related complexities of our region. I wish to place on record that successive governments continued to safeguard this option, demonstrate our capability, and take such steps as were necessary to ensure the viability of the option through weaponization.

Just as our conventional defense capability has been deployed in order to safeguard the territorial integrity and sovereignty of India against any use or threat of use of force, the adoption of our nuclear deterrent posture has also followed the same logic. We have announced our intention to maintain a

[1] Available at www.meadev.gov.in, accessed on 20 December 1998.

minimum nuclear deterrent, but one that is credible. Mindful of our global and enhanced responsibility to address concerns of the international community, and in order to reassure all countries about the defensive nature of our nuclear capability, we have engaged in bilateral discussions with key interlocutors. In international forums, like the United Nations, India is the only country possessing nuclear weapons to raise a call for negotiating a gradual and progressive elimination of all nuclear weapons, within a time-bound framework.

We also have an established tradition of consultation with friendly countries on all important international issues. Successive governments have pursued an open, positive and constructive approach in our foreign relations. This is in keeping with our national ethos. It is within this framework that India had been engaged, even before May 1998, in a wide-ranging and broad-based dialogue with the United States. This included discussions on disarmament and non-proliferation and on larger strategic issues.

Following the 11 and 13 May nuclear tests, apprehensions were expressed in some quarters. It was, therefore, decided to have more focused and intensive discussions. Accordingly, Shri Jaswant Singh, Deputy Chairman, Planning Commission was designated as our Representative, to carry forward this dialogue. Similarly, President Clinton designated Deputy Secretary of State, Strobe Talbott, as the US interlocutor.

This dialogue has been conducted on the basis of a set of comprehensive proposals, put forward by India, to the international community, soon after the May tests. As the House would recollect, these proposals comprise: a voluntary moratorium on underground nuclear test explosions; our willingness to move towards a de-jure formalization of this commitment, a decision to join negotiations on a treaty for a ban on future production of fissile material for weapons purposes; and, our determination to make more stringent the existing system of export controls over sensitive materials and technology.

Since the 11 June 1998 Washington meet, six rounds of discussions between Shri Jaswant Singh and Mr. Talbott have been held. Both teams have worked purposefully to narrow gaps of perception and to establish common ground. These exchanges have been marked by a sense of responsibility, candour and a sincere attempt to understand each other's concerns and points of view. The Government is entirely mindful that the issues involved touch upon matters of vital interest to both countries. In these talks, we have firmly put across our security concerns and the imperative of maintaining a minimum, credible, nuclear deterrent. I wish to inform the House that the talks are premised on this basis. Also there now exists some understanding of our security concerns and requirements.

The talks have focused on issues related to disarmament and non-proliferation. It is agreed that regional issues shall be kept distinctly apart. As Hon'ble Members are well aware, India's concerns in these matters go beyond the South Asian region, and involve a wider perspective.

After six rounds, talks have narrowed and are now focused on the following four issues:

CTBT

India remains committed to converting our voluntary moratorium into a *de jure* obligation. In response to the desire of the international community, as expressed to us in our bilateral and multilateral interactions, that the Treaty should come into effect in September 1999, in my address to the United Nations General Assembly on 24 September, I reiterated broadly what I had said in Parliament, that: 'India is now engaged in discussions with our key interlocutors on a range of issues, including the CTBT. We are prepared to bring these discussions to a successful conclusion, so that the entry into force of the CTBT is not delayed beyond September 1999. We expect that other countries, as indicated in Article XIV of the CTBT, will adhere to this Treaty without conditions.'

That remains our position. For the successful conclusion of the talks, the creation of a positive environment by our interlocutors is a necessary ingredient.

The House will be reassured that in the assessment of our scientists, this stand does not come in the way of our taking such steps as may be found necessary in future to safeguard our national security. It also does not constrain us from continuing with our R & D programmes, nor does it jeopardize in any manner the safety and effectiveness of our nuclear deterrent in the years to come.

FMCT

We have expressed our willingness to join the FMCT negotiations in the Conference on Disarmament at Geneva. It is our understanding, as that of many other countries, who have confirmed this to us, that the objective of these negotiations is to arrive at a non-discriminatory treaty, that will end the future production of fissile material for weapons purposes, in accordance with the 1993 consensus resolution of the UN General Assembly. We are willing to work for the early conclusion of such a treaty.

It was suggested to us that we might examine announcing a moratorium on fissile material production. We have conveyed that it is not possible to take such steps at this stage. We will, of course, pay serious attention to any negotiated multilateral initiatives in the course of the FMCT negotiations.

Export Controls

Discussions in this area have registered progress. An expert level meeting of officials from both sides was held in New Delhi on 9-10 November. In light of our additional capabilities, as a responsible state possessing nuclear weapons, and as earlier announced, we are taking steps to make more stringent our laws in this regard. We have also conveyed that India should be provided better access to dual-use and high technologies in view of India's impeccable record of effective control over sensitive technologies. The expert-level meeting was categorized as helpful by both, India and the US, to the prospects of continuing cooperation in this area.

Defence Posture

As Hon'ble Members are, no doubt, aware, matters relating to defence postures are sovereign functions, not subjects for negotiations. In fact, our talks are based on the fundamental premise that India will define its own requirements, for its nuclear deterrent, on its own assessment of the security environment. The US and other interlocutors, are interested in understanding our positions and our policies better.

We have formally announced a policy of No-First-Use and non-use against non-nuclear weapons states. As Hon'ble Members are aware, a policy of no-first-use with a minimum nuclear deterrent, implies deployment of assets in a manner that ensures survivability and capacity of an adequate response. We are also not going to enter into an arms race with any country. Ours will be a minimum credible deterrent, which will safeguard India's security—the security of one-sixth of humanity, now and into the future. The National Security Council, with the assistance of its subsidiary bodies, the establishment of which has been announced, will make important contributions to elaborating these concepts.

We have expressed our reservations about provisions of certain export control regimes that ostensibly seek to promote non-proliferation objectives, but are discriminatory in application. India's missile development programme is an indigenous programme, that was launched almost 15 years ago. This programme is regularly reviewed, taking into account our security environment, particularly missile acquisitions and deployments in our region. We have announced that a new version of the Agni, with an extended range is under development. Flight-testing of such an enhanced range Agni will be conducted fully in accordance with established international practice. While our decision is to maintain the deployment of a deterrent which is both minimum but credible, I would like to re-affirm to this House that the Government will not accept any restraints on the development of India's R & D capabilities. Such activity is an integral of any country's defense preparedness and essential for coping with new threat perceptions that may emerge in the years ahead. This Government remains unequivocally opposed to any suggestions that seek to place India at a technological disadvantage through intrusive or sovereignty violative measures.

At the same time, we will continue to take initiatives in the international forums towards fulfilling the objective of complete elimination of all nuclear weapons. At this year's UN General Assembly, we had taken the initiative for what could be an important first step, through a resolution on 'Reducing Nuclear Danger'. This initiative was intended to urge countries to move back from the nuclear hair-trigger response postures of the Cold War. If such initiatives are multilaterally accepted by other nuclear weapon states, they will, of course, be accordingly reflected in our own positions, too.

In the course of these discussions with the United States and other countries, I have kept in touch with leaders of various political parties. We have issued statements from time to time on pronouncements and declarations by various countries. This corpus of Statements in Parliament and through Official Spokesman conveys our position and is well known to Hon'ble Members. These issues have also been discussed, at considerable length, in meetings of the Standing Committee and the Consultative Committee of Parliament. The viewpoints expressed by Hon'ble Members in these discussions, have provided us valuable guidance in conducting discussions with the United States and other countries.

The dialogue with the United States will be continued at the next meeting scheduled to be held in the second half of January, in New Delhi.

While there is no time-frame for the conclusion of these talks, it is the intention of both countries, that a stable understanding should be reached on the remaining issues at an early date. This would provide a further momentum to bilateral relations, which is desired by both countries.

In addition to the talks between Shri Jaswant Singh and Mr. Strobe Talbott, we have had detailed exchanges with France and Russia. Discussions have also taken place with UK and China at the level of Shri Jaswant Singh and at official level with Germany and Japan as well as with other non-nuclear weapon states. I have been in regular correspondence with President Clinton. Our correspondence has touched not only upon issues under discussion between our Representatives but also on larger aspects of Indo-US relations. It is my view that the future of Indo-US relations is much larger than the four issues under consideration. President Clinton has also expressed to me, his desire for a broad-based relationship with India that befits the two largest democracies of the world. I have fully reciprocated these sentiments. Indeed, our ongoing dialogue with the United States is geared towards that end. I am confident this House will want to wish it all success.

APPENDIX 3

The Lahore Declaration, 21 February 1999

The Prime Ministers of the Republic of India and the Islamic Republic of Pakistan:

Sharing a vision of peace and stability between their countries, and of progress and prosperity for their peoples;

Convinced that durable peace and development of harmonious relations and friendly cooperation will serve the vital interests of the peoples of the two countries, enabling them to devote their energies for a better future;

Recognizing that the nuclear dimension of the security environment of the two countries adds to their responsibility for avoidance of conflict between the two countries;

Committed to the principles and purposes of the Charter of the United Nations, and the universally accepted principles of peaceful coexistence;

Reiterating the determination of both countries to implementing the Simla Agreement in letter and spirit;

Committed to the objective of universal nuclear disarmament and non-proliferartion;

Convinced of the importance of mutually agreed confidence building measures for improving the security environment;

Recalling their agreement of 23rd September, 1998, that an environment of peace and security is in the supreme national interest of both sides and that the resolution of all outstanding issues, including Jammu and Kashmir, is essential for this purpose.

Have agreed that their respective Governments:

- shall intensify their efforts to resolve all issues, including the issue of Jammu and Kashmir.
- shall refrain from intervention and interference in each other's internal affairs.
- shall intensify their composite and integrated dialogue process for an early and positive outcome of the agreed bilateral agenda.

shall take immediate steps for reducing the risk of accidental or unauthorized use of nuclear weapons and discuss concepts and doctrines with a view to elaborating measures for confidence building in the nuclear and conventional fields, aimed at prevention of conflict.

Reaffirm their commitment to the goals and objectives of SAARC and to concert their efforts towards the realization of the SAARC vision for the year 2000 and beyond with a view to promoting the welfare of the peoples of South Asia and to improve their quality of life through accelerated economic growth, social progress and cultural development.

Reaffirm their condemnation of terrorism in all its forms and manifestations and their determination to combat this menace.

Shall promote and protect all human rights and fundamental freedoms.

Signed at Lahore on the 21st day of February 1999.

Atal Behari Vajpayee Prime Minister of the Republic of India	Muhammad Nawaz Sharif Prime Minister of the Islamic Republic of Pakistan

Source: *The Hindu*, 22 February 1999.

Indo-Pak Joint Statement, 21 February 1999

The following is the text of the Joint Statement issued at the end of the Prime Minister, Mr. A.B. Vajpayee's visit to Lahore:

In response to an invitation by the Prime Minister of Pakistan, Mr. Muhammad Nawaz Sharif, the Prime Minister of India, Shri Atal Behari Vajpayee, visited Pakistan from 20-21 February, 1999, on the inaugural run of the Delhi-Lahore bus service.

The Prime Minister of Pakistan received the Indian Prime Minister at the Wagah border on 20th February 1999. A banquet in honour of the Indian Prime Minister and his delegation was hosted by the Prime Minister of Pakistan at Lahore Fort, on the same evening. Prime Minister, Atal Behari Vajpayee, visited Minar-e-Pakistan, Mausoleum of Allama Iqbal, Gurudawara Dera Sahib and Samadhi of Maharaja Ranjeet Singh. On 21st February, a civic reception was held in honour of the visiting Prime Minister at the Governor's House.

The two leaders held discussions on the entire range of bilateral relations, regional cooperation within SAARC, and issues of international concern. They decided that:

(a) The two Foreign Ministers will meet periodically to discuss all issues of mutual concern, including nuclear related issues.
(b) The two sides shall undertake consultations on WTO related issues with a view to coordinating their respective positions.

(c) The two sides shall determine areas of cooperation in Information Technology, in particular for tackling the problems of Y2K.
(d) The two sides will hold consultations with a view to further liberalizing the visa and travel regime.
(e) The two sides shall appoint a two member committee at ministerial level to examine humanitarian issues relating to Civilian detainees and missing POWs.

They expressed satisfaction on the commencement of a Bus Service between Lahore and New Delhi, the release of fishermen and civilian detainees and the renewal of contacts in the field of sports.

Pursuant to the directive given by the two Prime Ministers, the Foreign Secretaries of Pakistan and India signed a Memorandum of Understanding on 21st February 1999, identifying measures aimed at promoting an environment of peace and security between the two countries.

The two Prime Ministers signed the Lahore Declaration embodying their shared vision of peace and stability between their countries and of progress and prosperity for their peoples.

Prime Minister, Atal Behari Vajpayee extended an invitation to Prime Minister, Muhammad Nawaz Sharif, to visit India on mutually convenient dates.

Prime Minister, Atal Behari Vajpayee, thanked Prime Minister, Muhammad Nawaz Sharif, for the warm welcome and gracious hospitality extended to him and members of his delegation and for the excellent arrangements made for his visit.

Lahore,
February 21, 1999

Source: *The Hindu*, 22 February 1999.

Memorandum of Understanding, 21 February 1999

The following is the text of the Memorandum of Understanding signed by the Foreign Secretary, Mr. K. Raghunath, and the Pakistan Foreign Secretary, Mr. Shamshad Ahmad, in Lahore on Sunday:

THE FOREIGN SECRETARIES OF
INDIA AND PAKISTAN:

Reaffirming the continued commitment of their respective governments to the principles and purposes of the U.N. Charter;

Reiterating the determination of both countries to implementing the Shimla Agreement in letter and spirit;

Guided by the agreement between their Prime Ministers of 23rd September

1998 that an environment of peace and security is in the supreme national interest of both sides and that resolution of all outstanding issues, including Jammu and Kashmir, is essential for this purpose;

Pursuant to the directive given by their respective Prime Ministers in Lahore, to adopt measures for promoting a stable environment of peace, and security between the two countries;

Have on this day, agreed to the following:

The two sides shall engage in bilateral consultations on security concepts, and nuclear doctrines, with a view to developing measures for confidence building in the nuclear and coventional fields, aimed at avoidance of conflict.

The two sides undertake to provide each other with advance notification in respect of ballistic missile flight tests, and shall conclude a bilateral agreement in this regard.

The two sides are fully committed to undertaking national measures to reducing the risks of accidental or unauthorized use of nuclear weapons under their respective control. The two sides further undertake to notify each, other immediately in the event of any accidental, unauthorized or unexplained incident that could create the risk of a fallout with adverse consequences for both sides, or an outbreak of a nuclear war between the two countries, as well as to adopt measures aimed at diminishing the possibility of such actions, or such incidents being misinterpreted by the other. The two sides shall identify/establish the appropriate communication mechanism for this purpose.

The two sides shall continue to abide by their respective unilateral moratorium on conducting further nuclear test explosions unless either side, in exercise of its national sovereignty decides that extraordinary events have jeopardized its supreme interests.

The two sides shall conclude an agreement on prevention of incidents at sea in order to ensure safety of navigation by naval vessels, and aircraft belonging to the two sides.

The two sides shall periodically review the implementation of existing Confidence Building Measures (CBMs) and where necessary, set up appropriate consultative mechanisms to monitor and ensure effective implementation of these CBMs.

The two sides shall undertake a review of the existing communication links (e.g. between the respective Directors-General, Military Operations) with a view to upgrading and improving these links, and to provide for fail-safe and secure communications.

The two sides shall engage in bilateral consultations on security, disarmament and non-proliferation issues within the context of negotiations on these issues in multilateral fora.

Where required, the technical details of the above measures will be worked out by experts of the two sides in meetings to be held on mutually agreed dates, before mid 1999, with a view to reaching bilateral agreements.

Done at Lahore on 21st February 1999 in the presence of Prime Minister of India, Mr. Atal Behari Vajpayee, and Prime Minister of Pakistan, Mr. Muhammad Nawaz Sharif.

(K. Raghunath)	(Shamshad Ahmad)
Foreign Secretary of	*Foreign Secretary of the*
Republic of India	*Islamic Republic of Pakistan*

Source: *The Hindu*, 22 February 1999.

APPENDIX 4

Draft Report of National Security Advisory Board on Indian Nuclear Doctrine, 17 August 1999

1. PREAMBLE

1.1 The use of nuclear weapons in particular as well as other weapons of mass destruction constitutes the gravest threat to humanity and to peace and stability in the international system. Unlike the other two categories of weapons of mass destruction, biological and chemical weapons which have been outlawed by international treaties, nuclear weapons remain instruments for national and collective security, the possession of which on a selective basis has been sought to be legitimized through permanent extension of the Nuclear. Non-proliferation Treaty (NPT) in May 1995. Nuclear weapon states have asserted that they will continue to rely on nuclear weapons with some of them adopting policies to use them even in a non-nuclear context. These developments amount to virtual abandonment of nuclear disarmament. This is a serious setback to the struggle of the international community to abolish weapons of mass destruction.

1.2 India's primary objective is to achieve economic, political, social, scientific and technological development within a peaceful and democratic framework. This requires an environment of durable peace and insurance against potential risks to peace and stability. It will be India's endeavour to proceed towards this overall objective in cooperation with the global democratic trends and to play a constructive role in advancing the international system toward a just, peaceful and equitable order.

1.3 Autonomy of decision making in the developmental process and in strategic matters is an inalienable democratic right of the Indian people. India will strenuously guard this right in a world where nuclear weapons for a select

[1] Available at http://www.meadev.gov.in/govt/indnucld.htm, accessed on 17 August 1999.

few are sought to be legitimized for an indefinite future, and where there is growing complexity and frequency in the use of force for political purposes.

1.4 India's security is an integral component of its development process. India continuously aims at promoting an ever-expanding area of peace and stability around it so that developmental priorities can be pursued without disruption.

1.5 However, the very existence of offensive doctrine pertaining to the first use of nuclear weapons and the insistence of some nuclear weapons states on the legitimacy of their use even against non-nuclear weapon countries constitute a threat to peace, stability and sovereignty of states.

1.6 This document outlines the broad principles for the development, deployment and employment of India's nuclear forces. Details of policy and strategy concerning force structures, deployment and employment of nuclear forces will flow from this framework and will be laid down separately and kept under constant review.

2. Objectives

2.1 In the absence of global nuclear disarmament India's strategic interests require effective, credible nuclear deterrence and adequate retaliatory capability should deterrence fail. This is consistent with the UN Charter, which sanctions the right of self-defence.

2.2 The requirements of deterrence should be carefully weighed in the design of Indian nuclear forces and in the strategy to provide for a level of capability consistent with maximum credibility, survivability, effectiveness, safety and security.

2.3 India shall pursue a doctrine of credible minimum nuclear deterrence. In this policy of 'retaliation only', the survivability of our arsenal is critical. This is a dynamic concept related to the strategic environment, technological imperatives and the needs of national security. The actual size components, deployment and employment of nuclear forces will be decided in the light of these factors. India's peacetime posture aims at convincing any potential aggressor that:

(a) any threat of use of nuclear weapons against India shall invoke measures to counter the threat: and (b) any nuclear attack on India and its forces shall result in punitive retaliation with nuclear weapons to inflict damage unacceptable to the aggressor.

2.4 The fundamental purpose of Indian nuclear weapons is to deter the use and threat of use of nuclear weapons by any State or entity against India and its forces. India will not be the first to initiate a nuclear strike, but will respond with punitive retaliation should deterrence fail.

2.5 India will not resort to the use or threat of use of nuclear weapons against States which do not possess nuclear weapons, or are not aligned with nuclear weapon powers.

2.6 Deterrence requires that India maintain:

(a) sufficient, survivable and operationally prepared nuclear forces,
(b) a robust command and control system,
(c) effective intelligence and early warning capabilities, and
(d) comprehensive planning and training for operations in line with the strategy, and
(e) the will to employ nuclear forces and weapons.

2.7 Highly effective conventional military capabilities shall be maintained to raise the threshold of outbreak both of conventional military conflict as well as that of threat or use of nuclear weapons.

3. Nulear Forces

3.1 India's nuclear forces will be effective, enduring, diverse, flexible, and responsive to the requirements in accordance with the concept of credible minimum deterrence. These forces will be based on a triad of aircraft, mobile land-based missiles and sea-based assets in keeping with the objectives outlined above. Survivability of the forces will be enhanced by a combination of multiple redundant systems, mobility, dispersion and deception.

3.2 The doctrine envisages assured capability to shift from peacetime deployment to fully employable forces in the shortest possible time, and the ability to retaliate effectively even in a case of significant degradation by hostile strikes.

4. Credibility and Survivability

The following principles are central to India's nuclear deterrent:

4.1. *Credibility*: Any adversary must know that India can and will retaliate with sufficient nuclear weapons to inflict destruction and punishment that the aggressor will find unacceptable if nuclear weapons are used against India and its forces.

4.2. *Effectiveness*: The efficacy of India's nuclear deterrent be maximised through synergy among all elements involving reliability, timeliness, accuracy and weight of the attack.

4.3. *Survivability*:

(i) India's nuclear forces and their command and control shall be organized for very high survivability against surprise attacks and for rapid punitive response. They shall be designed and deployed to ensure survival against a first strike and to endure repetitive attrition attempts with adequate retaliatory capabilities for a punishing strike which would be unacceptable to the aggressor.

(ii) Procedures for the continuity of nuclear command and control shall ensure a continuing capability to effectively employ nuclear weapons.

5. Command and Control

5.1 Nuclear weapons shall be tightly controlled and released for use at the highest political level. The authority to release nuclear weapons for use resides in the person of the Prime Minister of India, or the designated successor(s).

5.2 An effective and survivable command and control system with requisite flexibility and responsiveness shall be in place. An integrated operational plan, or a series of sequential plans, predicated on strategic objectives and a targeting policy shall form part of the system.

5.3 For effective employment the unity of command and control of nuclear forces including dual capable delivery systems shall be ensured.

5.4 The survivability of the nuclear arsenal and effective command, control, communications, computing, intelligence and information (C412) systems shall be assured.

5.5 The Indian defence forces shall be in a position to, execute operations in an NBC environment with minimal degradation.

5.6 Space based and other assets shall be created to provide early warning, communications, damage/detonation assessment.

6. Security and Safety

6.1. *Security*: Extraordinary precautions shall be taken to ensure that nuclear weapons, their manufacture, transportation and storage are fully guarded against possible theft, loss, sabotage, damage or unauthorized access or use.

6.2. Safety is an absolute requirement and tamper proof procedures and systems shall be instituted to ensure that unauthorized or inadvertent activation/use of nuclear weapons does not take place and risks of accident are avoided.

6.3. *Disaster control*: India shall develop an appropriate disaster control system capable of handling the unique requirements of potential incidents involving nuclear weapons and materials.

7. Research and Development

7.1. India should step up efforts in research and development to keep up with technological advances in this field.

7.2. While India is committed to maintain the deployment of a deterrent which is both minimum and credible, it will not accept any restraints on building its R&D capability.

8. Disarmament and Arms Control

8.1. Global, verifiable and non-discriminatory nuclear disarmament is a national security objective. India shall continue its efforts to achieve the goal of a nuclear weapon-free world at an early date.

8.2. Since no-first-use of nuclear weapons is India's basic commitment, every effort shall be made to persuade other States possessing nuclear weapons to join an international treaty banning first use.

8.3. Having provided unqualified negative security assurances, India shall work for internationally binding unconditional negative security assurances by nuclear weapon states to non-nuclear weapon states.

8.4. Nuclear arms control measures shall be sought as part of national security policy to reduce potential threats and to protect our own capability and its effectiveness.

8.5. In view of the very high destructive potential of nuclear weapons, appro-priate nuclear risk reduction and confidence building measures shall be sought, negotiated and instituted.

APPENDIX 5

Securing Nuclear Peace

Aga Shahi, Zulfiqar Khan and Abdul Sattar, *The News International*, 5 October 1999

New questions about deterrent stability have arisen since May 1998 when first India and then Pakistan conducted multiple tests and embarked on overt nuclearization. More recently, in August 1999, India released a draft nuclear doctrine which envisages, in the guise of 'credible minimum nuclear deterrence' a massive expansion of strategic as well as conventional forces. With a large land-, air- and sea-based strike force of bombers and missiles capable of reaching every nook and corner of Pakistan, India would pose a threat far more serious in future than at present.

So far Pakistani spokesmen have indulged in denunciation of the threatening Indian nuclear posture. That is an exercise in futility and frustration. Such vociferation will have no effect in New Delhi. Nor should we expect major powers to prevail on India to abandon its ambitious plans. Their capacity if not also the desire to promote nuclear restraint in South Asia has ebbed. They do not have effective leverage or lack the will to use it for fear of detriment to their economic and political interests in India.

What is needed is focus on objective analysis and assessment of the implications of India's plans for Pakistan's defence and security. How long will India take to realize the projected force goals? To what extent might our minimal deterrent capability become vulnerable to a surprise attack by Indian missiles and strike aircraft? Might India conclude that its pre-emption and interception capability, enhanced by the anti-ballistic missile system New Delhi is planning to acquire, make it immune from a Pakistani response? If so, what concrete steps should Pakistan take to ensure the survivability and credibility of its deterrence force?

Restoration of the credibility of Pakistan's deterrence capability has therefore emerged as an urgent issue. In the face of widening power disparity, priority needs to be given to formulation of our plan of action to ensure the continued efficacy of Pakistan's deterrence force. As we embark on development of a counter-strategy, it should be necessary to bear in mind the rationale of Pakistan's policies and the lessons that have been learnt from our experience. Based on proven premises, projections into the future will be more reliable.

Nuclear deterrence: So great is the magnitude of the havoc a nuclear bomb can inflict that even a small number can achieve the effect. As Kenneth Waltz argued, their awesome destructive power invests nuclear weapons with unequalled capacity for deterrence. These weapons, he averred, 'make the cost of war seem frighteningly high and thus discourages states from starting any wars that might lead to the use of such weapons'. A state should shrink from resort to aggression because no potential gains would be worth the havoc a nuclear response would entail. Such a conclusion is not obvious in a conventional environment.

Fortunately, our leaders instinctively assimilated the deterrence rationale and embarked on a programme to acquire the nuclear weapons option. Conceived in the wake of the 1971 disaster when neither conventional military strength, alliances, nor the United Nations proved equal to the task of preventing Indian aggression and intervention, the object was solely to deter another Indian onslaught aimed at the territorial integrity of residual Pakistan. That purpose has been well served so far. Despite recurrent crises in Pakistan-India relations over the past two decades, another war has been averted. Even though nuclear weapons were not assembled, the recessed capability was credible enough to induce restraints against escalation.

The value of nuclear capability was illustrated on at least three occasions.

The first, somewhat ambiguous, instance of a hint of possible use of nuclear weapons arose in the mid-1980s when Islamabad received reports that India was contemplating, by itself or in collusion with another state then inimical to Pakistan, an air attack aimed at the destruction of the uranium enrichment plant at Kahuta. The Pakistan government is said to have conveyed a warning to New Delhi that it would hold India responsible for any such aggression and retaliate with 'all means at its disposal'. Use of nuclear weapons was neither specifically mentioned nor excluded, however.

The second crisis with nuclear undertones was triggered by the largest combined military exercise in India since independence, in the Rajasthan salient on Pakistan's border in the winter of 1986-7. Code-named Brasstacks, its aim, according to exercise documents obtained by Pakistani intelligence, was to cut off southern Pakistan from the north. Whether Indian military planners projected the conversion of the exercise into a cross-border operation and whether Pakistan intended in that event to use nuclear weapons has been conclusively established by research. But both assumptions are considered to be more than mere speculation.

The third crisis during which the spectre of a nuclear war arose was in April-May 1990. It was precipitated by reports that, unnerved by the mass uprising for freedom in occupied Kashmir, Indian GHQ had recommended air raids on training camps allegedly established in Azad Kashmir. Such aggressive action, American analysts concluded, would provoke a Pakistani response with a high probability of escalation to general war in which Pakistan, unable to defend its territory by conventional means, would be forced to use the weapon of last resort. So grave was the concern that the United States President sent Robert Gates as his personal emissary to Pakistan and India on a successful mission of preventive diplomacy in April.

The Kargil crisis both tested and illustrated the deterrence assumption. In 1965, actions provoked disproportionate reactions, with each side raising the ante leading to a general war that neither had contemplated. In 1999 India did not open a new front even in Kashmir, Pakistan did not bring its air force into action and the armed forces refrained from general mobilization. The crisis was contained.

Minimum deterrence: Although the precise contingencies in which Pakistan might use nuclear weapons have not been articulated or perhaps even defined by the government, the assumption has been that if the enemy launches a general war and undertakes a piercing attack threatening to occupy large territory or communication junctions, the 'weapon of last resort' would have to be invoked. That possibility cannot be ignored and hence acts as a deterrent.

Deterrence was the sole aim, and a small arsenal was considered adequate. At no time did Pakistan contemplate use of nuclear weapons for war-fighting or seek to develop capability for a pre-emptive attack. Apart from the obvious constraint of resources, it was not so unrealistic as to entertain such thoughts. India is too large and too well armed to be vulnerable to a disabling strike. Besides, any such attempt would provoke retaliation with disastrous consequences.

Pakistan's purpose warranted no more than a minimalist approach. Consistently with that purpose, Pakistan was satisfied with nuclear capability. For years after achieving that capability, it relied on recessed deterrence, refraining from a test explosion. Islamabad was willing, indeed keen, to consider and promote mutual restraints. Pakistan's approach was eminently rational. As General Krishnaswamy Sundarji later said in a vivid phrase: 'More is unnecessary if less is enough.'

Believing that its minimal capability was then sufficient for deterrence, it even discontinued further production of fissile uranium in 1989. That decision had to be revised in 1990 when India was reported to be considering air raids on sites in Azad Kashmir. Still, Pakistan did not embark upon weaponization. Only after India conducted multiple test explosions, Pakistan followed suit mainly because influential opinion in India seemed to discount Pakistan's nuclear capability.

Even as between great powers, purely deterrent forces 'can be relatively modest', provided their survivability can be assured against a surprise attack, continued build-up of nuclear weapons should be unnecessary. Nor does a strategic arsenal have to match the adversary's arsenal. For, nuclear weapons are not meant for war-fighting. Nuclear deterrence, unlike the conventional one, is not degraded by quantitative or qualitative disparity.

Fear of retaliation probably deterred proposals for a pre-emptive American and/or Soviet strike on China's fledgling nuclear facilities around the 1970s. Andrei Gromyko alleges in his autobiography that the idea was broached with him by Henry Kissinger. Even if the suggestion came from the other side, what is relevant in the context of deterrence is that the idea was abandoned. For, no one could guarantee that such aggression would not provoke a nuclear response. Even though China's nuclear force was a small fraction of the bloated arsenals of the United States and the Soviet Union, its self-appointed adversaries, it served to deter aggression. Similarly, at the time of the Cuban crisis in 1962, the Soviet nuclear arsenal was much smaller than that of the United States; yet it provided deterrence.

Upgrading deterrence: Obviously, our deterrence force will have to be upgraded in proportion to the heightened threat of pre-emption and interception. Augmentation of the quantum and variety of our strategic arsenal is unavoidable. That will involve expenditures. Equally important are questions about adequacy of conventional forces. A nuclear response cannot be involved to deal with local contingencies. Given the consequences, the nuclear threshold should be maintained at a high level. Can Pakistan cope with the budgetary burden? We should not, however, presume that the task cannot be managed within the limits of our resources. Innovative planning should have to restructure the defence forces, integrating conventional and nuclear deterrence within the limits of Pakistan's financial capacity and without compromising prospects of economic growth, which is indispensable if the country is to sustain its ability to maintain long-term defence needs.

Minimum deterrence has been and should continue to be the guiding principle of Pakistan's nuclear pursuit. Of course the minimum cannot be defined in static numbers. In the absence of an agreement on mutual restraints, the size of Pakistan's arsenal and its deployment pattern have to be adjusted to ward off dangers of pre-emption and interception. Only then can deterrence remain efficacious.

The concept of a nuclear race is fundamentally flawed. It eclipses the basic point that nuclear deterrence is not dependent on parity of arsenals. Pakistan does need to enter into a competition with India. Invocations of an impending nuclear race are not only irrelevant but also counterproductive. Given the disparity in size and resources, the implicit threat of Pakistan challenging India into a competitive build-up lacks credibility. Worse, by conjuring up the prospect of such a competition and of enormous additional expenditures, statements by government spokesmen succeed only in frightening us into the false impression that the task of maintaining deterrence is beyond our means.

Not only foreign but also some concerned Pakistani critics invoke the US-USSR strategic arms race as an example of the burdens it imposed on both superpowers, especially the USSR. While recognizing the validity of Paul

Kennedy's thesis of imperial overstretch as the main factor in the fall of great powers, it is a gross oversimplification to attribute the disintegration of the Soviet Union to expenditures on strategic arms alone. Equal if not more fatal flaws were the repressive system, egregious pursuit of ideological rivalry and the attempt to perpetuate and enlarge the Russian empire.

Of lessons for us in the Russian experience, the one that we need to assimilate is the indispensability of good governance. The writer who was stationed in Moscow during the 1988-90 period was struck by the erosion of the popular will. So disillusioned had people become with the empty promises of the Soviet system and disgusted with political misrule and rampant corruption that they seemed not only to have lost faith in the Soviet Union's right to survival but actually to wish for its collapse. Relevant too is the fact that massive reductions in strategic arms alone have not availed the Russian state.

To be sure, we cannot afford to burn our candle at both ends. Prevalent corruption and misrule have crippled our state's capacity and excessive diversions to defence historically starved our country's development. But both are remediable. The nation will have to get rid of incompetent and dishonest leaders. Military expenditure have to be contained through more innovative planning. Fortunately, that is being done. Already, allocations for defence have been reduced from over six per cent of GDP to under five.

Every nuclear state has determined its nuclear posture in the light of its own objectives and assessment of the security environment. The US-USSR paradigm has no relevance for us. Nor India, with its anachronistic ambitions to hegemony, great power status and pathological rivalry with China, can be an exemplar for Pakistan. Our objective is limited and specific. On that solid foundation we can erect an appropriate nuclear posture within our limited means.

Policy and posture: Implicit in nuclear deterrence is the assumption that nuclear weapons are intended to prevent wars, and not for fighting wars. The contingencies in which nuclear weapons may have to be used have not been articulated and may even be difficult to define. It is obvious, however, that a weapon of last resort is by definition not a weapon to be used for conquest or expansion. Pakistan can therefore declare that it will never resort to the threat or use of nuclear weapons, or for that matter conventional force, for aggression. A unilateral non-aggression proclamation automatically rules out the first use of nuclear or conventional weapons.

No-first-use: India's declaration that it would not be the first to launch a nuclear strike is a cost-free exercise in sanctimonious propaganda. In the first place, India is not threatened with aggression. Secondly, enjoying superiority in conventional forces, India can cope with local wars without invoking the nuclear threat. It is, besides, flawed in logic: renunciation only of first use of nuclear weapons seems like a subterfuge to camouflage the intention to resort to first use of conventional weapons. From Pakistan's viewpoint, such a thought needs to be deterred. A no-first-use nuclear posture could invite aggression. Faced with the prospect of destruction at the hands of an aggressor with superior conventional forces, a victim cannot foreswear retaliation with any means at its disposal. That would make nonsense of the concept of nuclear deterrence.

It is for that sound reason that NATO's military doctrine of 'flexible response' envisaged the use of nuclear weapons in defence against an attack by Warsaw Pact powers even with conventional forces. The warning implicit in this posture is widely regarded to have prevented an attempt to exploit theatre superiority in conventional forces. The same logic was at work during the Pakistan-India crises in the 1980s and 1990s. Implicit in the possession of nuclear capability was a warning of their actual use. That was a key factor in defusing the crises.

Size of strategic arsenal: Sound in logic, the concept of minimum deterrence has been efficacious in the past and there is no reason to change it. However, the minimum cannot be described in static numbers. Credibility of the deterrence force does not depend on the number of nuclear bombs in the arsenal but on the survivability of the minimum number necessary for deterrence and the ability to deliver them on predetermined value targets.

Obviously, the adversary's capacity for pre-emption and interception has to be taken into account. As a rule of thumb, if 50 per cent of the counterforce becomes vulnerable, its size should have to be doubled. Delivery systems, too, have to be upgraded in proportion to their vulnerability. The induction of mobile missiles with adequate range is a sound response to the mounting threat to Pakistan's minimum deterrence.

Nuclear threshold: Given the catastrophic consequences of a nuclear exchange, these weapons of last resort cannot be invoked in every contingency. Adequate conventional forces, too, should have to be maintained so that local challenges can be dealt with locally by conventional forces. For that purpose, the determining factor is not the overall size of adversary forces but the capacity to concentrate requisite forces in order to defend against local challenges. A modern, mobile force has to be maintained and strengthened.

Defence budget: The key issue for Pakistan is how to ensure defence and deterrence within the available means. A responsible approach cannot ask for allocations that would undermine prospects of economic development. On the other hand, governance has to be improved so that resources are not dissipated by mismanagement and corruption.

Command, control and intelligence: Precautions against accidental or unauthorized launch of nuclear weapons are obviously imperative. Pakistan is in the process of establishing institutional controls. Co-operation of more experienced nuclear states should be solicited. Early warning capability may be more problematic. Even if Pakistan could afford satellite monitoring, the warning will be no more than a few minutes. A high state of alert will become more necessary as India proceeds with deployment of nuclear weapons

APPENDIX 6

A Concise Report of a Visit by Landau Network Centro Volta, *Nuclear Safety, Nuclear Stability and Nuclear Strategy in Pakistan,*[1] January 2002

Introduction

Landau Network, an Arms Control Italian institution that is regularly been consulted by the Italian Ministry of Foreign Affairs, proposed to organize a visit to Pakistan, with the purpose of having a better understanding of the security problems concerning nuclear weapons and nuclear material, of the situation of nuclear scientists and experts, of the development of Pakistani nuclear strategy, and of Pakistani approach to arms control and confidence building measures. More generally, the idea was to have a better understanding of the prospects of nuclear disarmament in the Indian subcontinent. After September 11th Pakistan has been at the epicenter of the anti-terrorist campaign and collaborated with the anti-terrorist coalition. But the impact of the Afghan war has been profound on Pakistan, and such issues such as the presence of radical Islamic movements, the existence of a relevant support for the Talibans inside Pakistan and, at the same time, the continuing confrontation with India may have serious effects on the nuclear situation in Pakistan and in the subcontinent. This is the reason for the timing of this visit.

The visit to Pakistan by Paolo Cotta-Ramusino and Maurizio Martellini of Landau Network was organized as follows. In Islamabad, we had meetings (in chronological order) with the Islamabad Policy Research Institute (IPRI) chaired

[1] Landau Network Centro Volta, Villa Olmo, Via Cantoni 1, 22100 Como (Italy). Home page: http://www.mi.infn.it/-landnet. This report was prepared by Paolo Cotta-Ramusino and Maurizio Martellini Paolo Cotta-Ramusino is Professor of Theoretical-Mathematical Physics at the University of Milan, Secretary General of the Italian Union of Scientists for Disarmament (USPID) and Director of the Program in Science Technology and International Security of Landau Network—Centro Volta. Maurizio Martellini is Professor of Theoretical Physics at the Universita' dell'Insubria (Como), Secretary General of Landau Network Centro Volta and member of the Scientific Council of USPID.

by Dr Pervaiz I. Cheema; the Foreign Office, where we were very kindly received by Honble Abdul Sattar (Foreign Minister) and by Additional Foreign Secretary Riaz Mohammad Khan; the Institute for Regional Studies (IRS), chaired by Brig. Bashir Ahmad the Institute for Strategic Studies (ISS), chaired by Min. Agha Shahi and directed by Dr. Shireen M. Mazari the Foundation for Research on International Environment, National Development and Security (FRIENDS), chaired by General Mizra Aslam Beg; the Strategic Planning Division (SPD) of the Pakistani Army, where we were kindly received by the Director, General Khalid Kidwai, and by Brig. Salik (Head of the Arms Control Division); the Foreign Service Academy Islamabad, with Ambassador Niaz A. Naik; the Sustainable Development Policy Institute (SDPI) directed by Dr Shahrukh Rafi Khan. One of us (PCR) later had meetings with some journalists in Lahore (Ejaz Haider, Khaled Ahmed, Abbas Rashid). Altogether the total number of people that participated in the meetings and talked to us was between 70 and 80.

First of all, we thank very much all our Pakistani friends for being so generous with their time and their efforts to make us understand the situation there. In particular we appreciated very much the fact that Foreign Minister Hon. A. Sattar and Gen. K. Kidwai took time from their very busy schedule to talk with us.

Prof. A. Nayyar of SDPI and of Quaid-i-Azam University and Ms Ayesha Inayat of SDPI, organized all our meetings and helped us to find our way in Islamabad. We are very happy to express to them our sincere gratitude. Also special thanks to Prof. Pervez Hoodbhoy and Dr Ejaz Haider

This visit has been suggested and encouraged by the Italian Ministry of Foreign Affairs, and particularly by Secretary General Ambassador G Baldocci and by the General Direction for Asia and Oceania, that also supported also part of the expenses. We want to thank in particular Min. I. Di Pace, Min. R. Miniero and Counc. R. Rosso. This report is part of a comprehensive case study for the General Direction of Political Affairs; warm thanks go to Counc. A. Cevese and to Counc. G. Iannuzzi. Discussions with the Head of the Policy and Analysis Planning Unit, Min. R. Toscano have been very useful.

The Department of Physics of the University of Milan supported the expenses of one of us (PCR) and this support is gratefully acknowledged. We thank also the Italian Embassy, and particularly Amb. G. De Ceglie and Counc. G. Cutillo for their help in Islamabad.

Few words of caution about this report are needed. We tried to report here some of what we learned from the meetings and from talking informally with people. When we use quotation marks we intend to reproduce the precise meaning, if not the exact letter of what has been said. In the comments we try to distinguish our personal opinion from the general feeling we got from the discussions. We hope to have made this clear. We will gladly accept comments and corrections, being understood that the responsibility for the mistakes is only our own.

Pakistani Motivation for Acquisition and Retention of Nuclear Weapons

In all the meetings we participated in, it has been repeatedly stressed that the motivations for Pakistan to acquire nuclear weapons had to do almost exclusively with India's analogous decision and with the fact that India represents a security threat to Pakistan. Motivations based on prestige have been mentioned and denied, even though, on this point, we maintain legitimate doubts.

It has been also stressed that India's nuclear program predates the corresponding Pakistani programme. India established the Atomic Energy Commission in 1948 while Pakistan established PAEC (Pakistan Atomic Energy Commission) in 1956; India tested a nuclear device in 1974, while Pakistan became nuclear capable around 1984 and tested its nuclear weapon only 17 days after India began its most recent series of nuclear tests in May 1998. It has also been said in the ISS meeting that Pakistan was ready to test years before 1998 (1984 has been suggested in the ISS meeting and 1987 has been written in a 1994 paper by Former Chief of the Army Staff, General Aslam Beg[2]), but refrained from doing so. Additional Foreign Secretary Riaz Mohammad Khan added in this respect that the international community underestimated the nuclear capabilities of Pakistan and believed that Pakistan, immediately after the Indian tests of May 1998, was not ready for its own nuclear test. As for the history of the Pakistani nuclear programme, it has been pointed out by Gen. Aslam Beg that by 1989 Pakistan had 6 devices and by 1991 it had 15 delivery systems, that the costs of the nuclear programme in the period 75-89 has been of the order of 200 ml. US$. We recall that foreign assistance to Pakistan came, among other things, from a 137 MW Canadian power reactor, US maraging steel for encasing uranium cores, Flash X rays machines from the Swedish firm Scandiflash, computers from Norway and a complex assistance from China.[3]

Opposition to the Pakistani nuclear programme seems rather weak, at least by looking at the group of people we met. In fact some previous opponents of the nuclear programme seem now to accept and justify the decision of testing. As an example, at the meeting with IRS, the director Brig. (ret) Ahmad told us that he initially disagreed with the nuclear programme, but he feels now that nuclear testing was a necessary step, and that further testing is not necessary any more. The argument here was that Pakistan had to show India and the rest of the world that it was able to match India's nuclear capabilities. This last sentence was essentially agreed upon by most people we met.

There are of course people who believe that Pakistan (as well as India) should give up nuclear weapons as they require costly programmes and provide basically

[2] Gen. Aslam Beg, *Pakistan Nuclear Propriety*, National Security (Rawalpindi: FRIENDS, 2000).

[3] See K. Matinuddin, *The Nuclearization of South Asia* (Karachi: Oxford University Press, 2002) and, as far as China's assistance is concerned, see the Monterey Institute for International Studies, Center for Non-proliferation Studies database.

no extra security. But a unilateral Pakistani nuclear disarmament was generally rejected and not even really discussed, since it appeared to lay outside the political reality.[4] A different question was whether Pakistan could abandon nuclear weapons jointly with India. The attitude here was more open; only once during our stay in Pakistan, one expert stated that Pakistan should retain nuclear weapons even if India decides to give up its nuclear capability. This opinion by ISS Director Dr. Shireen Mazari, was motivated on the basis of 'security', but there was no further elaboration. On the contrary, during our discussion with Gen. Kidwai of SPD it was stated that if India renounces the possession of nuclear weapons, Pakistan will follow suit.

The general attitude in dealing with India has been that Pakistan is interested in discussing with India issues related to nuclear weapons and other security matters, but it will not do so if the issue of Kashmir will be intentionally excluded from the agenda (see below the point 'Kashmir'). Anyway, the prospect of removing nuclear weapons from the subcontinent did not appear a realistic perspective for the foreseeable future.

One of the questions that were discussed a few times was whether the Pakistani nuclear capability had to be seen as an *Islamic Bomb.* This point of view has been generally referred to be a prejudice/misconception present in the West and particularly in Israel. It has been pointed out a few times that no Islamic alliance centred around Pakistani nuclear capability has been established or even proposed. Pakistani nuclear weapons are not seen as a nuclear guarantee by any other state (Islamic or not Islamic). Furthermore, no support for Pakistan has been expressed by Islamic countries when sanctions were in force after the nuclear tests of May 1998. Finally, Pakistan did not commit itself to the nuclear defence of any other country, be it Islamic or not Islamic. Leaving the issue of the Islamic bomb aside, there are nevertheless concerns to relating the nuclear infrastructure and the nuclear experts with the spread of Islamic radicalism in Pakistan. These problems will be addressed separately below.

Nuclear Control and Nuclear Structure

None of the people we discussed with had any doubt that nuclear materials and bombs are under tight control. There is a general agreement that no leak has ever been reported for any quantity (even grams) of Pakistani fissile materials. In fact no leak apparently happened, even though 'the risk of nuclear proliferation has been in Pakistan for over 15 years' (Add. Secr. R.M Khan). Again there appear to be a general consensus that all nuclear weapons are under strict control, or, to use an expression by Foreign Minister Abdul Sattar, under 'ironclad' control.

As a matter of caution, we would like to add that if and when nuclear weapons

[4] This is consistent with the survey of Pakistani public opinion discussed in S. Ahmed and D. Cortright (eds.), *Pakistan and the Bomb* (University of Notre Dame Press, 1998).

and nuclear materials are moved around into different locations, this poses a significant extra stress on the security system, requiring a tight control of multiple locations and means of transportation. So security may differ in ordinary times and in times of crisis. For instance, reports have been made that after the beginning of US bombing of the Afghanistan (different components of) nuclear weapons have been moved to (possibly 6) separate locations of the country.[5] Conjectures were also made about transfers of nuclear weapons through Gilgit in Northern Pakistan. The exact amount of bombs and/or nuclear material was obviously not known by most of the people we met and those who know did not disclose any exact number. As a general reference we can consider the estimates of David Albright who says that the total amount of Pakistani fissile materials is roughly enough to produce 30–50 bombs.[6] Gen Aslam Beg in the FRIENDS meeting made some reference to keeping (in the future) the total number of devices between 75 and 90 just to readdress the conventional balance *vis à vis* India, that possesses an army three times as big as Pakistan, an air-force five times as big as Pakistan, and a navy six times as big as Pakistan. The bombs have been declared by Gen. Musharraf to be in a 'disassembled state', meaning probably that the fission core is kept separately from the non-nuclear (ignition) components. Nevertheless, according to General Kidwai of SPD, the bombs can be assembled 'very quickly'. The same General Kidwai stated that Pakistan has 'ground and air capability for the delivery of nuclear weapons'. This apparently means that bombs/warheads can be delivered by airplanes and/or missiles. Gen. Kidwai said explicitly that nuclear artillery is not part, at the moment, of the Pakistani nuclear programmes.

According to the same Gen. Kidwai, there are now no such things as Permissive Action Links (PALs) to prevent the unauthorized use of nuclear weapons. It has been pointed out by some participants in the IPRI meeting that keeping the weapons in an unassembled state makes PALs unnecessary. In fact, it has been said, again in the IPRI meeting, that the emplacement of PALs would be needed only if the weapons themselves are assembled and, as a consequence, the emplacement of PALs could be interpreted as a sign that Pakistan is moving towards a quicker nuclear reaction capability. According to Foreign Minister Sattar there was the possibility that a group of Pakistani officials may visit the US to discuss issues concerning such issues as PALs and control of nuclear devices.

There is some grey area here, according to us. PALs do not exist, but, at the same time, weapons can be assembled 'very quickly' and so also the reaction in a situation of crisis can be relatively 'very quick'. This raises some important questions about the effective control of nuclear weapons in moments of crisis.

[5] See e.g. M. Ijaz and R.J. Woolsey, 'How Secure is Pakistan's Plutonium. *The New York Times*, 28 November 2001.

[6] David Albright, *Securing Pakistan's Nuclear Weapons Complex*, October 2001. www.isisonline/publications/terrorism/stanleypaper.html.

This is an important area in which, according to us, international cooperation with nuclear and non-nuclear weapons states could be developed. The impression is that an offer of cooperation to technically improve security and safeguards of nuclear materials and nuclear weapons can be and probably will be positively considered by Pakistan, provided that some obvious conditions are met, such as the protection of classified data and the absence of intrusive activities.

General Kidwai stated further that the safe control of nuclear weapons is guaranteed by a '3-men rule', namely any procedure involving nuclear weapons requires the concurrent decision by 3 persons. This has been contrasted to the 2-men rule that apparently exists in various US nuclear operations. In the US though, multiple devices to prevent unauthorized use are ubiquitous and, most of them, quite sophisticated.

In February 2000 the Strategic Planning Division (SPD) has been established in order to improve the control of nuclear operations. As explained by Gen. Kidwai and Brig. Salik of SPD, the SPD itself acts as a secretariat for the National Command Authority (NCA), headed by the Head of the Government that deals with all aspects of nuclear weapons. More precisely, the NCA is a 'military-political-scientific forum' assisting the Head of Government in all nuclear matters. Here follows a brief description of the structure of NCA.

The NCA is divided into two committees: the Employment Control Committee (that supervises the employment policy and the possible actual use of nuclear weapons) whose Deputy Chair is the Minister of Foreign Affairs and the Development Control Committee that supervises the nuclear development programme, whose Deputy Chair is the Chairman of the Joint Chiefs of Staff Committee (CJCSC). In both committees it is understood that the chairman is the Head of the Government.

Besides the Chairman and the Deputy Chair, the members of the Employment Control Committee are: the Minister of Defence, the Minister of Interior, the CJCSC, the Services Chiefs and the Director of SPD who has the role of Secretary of the Committee. Other people can be invited according to specific needs.

Besides the Chairman and the Deputy Chair, the members of the Development Control Committee are: the Services Chiefs, the Heads of concerned strategic organizations (such as the Scientists), the Director of SPD who has the role of Secretary of the Committee, the Services Strategic Forces (for the operational control).

As the names suggest the Development Control Committee deals specifically with the planning and development of nuclear forces, while the employment Control Committee deals with what can be defined broadly as 'nuclear strategy' including targeting policy and the conduct of nuclear operations. The issue of Pakistani nuclear strategy is discussed below as a separate point.

Gen. Kidwai stated that practically all (99 per cent) of the nuclear decisions pertain to the Head of Government and that no 'delegation of authority concerning nuclear weapons is planned'. After 1998, the management of nuclear weapons, with the establishment of NCA and SPD became a 'transparent institutionalised capability'. This has also the purpose of 'reassuring the world that everything is under control'.

The SPD itself has 35 officers[7] and is divided into 4 directorates: 1. Operations and Planning, 2. Strategic Weapons, 3. Arms Control and Disarmament (headed now by Brig. Salik), 4. C^4-I^2-S-R which stands for Command–Control-Communications–Computer–Intelligence–Information–Surveillance–Reconnaissance.

Control of Nuclear Scientists and Personnel Dealing with Nuclear Weapons

A delicate question in any organization dealing with nuclear weapons and fissile material concerns the reliability and the trustworthiness of scientists, technicians and military people that have the responsibility of handling the weapons and the fissile material.

Gen. Kidwai reminded us that before 1998 the Pakistani nuclear programme has been initiated and handled by few people at the top level. After Pakistan nuclear capability was made public in 1998, the need of creating a controlled, transparent (and presumably much larger) structure became apparent.

We discussed in the SPD meeting the screening and control of personnel. We learned that key people are screened and controlled by 4 agencies (ISI, Military Intelligence, Intelligence Bureau, SPD). Every aspect of each person's life is reportedly controlled, including families and relatives. Such screenings are repeated every 2 years. We also learned that military people (of lower levels) involved with nuclear operations are professionally selected by ISB (Interservice Selection Bureau) with an average success of 5 per cent, and screened by professional psychiatrists. Top-level people (including scientists) are controlled by their organizations and not psychologically screened. In this sense there is no such thing in Pakistan as an American PRP (Personal Reliability Programme).

While we were in Pakistan, there was much debate about two nuclear scientists Sultan Bashiruddin Mehmood and Abdul Majeed were arrested for alleged cooperation with the Talibans. Gen. Kidwai acknowledged that these arrests created much problems for Pakistan in terms of public image. In all the meetings we participated, there was though a general consensus that these scientists did not have (at least recently) direct responsibilities in the nuclear programme. This is not the same as saying that they were incompetent in nuclear matters, as has been reminded to us by some physicists.

A key issue surfaced here especially during our private discussions with our colleagues physicists. There is a large sector of physics graduated and physics scholars that are involved in the nuclear programme, at various levels of responsibility. For the classes of Quaid-i-Azam University, in some specific years,

[7] According to Gen. Kidwai, most officers of SPD have graduated from Quaid-i-Azam University.

the majority, if not the totality, of the students graduated in physics ended up in the nuclear programme. Political and religious attitudes in the Pakistani scientific community are certainly diversified, but there is a growing influence of Islamic radicalism. This influence needs not to be dominant in the scientific community to create problems. It is enough that few people with some critical knowledge decide to help some terrorist organization to build even a crude nuclear device. As an example we were told about scientists with experience in cold implosion (implosion of spheres possibly of U^{238} that will not create a nuclear detonation). A physicist with this experience will be very useful (possibly essential) in preparing a plutonium implosion bomb for any organization/state that illegally acquired plutonium from anywhere (e.g. originating from the former Soviet Union). And there are physicists with this kind of experience, having political attitudes bordering to Islamic radicalism, which could in principle answer yes to a request of help from a radical organization.

In conclusion it seemed to us that the risks of nuclear proliferation in Pakistan may be more significantly linked to the acquired nuclear expertise combined with pro-radical political attitudes, than with the actual risk of leakage of fissile material or of nuclear weapons (at least at the present quantitative level of material and weapons). This is the conclusion that was suggested to us by some key physicists, even though it should be pointed out that many people in the various meetings tried to reassure us that no scientist will be in position to work for a non-state organization in the development of nuclear weapons. There appeared to be anyway a general consensus that the international community should keep increasing the level of the security of all nuclear infrastructures worldwide.

Pakistani Nuclear Strategy

It is well known that Pakistan does not have a 'No First Use Policy'.[8] Pakistani nuclear weapons will be used, according to Gen. Kidwai, only 'if the very existence of Pakistan as a state is at stake'. This has been detailed by Gen. Kidwai as follows:

'Nuclear weapons are aimed solely at India. In case that deterrence fails, they will be used if

(a) India attacks Pakistan and conquers a large part of its territory (space threshold);
(b) India destroys a large part either of its land or air forces (military threshold);
(c) India proceeds to the economic strangling of Pakistan (economic strangling);[9]

[8] In the ISS meeting, the *no-first-use policy* has been defined as 'totally illogic' by one participant.

[9] Examples of economic strangling of Pakistan included a naval blockade and the stopping of the waters of the Indus river.

(d) India pushes Pakistan into political destabilization or creates a large scale internal subversion in Pakistan (domestic destabilization).'[10]

We in turn asked Gen. Kidwai if he did not think that the above conditions for the use of nuclear weapons were at the same time too broad and too vaguely defined and how he considered the risk of inadvertent nuclear conflict in the subcontinent. The answer has been that there will be no risk of nuclear conflict assuming 'rational decision making' by the interested parties. The example of the Cold War, when no nuclear conflict was initiated, has been quoted few times to support the idea that India—and Pakistan—will stay clear of the nuclear threshold and restrain from an aggressive behaviour that could trigger a nuclear reaction. Asked if Pakistan has prepared something like a ladder of nuclear escalation, Gen. Kidwai answered that of course there were options available in the nuclear response, but he re-emphasized few times that nuclear war will not happen since India and, for that matter, Pakistan will avoid getting close to the nuclear threshold. Also there has been no discussion about the possible consequences of Pakistan nuclear attack on India, namely on the effects of Indian nuclear retaliation. This possibility has been discarded again on the basis of the fact that rational decision making will keep both countries away from the nuclear brink. Anyway, Pakistan does not intend to develop (and make public) for the time being, a 'nuclear doctrine' in a fashion analog to the nuclear doctrine considered in India.

Let us add now a brief comment of ours: it seems that the combination of the diversity and broadness of the motivations that may justify the use of nuclear weapons, on one side, and the use of the nuclear threat to enforce a rational decision making, i.e. a not too aggressive behaviour, by the opponent, on the other side, is suggesting a vision of the type *doomsday machine* (to use a well-known expression by H. Kahn) for Pakistani nuclear weapons, that is not reassuring. It is also clear that nuclear weapons are perceived in Pakistan as an instrument to countervail a manifest conventional inferiority[11] *vis à vis* the Indian military force. Presumably Pakistan feels or will feel compelled to enlarge and diversify its nuclear arsenal so to increase the nuclear options[12] and make the threat of nuclear retaliation more credible. If this diversification will move Pakistan away from a doomsday machine vision, it will also increase the likelihood of the use of nuclear weapons in a situation of crisis. Thus the Indian subcontinent

[10] The political destabilization and the internal subversion scenarios are considered as distinct possibilities.

[11] As a general reference, let us recall that the NATO doctrine of extended deterrence in the Cold War Period made constant reference to the possible use of nuclear weapons to countervail conventional inferiority *vis à vis* the Warsaw Pact military forces and refused to issue any *no-first-use* declaration (and still does). Pakistani position is tuned along these lines.

[12] In the IPRI meeting, an explicit reference to the need for Pakistan to acquire a *second strike capability* has been made.

may follow on a reduced scale (but not necessarily on a reduced risk) the pattern of the US-USSR nuclear race during the Cold War. The alternatives may come from dialogue and the development of arms control negotiations directly between India and Pakistan on one side and from some kind of international constraint and pressure on the two nuclear programmes in the subcontinent, on the other side.

In the IPRI meeting it has been pointed out that public discussion on nuclear strategy, and, more generally, on all things pertaining to nuclear weapons, is scarce. The motivation for this has been directly ascribed to the existence of a military regime. The perception has been also expressed that the military regime is also responsible for the strict control over nuclear assets and nuclear scientists and for the fact that there has been no loss of either material or scientists.

Pakistan and Arms Control

Nobody denied that Pakistan is in principle interested in the broad spectrum of arms control initiatives (be they local or general). Let us have a quick review of the various arms control issues that have been mentioned or discussed. We express here just the general agreed position that surfaced in the meetings and not necessarily the official Government position.

a. *CTBT*
The CTBT has been killed by the US. Nevertheless if India agrees to sign it, Pakistan will follow suit. Pakistan does not intend, for the time being, to restart nuclear testing.

b. *NPT*
Pakistan is interested in keeping some basic provisions of NPT (such as safeguards), but will not accept to adhere to a discriminatory regime.

c. *FMCT*
Pakistan agrees to a ban of production of fissile material not limited to weapon-grade material.

d. *CBMs*
Pakistan is interested in developing CBMs with India. Reference has been made (by Gen Kidwai) to missile test notifications and to the fact that Pakistan did notify India, while the contrary has not been always true.

e. *NWFZ*
Has been proposed by Pakistan in 1974, with no success.

f. *Missile Proliferation and BMD*
Pakistan will not transfer missile technology to other states following MTCR criteria. No discussion has been made about transfer of missile technology to Pakistan. A question in this sense by us got the answer that Pakistani missile production is indigenous. On BMD, Pakistan is seriously concerned about possible acquisition by India of BMD technology.

KASHMIR

The Kashmir situation is at the core of India-Pakistan relations. According to Additional Foreign Secretary R.M. Khan, the main concern of the Foreign Office are Kashmir, Security and Terrorism (in that order). Both Add. Secretary R.M. Khan and Gen Kidwai stressed that 'any solution that will be acceptable to Kashmiri people will be acceptable to Pakistan'. This is reportedly the official Pakistani position, as expressed by Gen. Musharraf.

The Kashmir issue is not what motivated Pakistani nuclear weapons, according to Add. Secretary R.M. Khan, but still being Kashmir at the center of India-Pakistani dispute and being India's security threat, as perceived by Pakistan, it is true that any shift in the Kashmir issue, either positive or negative, will affect substantially the security and the nuclear stability of the subcontinent.

We heard (e.g. from Add. Foreign Secetary Khan) that Pakistan is interested in discussing with India on Kashmir and other issues, with no preconditions. In particular Pakistan is prepared to discuss issues of nuclear safety and stability. But Pakistan will not accept to open a discussion table with India that will intentionally exclude Kashmir. In Pakistan, Kashmir is seen as an outstanding problem, a proof that 'the agenda of partition with India has not yet been completed' (as said by Gen. Kidwai).

Let us recall that Kashmir is a very emotional issue for Pakistan (as is for India). It is a direct reminder of the tragically painful separation between India and Pakistan, it brings with it all the tensions that are generally associated to regions that are forcibly divided in two parts with no possible communication, it triggers national pride and national hostility towards the opponent. It is an issue of religious identity where the strong Islamic identity of Pakistan has to deal with the fact that the Islamic majority of Kashmir is under Indian rule. This help explaining the level of political support that even extremist groups can obtain in Pakistan. Supporting insurgents in Kashmir has been for the past Pakistani governments a relatively convenient position in terms of domestic policy, but a dangerously risky one in terms of confrontation with India. Containing extremist groups (such as Lashkar-e-Taiba) and radical religious organizations, has been on the contrary objectively not an easy task for Pakistani governments and, over all, a task, up to recent times, seldom undertook. The situation did not become better after the nuclearization of both India and Pakistan. In fact the dramatic consequences of a nuclear confrontation and the belief that nuclear weapons will be not used or will be only used as a weapons of last resort (as the rule of rational decision making dictates) may encourage more aggressive postures, as far as conventional confrontation is concerned. So nuclear weapons do not necessarily bring stability at the conventional level, as the Kargil experience,[13] or

[13] See e.g. W.P.S. Sidhu, *Nuclearization of South Asia: The Kargill Experience*, in USPID, *New Challenges in the Spread of Weapons of Mass Destruction*, Castiglioncello Conference, 1999.

the more recent confrontation between India and Pakistan, shows. In fact Kashmir may be very well the trigger that may start a nuclear exchange between India and Pakistan.[14]

There has been little discussion in our meetings on the necessary concrete steps that would allow a better relation with India and hence a return to the spirit and the letter of the Lahore declaration, but the general feeling is that this return is considered necessary. The impression we got also was that international initiatives aimed at resurrecting a serious dialogue between India and Pakistan on nuclear stability, Kashmir and other contentious issues between the two countries would be welcomed at least on the Pakistani side.

Islamic Radicalism and Terrorism

Inevitably in many of our discussions we dealt with the spread of Islamic radicalism in Pakistan. The concerns in this connection were:

1. Fear that radical Islamic movements may destabilize Pakistan and possibly transform Pakistan into the first radical Islamic country possessing nuclear weapons.
2. Fear that radical Islamic movements may influence military people and/or scientists dealing with nuclear weapons and fissile materials.

In particular, we were interested in understanding how our Pakistani colleagues view the impact of the Afghan war and the campaign against Al Qa'ida on the internal political situation of Pakistan.

As for the first question concerning the relation between radical Islam and Pakistan and the risk of Pakistan being 'Talibanized' or transformed into a radical Islamic society, some basic data have been reminded to us by many people, including Foreign Minister Sattar and Brig. Ahmad of IRS. The Islamic parties or groups (including Jama'at-i-Islam [Party of Islam], the fractions of Jami'at-i-Ulema-i-Islam [Gathering of Religious Scholars of Islam] and of Jami'at-i-Ulema-i-Pakistan [Gathering of Religious Scholars of Pakistan]) have an electoral consensus of the order of 5-6 per cent which maybe a higher political influence (of the order of 10 per cent) and certainly a lower political representation (few seats) due to the structure of the electoral system. On the role of the madrassas in the education systems and hence in the shaping of the society, we have been reminded that there are about 6500 madrassas in Pakistan. Children who go to madrassas (and study the Qu'ran in Arabic while doing most of the readings in Urdu) belong generally to the lower classes of the population and represent no more than 10-12 per cent of the population of children. Middle class children go to public schools and higher class children go to private schools. Madrasas-

[14] On the risks of nuclear confrontation between India and Pakistan, see M.V. Ramana and A.H. Nayyar, 'India, Pakistan and the Bomb', *Scientific American*, December 2001.

educated people do not go in the Army, not even into the lower levels. Moreover, Army officers have all received a higher education (and speak English).

It has been stressed that the majority of the Pakistani population is moderate, as far as religious beliefs and practice are concerned. Many are 'Sufi-oriented' (Brig. Ahmad, IRS). Still the influence of Islamic radical movements is probably higher that what the above numbers and the above arguments suggest. Gen Zia-ul-Haq was a devoted Muslim, trained in Saudi Arabia and heavily supported by the United States. He pushed ahead the process of Islamization of the society, introducing and/or enforcing strong laws aimed at putting the Shari'iah at the centre of many regulations and codes of conduct. For example, we discussed with Foreign Minister Sattar the well-known blasphemy law that mandates capital punishment for blasphemy offenders. There have been 395 people accused and 134 charged of blasphemy. Actually there are 122 pending cases of blasphemy. These people cannot be paroled since the felony they are accused implies capital punishment. There is a laws forbidding bank interests, which is troublesome for the economic system, and, on a less dramatic side, there are laws forbidding eating lunch during Ramadan. More generally, the strict adherence to Islamic rules is required by law in many instances and there is hardly political support for repealing these laws. Apparently even the present Government would have difficulties in eliminating them.

Religious feeling was and is very high in Pakistan and religion has been seen as the defining cultural and ideological glue of the society. Moreover the contentious relation with India and the religious identification of Pakistan feed each other since 1947. A more secular attitude has a rather limited diffusion in the Pakistani society, one notable exception being made by sectors of the upper class and of the intellectuals. One of the reasons is that, in order to gain ground, a more secular vision of the society should be matched with economic and social opportunities and perspectives, with interaction with other parts of the world. All of this is scarcely available to the bulk of the Pakistani society.

The Afghan war and the anti-terrorist campaign brought conflicting results. To start with, a significant number of radical Pakistanis went to Afghanistan to support Al Qa'ida and the Taliban. Possibly hundreds up to one thousand of them died in the Afghan war. Foreign Minister Sattar suggested that these dramatic events gave a fatal blow to the credibility of those radical religious leaders who sent these young people to fight in Afghanistan. But, according to us, it could also be pointed out that the families, friends, and co-workers of the many dead people could be very well also upset with a Government that cooperated with the US in the destruction of the Taliban forces and that, apparently, appears to care very little about the destiny of these young (deceived) 'freedom fighters'.

The Taliban government has been supported by Pakistan in the past for reasons that have to do primarily with the need of having a relatively friendly neighbour on the western border and with the need of protecting communication routes to Central Asia. The official support to the Talibans stopped after

September 11th, as is well known, but ideologically motivated sympathies were not erased as pointed out, e.g. by Zafar N. Jaspal in the FRIENDS meeting.[15]

Again it has been pointed out to us (by Foreign Minister Sattar) that the demonstrations in support of the Taliban were much more modest than what appeared in the western press. On 8 October, the peak of pro-Taliban demonstrations was reached with a total of 1,65,000 demonstrators in the whole of Pakistan (of which 30,000 were in Karachi, 10,000 in Quetta, 10,000 in Peshawar). The consequence of these data, as has been pointed out to us, is that the majority of the population is far from being fanatic about the Talibans. It is also true that after September 11, Gen. Musharraf increased the repression of radical Islamic groups and so any open support for the Taliban may endow some risk.

There has been a discussion, of the risk—before and after September 11th—for Pakistan to be Talibanized,[16] or transformed into a radical Islamic country. Whenever this subject was touched even marginally in the meetings, this possibility has been outrightly rejected: We heard again and again that Pakistan is a responsible country and that would not fall into the trap of Talibanization. In private conversations (*not* with actual or retired Government officials and military) we had at times a different impression. During the Government of Nawaz Sharif there has been a push for further Islamization, some clerics have been very vocal and active in the push for Talibanization and there were even high ranking officials reportedly favouring Talibanization. A downturn of Pakistan towards a radical Islamic society could possibly have happened then. One impression we got is that such a downturn could be considered as an option by a weak leader in order to contain the opposition and gain support among particularly aggressive sectors of the population.

As a side remark, let us point out that radical Islamic groups may be very aggressive when nuclear capabilities are concerned. Foreign Minister told us that the Jamaat-i-Islam party defined a *traitor* as one who ever supports the signing of the CTBT by Pakistan.

Given the present position of Gen. Musharraf, radical Islam is now under pressure. The forced retirement of some Generals, the partial disempowerment of ISI, are symptoms of this pressure. But, speaking about the retirement of 3 Generals, Foreign Minister Sattar, emphasized that, due to a change in the organizational structure of the Army, they have been superseded in their normal carrier and, hence, as customary in these cases, they took retirement. In this, Foreign Minister Sattar did not see at all the repression of a political dissent.

In conclusion the possibility of a Talibanization of Pakistan seems not to be a real danger now, but opinions vary about the risk in the past and in the future.

Having said that, one should not infer that there is a widespread support for American intervention in Afghanistan and that the status of the relation between

[15] He also added that [ideologically] dedicated scientists and nuclear weapons could create a 'lethal mix'.

[16] Read also Khaled Ahmed in *Was Pakistan being Talibanized*, *The Friday Times*, 7–13 December 2001.

Western and the Islamic world is considered to be a positive one.[17] On the contrary, in all the meetings we participated, it has been pointed out, by about everybody, that the relation between the Western and the Islamic world were critical, that the general perception is that Islamic countries are on the 'losing side'. The most common expression used was the feeling of being 'hurt'. Examples of this 'being hurt' ranged from Palestine (to which everybody referred to), to Kashmir and to Bosnia. The perception of Pakistan being on the side of the humiliated Islamic countries is reinforced by the difficult economic situation. To use an expression of Foreign Minister Sattar, the general perception is that the 'economy is declining in this part of the world'.

We now come back to the second question we began this section with, namely the possibility of radical Islam influencing scientists and technicians dealing with nuclear weapons. Much about this has been discussed above (in Section 4): in order to have nuclear scientists and technical experts to work for the construction of nuclear weapons for other states or for non-state actors there is no need for Islamic groups to gain full control of Pakistan: much less is needed. One of the question that was widely discussed in various meetings was, in fact, how many people and what kind (and size) of laboratory structures will be necessary to develop a clandestine nuclear programme (*not* supported by a State). Here again opinions were diversified. Some people stressed that possessing fissile materials and good basic knowledge (and on top of that *experience*) would allow a very small group of people to build a crude nuclear device (e.g. of the gun-assembly type). Other people (including some physicists) believed on the contrary that, besides the acquisition of fissile materials, good size laboratories would probably be needed in order to start a primitive clandestine nuclear programme.

A Final Note on Improving Relations between Pakistan and Western Countries

As a final remark, let us start with some considerations by Foreign Minister Sattar on the basic priorities for Pakistan. These are (i) Revival of the Economy, (ii) Improvement of Government, (iii) Eradication of Corruption.

In fact Minister Sattar added that the elimination of corruption could be considered as the top priority, given the tragic record of previous Pakistani governments (between B. Buttho and N. Sharif about $ 34 bn. were drained, during ten years, in the corruption vortex). Dealing with these priorities will be anything but easy,[18] different kinds of external help and support will be needed and European countries and the US should take their responsibility.

[17] To have a feeling of the degree of anti-Western hostility even among intellectuals, see, e.g. Pervez Hoodbhoy, 'Muslims and the West After September 11', to be published in the proceedings of the 2001 Castiglioncello Conference.

[18] Incidentally, constitutional changes will probably precede the general elections that are scheduled for autumn 2002.

The combination of radical extremism, economic impoverishment—and lack of perspectives, national humiliation, territorial disputes, critical governmental structures and nuclear weapons is a dangerous cocktail and no western country should feel exempt from taking their shares of responsibility in this part of the world. Western countries should invest here for the sake of guaranteeing peace in a very critical area. A message that we heard during our meetings and outside them, has been about the importance and the usefulness of keeping contacts (economic, cultural, scientific, also military, etc.) with the rest of the world and particularly with Western countries. Moreover contacts and relations with India are plagued by all sorts of disputes and by a deeply sedimented animosity. Pretending that India-Pakistani relations are something that pertains only to the two countries and that they are to be resolved only by them without any cooperation from the outside world could be a shortsighted attitude.

Postscript, 11 February 2002

We received few comments about our report coming from Pakistani officials. They do not put in question the content of our report, but still we would like to share them with the readers:

- It has been pointed out to us that the four thresholds considered in section 5, that would trigger a Pakistani nuclear reaction were 'purely academic'. The comments go on saying, 'These are matters which as elsewhere, are primarily the responsibility of the political leadership of the day. . . . The elaborate command and control mechanisms introduced with the establishment of the National Command Authority which is Chaired by the Head of State and assisted by political and civilian leaders . . . ensure the highest level of responsibility and due deliberation on all matters of strategic importance.' Still we underline that the four thresholds were explicitly mentioned to us and this has not been denied.
- It has been pointed out that 'Pakistani assets are not on hair-trigger status' and that Gen. Kidwai had not denied the existence of PALs. The difference here is minor: still to the best of our recollection we were told that only the 3-men system was in place as a guarantee against unauthorized use. But again we have to remember that weapons are (were) still in an unassembled state.
- The only 'factual error' that is ascribed to our report is 'the suggestion that even the lives of families and relatives of persons working in sensitive organizations are "controlled" '. We remember that the screening of families and relatives of people to be included in the nuclear structure was referred to as a part of the security procedures. This would be a common practice in all the nuclear countries.

Contributors

P.R. CHARI, former member of the Indian Administrative Service, is currently the Director of the Institute of Peace and Conflict Studies, New Delhi. He has worked extensively on nuclear disarmament, non-proliferation and Indian defence issues and has authored many books on these subjects.

SONIKA GUPTA is Research Officer at the Institute of Peace and Conflict Studies and a doctoral student at the Chinese Studies division, Centre for East Asian Studies, School of International Studies, Jawaharlal Nehru University. Her publications include several newspaper and website articles on Chinese foreign policy, and co-edited book *Human Security in South Asia* (2003).

ARPIT RAJAIN has been working as Research Officer in the Institute of Peace and Conflict Studies since 1997 on WMD issues. He has co-edited *Working Towards a Verification Protocol for Biological* Weapons (2001), and co-edited *Biological Weapons: Issues and Threats* (2003).

ASHLEY J. TELLIS is Senior Advisor to the US, New Delhi. Prior to joining the State Department, he was a Senior Policy Analyst at RAND, Washington, D.C., and Professor of Policy Analysis at the RAND Graduate School. He has authored: *Interpreting China's Grand Strategy: Past, Present, and Future* (2000, co-authored with Michael Swaine), and *India's Emerging Nuclear Posture* (2001). His academic publications have appeared in the *Journal of Strategic Studies, Asian Survey, Orbis, Comparative Strategy, Naval War College Review* and *Security Studies.* His RAND publications include *The United States and Asia: Toward a New U.S. Strategy and Force Posture (2001); Limited Conflicts Under the Nuclear Umbrella: Indian and Pakistani Lessons from the Kargil Crisis* (2001); and, *Stability in South Asia.*

KARL-HEINZ KAMP is heading the International Planning Staff of the Konrad Adenauer Foundation, Sankt Augustin, near Bonn. He holds a Ph.D. from the University of the German Armed Forces. He was research fellow with the Center for Science and International Affairs (CSIA), John F. Kennedy School of Government, Harvard University, USA (1988). From 1992 to 2000, he was Head of the Foreign- and Security Policy Research Section at the Konrad Adenauer Foundation and was appointed as the head of the International Planning Staff of the Foundation in 2000.

He has published extensively on security policy issues—particularly on NATO and on nuclear questions—including articles in *Foreign Policy, Financial Times, Survival, Frankfurter Allgemeine Zeitung, Washington Quarterly, Internationale Politik, Strategic Review, International Defense Review, Die Welt, Christian Science Monitor, Defense News, Neue Zuercher Zeitung, Focus.*

RAJEN HARSHE is Professor of International Relations at the Department of Political Science, University of Hyderabad. A Ph.D from Jawaharlal Nehru University, he was also a Fulbright scholar at the Columbia University, New York, during 1985–6. His has published *Twenthieth Century Imperialism Shifting Contours and Changing Conceptions* (1997), and written extensively for prestigious academic journals and anthologies on areas related to theories, concepts and processes in international relations. He has been associated with the Indian Council of Social Science Research, the University Grants Commission, Ford Foundation, National Assessment and Accreditation Council, the Ministry of External Affairs and the World Bank.

RAJESH M. BASRUR. He taught in Ramnarain Ruia College, Mumbai, from 1978 to 1996, and in Mumbai University's Department of Politics from 1996 to 2000. Currently he is Director, Center for Global Studies, Mumbai and is a Visiting Postdoctoral Fellow at Stanford University's Center for International Studies and Cooperation. He has been a Fulbright Fellow at the University of Illinois at Urbana-Champaign Visiting Fellow/Scholar at the Stimson Center, Brookings Institution, and Cooperative Monitoring Center, Sandia.

He has specialised in the politics of nuclear weapons, terrorism, and the theory of international relations. He has published/edited *Security in the New Millennium: Views from South Asia (2001)*; *India's External Relations: A Theoretical Analysis (2000)*; and *Perspectives on India's*

Defence and Arms Control (1999). He is currently working on minimum deterrence and Indian nuclear strategy, and on nuclear-terrorism threats.

AIR COMMODORE JASJIT SINGH, AVSM, VrC, VM, IAF (Retd), is Director of the New Delhi-based Centre for Strategic and International Studies. He headed the Institute for Defence Studies and Analyses (IDSA), New Delhi (1987-2001). He has published extensively on strategic and security issues and is the author/contributing editor of two dozen books which include: *Air Power in Modern Warfare* (1985); *AWACS, the New Destabiliser* (1987); *Non-provocative Defence* (1989); *Nuclear India* (1998); *Kargil 1999* (1999); and *India's Defence Spending* (2000).

Visiting lecturer at defence and war colleges in India and abroad. Former Member of International Commission for Peace. Former Member International Commission for New Asia. Was Convenor of the Task Force to establish the National Security Council in 1998. Former Member of National Security Advisory Board. Currently Editorial Adviser (Defence and Strategic Affairs) to the *Indian Express* Group of newspapers.

R. ADM RAJA MENON (Retd) retired from the Indian Navy as the Assistant Chief of Naval Staff (Operations). After retirement he was senior research fellow at the Institute of Defence Studies and Analysis. He was Deputy Director General, Defence Planning Staff, Head of submarine Acquisitions from USSR and Chief Instructor at the Defence Service Staff College. He was on the Arun Singh Committee for restructuring the management of defence, and is currently on the committee to establish a National Defence University in India.

He has written for professional journals and published in the United States Naval Institute Proceedings and the British Naval Review. He presently writes for *The Times of India* and the weekly magazine *Outlook* His books include *Maritime Strategy and Continental War* (1988) and *A Nuclear Strategy for India* (2000), *The Indian Navy: A Photo Essay* (2002), and *Weapons of Mass Destruction: Questions and Answers for India* (forthcoming).

G. BALACHANDRAN is an independent economist/ analyst specializing in country risk analysis, security issues, industry and trade issues. He was the Director of the India center of a UNDP project, which set up a trade promotion computer-linked trade information network in the late 1980s. He was a Senior Visiting Scientist at the Carnegie Mellon University in the early 1990s. His other stints include: Development Correspondent of *The Hindu*; consultant in S&T to the Brazilian Embassy in India and consulting editor *The Business Standard.*

Index